PENGUIN BOOKS
# LEOPARD DIARIES

Sanjay Gubbi is a scientist, conservationist and writer. His work integrates science, contemplative studies of the natural world, and society. His conservation work has been consistently of the highest quality and exhibits an infectious enthusiasm that few in the country have been able to match.

Working on leopards has been central to his research work. The complex and ambivalent world of leopards is sometimes marked by horrifying tension between humankind and the natural world. This, he writes about in a sharply observant style, lucidly and at times wittily.

Gubbi holds a doctorate in leopard ecology and conservation. Along with his scholarly research, Gubbi has also written extensively in the popular press. A self-taught conservationist, he was the winner of the Whitley Award (popularly known as the Green Oscars) in 2017. He was listed as one of 'Tomorrow's 25 Leaders' by the *Times of India* and is the recipient of the Co-existence Award, the Carl Zeiss Conservation Award and various others.

# PRAISE FOR THE BOOK

'With over a billion people and more leopards than any other country in Asia, India is a fascinating test case of humanity's ability to live with large carnivores. Through the lens of rigorous science, Sanjay Gubbi shines a revealing light on this grand experiment, showing how both big cats and conservationists must navigate an intricate landscape of obstacles, setbacks, and danger. As the only researcher I know who has experienced first-hand the terrified fury of a leopard hemmed in by people, his narrative is unique. This is a captivating and valuable contribution to the growing literature on the leopard in India.'

—Luke Hunter, Ph.D., Executive Director,
Big Cats Program, Wildlife Conservation Society

'*Leopard Diaries* is a captivating read that deftly mixes personal narrative with research insights and critical analysis of current challenges, drawn from Gubbi's years of work on leopard research and conservation.'

—*India Today*

'This book is a 360-degree view of the leopard, its ecological context, and its fraught relationship with the human world.'

—*Hindustan Times*

# LEOPARD DIARIES

## THE ROSETTE IN INDIA

## SANJAY GUBBI

**PENGUIN BOOKS**

An imprint of Penguin Random House

PENGUIN BOOKS

USA | Canada | UK | Ireland | Australia
New Zealand | India | South Africa | China

Penguin Books is part of the Penguin Random House group of companies
whose addresses can be found at global.penguinrandomhouse.com

Published by Penguin Random House India Pvt. Ltd
4th Floor, Capital Tower 1, MG Road,
Gurugram 122 002, Haryana, India

Penguin
Random House
India

First published in Penguin Books by Penguin Random House India 2022

10 9 8 7 6 5 4 3 2

ISBN 9780143459323

Typeset by SÜRYA, New Delhi
Printed at Replika Press Pvt. Ltd, India

www.penguin.co.in

MIX
Paper from
responsible sources
FSC® C016779

# CONTENTS

# FOREWORD

It is believed that the environment in which a child grows and the activities in which it participates influence the child's future. This seems to be particularly applicable to the lives of many of the famed conservationists we are familiar with. Jim Corbett grew up in Kaladhungi in the Himalayan foothills with tigers and leopards, and as a boy he learnt about the jungle as he roamed around hunting with catapult, bow and arrow and a muzzle-loading gun. Later, he became a great slayer of man-eaters and a renowned author. George B. Schaller, the eminent wildlife biologist, fondly remembers his childhood wanderings in the German countryside. The childhood hobby of Rachel Carlson was to wander in the fields and hills and her mother instilled in her a love of nature and the living world. Aldo Leopold, a keen observer of nature, learnt woodcraft and hunting from his father.

As examples from the native Indian landscape, I will mention T. Antony Davis who grew up in the picturesque Kanyakumari district, obtained his doctoral degree in genetics from the eminent J.B.S Haldane and is known for his interesting observations on the Nicobar meagapods and the nesting behaviour of crows in Calcutta. His ambition was to grow dwarf varieties of palmyra trees (*Borassus flabellifer*) and with that goal in mind, he had even established the Haldane Research Institute in the foothills of Western Ghats on the way to Cape Comorin. Dhritikanta Lahiri Choudhury, born in a zamindar family in Kalipur village, Mymensingh district in what is now Bangladesh, which maintained a large number of captive elephants, became a renowned elephant expert although he was a professor of English in Rabindra Bharati University, Calcutta.

Sanjay Gubbi, passionate and dedicated to conservation in his home state of Karnataka, is a native of Gubbi in Tumkur district about 90 kms from Bengaluru. The landscape in Tumkur district where Sanjay grew up (Tumkuru officially, altitude 835m) has low lying hills, part of the Eastern Ghats, and patches of forests such as Devarayanadurga, Madhugiri, Siddarabetta, Ujjini, Maidenahalli, and Bukkapatna and the landscape is home to species such as wolf, leopard, sloth bear, Bengal fox, wild pig, four-horned antelope, chinkara and blackbuck. Naturally, Sanjay even as a child had developed a liking for these animals and was aware of the conflict situation that was prevalent around his home between humans and wildlife such as wild pig, sloth bear and leopard.

The species that had attracted his attention most was the leopard which has given him a doctoral degree. Getting the needed permissions from the Karnataka Forest Department, Sanjay started his leopard work in 2011 which continues till date and therefore can be said to be the longest study carried out on the leopard in India. Sanjay has been affiliated with Nature Conservation Foundation, a dedicated non-governmental organisation, which works for conservation through research and in close collaboration with the local people where the research is being carried out. Sanjay also has a small, passionate and talented team to work on his various conservation programmes and the leopard project.

His research on leopards primarily had three components: camera-trapping to assess the number of leopards, occupancy surveys to quantify leopard distribution, prey availability and biotic pressures and radio-telemetry of selected individuals. During the nine-year period in which his research has been conducted, camera-trapping was carried out in twenty-four areas including protected areas such as BRT Tiger Reserve, Cauvery and MM Hills Wildlife Sanctuaries and the Bannerghatta National Park and the total area covered for this effort was 4,500 sq kms. The images of leopards obtained were 7,658 and a careful study of the images showed that the minimum number of leopards present in these images was 600. In one patch of reserved forest, known as Kukwadi-Ubrani which had an area of 370 sq kms, fifty-two individual leopards were camera trapped which is one of the high densities of leopards recorded so far (14/100 sq kms). The occurrence of leopards in many places between Bannerghatta National Park and the outskirts of Bangalore has also been established. Camera-trapping in Chamundi hills initially showed six leopards and the number rapidly came down to two as a result of death on the roads due to collision with speeding vehicles and other reasons. This highlights one of the serious conservation problems faced by the leopard and other wildlife in the country and this is a global problem.

Camera-trapping not only brought the presence of leopards but also several other rare species. Honey badgers were camera-trapped in the Cauvery Wildlife Sanctuary, the rusty-spotted cat in several areas, the brown mongoose in the BRT Tiger reserve, the wolf in the Cauvery Wildlife Sanctuary and the chinkara in the Bukkapatna Reserved forest which led to the formation of 148 sq km Bukkapatna Chinkara Wildlife Sanctuary, which has the southernmost distribution of chinkara in India. Cameras also caught poachers and timber smugglers. Also, sometimes the cameras were stolen and elephants became curious about the cameras and destroyed them.

Besides camera-trapping Sanjay and his team walked nearly 3,000 kms and embarked on an occupancy survey in the southern part of Karnataka covering 23,900 sq km quantifying leopards and other related wildlife signs. Based on all the information gathered, Sanjay believes that the number of leopards in Karnataka could be 2500 and if such a dedicated exercise is carried out all over India one would get a population of at least 20,000 leopards. The survey also brought to light the presence of dinosaur-era cycad *Cycas indica* (*Cycas swamyi*) in the dry forests of Mandya, Ramanagara and Tumkur.

Sanjay also gives us information on the importance of predators in an ecosystem, the origin and distribution of the different subspecies of leopards, the biology of leopards, black and strawberry leopards, the co-existence of leopards with other predators, diet and caching behaviour, mating, reproductive strategies and dispersal of sub-adults, man-eating leopards, problems faced by the leopards and their future. Details of the incident of Sanjay getting attacked by a leopard in February 2016 in a school in Bangalore and his admission to a hospital are provided in one chapter. Fortunately for him, maybe because the leopard was not a man-eater, it did not go for his throat which is the killing bite of a leopard.

Sanjay has a way of helping conservation in Karnataka which is explained well in his earlier book *Second Nature: Saving Tiger Landscapes in the Twenty First Century.* Two achievements are worth mentioning. One is his success in increasing the geographical area under protection in Karnataka from 3.8 per cent to 5.5 per cent and the other was securing a hardship allowance of Rs. 3,500 per month along with a basic salary for the frontline staff. These achievements were not accomplished overnight and he had to single-mindedly work for several years securing the support of higher officials and politicians.

Conservation is like rope climbing. Both the arms and all the ten fingers have to give support to the one climbing the rope. Similarly, to achieve conservation success in the field, full-fledged support of the field staff, officers and politicians is needed and if one group fails to give support then success will only be a dream. Sanjay is well aware of this.

His other important conservation achievement is the establishment of the Holematthi Nature Information Centre in 2018 in Cauvery-MM Hills landscape which is being visited by a large number of people, primarily by students. The Centre is also used for various training programmes for the local villagers and the forest staff. The centre derives its name from the 'Holematthi' (*Terminalia arjuna*) tree, which grows to a magnificent size along the riverine tracts of the Cauvery River. Cauvery-MM Hills is going to be the primary study and conservation area of Sanjay and his goal is, by controlling all biotic disturbances, including poaching, to have about fifty tigers in this landscape.

**DR A.J.T. JOHNSINGH, Nature Conservation Foundation, WWF-India and The Corbett Foundation**

# PREFACE

Large predators and human beings have shared the land since ancient times, usually in an uneasy proximity. Many predators were and are worshipped in cultures across the world. The teeth of big predators, their claws and their ferocity are all grim realities. Similarly, their beauty, agility and obscurity have fascinated humans since times immemorial. Though historically, large carnivores have predated on humans, the tables have turned in the last two centuries with the invention of firearms, advanced tools, vehicles and the colossal growth of human population. Carnivore numbers and habitats have gone through enormous transformation due to the unprecedented growth of human population. It is estimated that by the year 2150 when the human population peaks at around 11 billion, alpha predators will cease to exist. But if there is one species which could make this prophecy wrong, it could be the leopard.

Today, leopards are found in tropical forests, scrub jungles and humid rainforests as well as cold deserts and coniferous forests that reach temperatures 40 degrees below zero. Besides these, leopards are also at times found in areca nut plantations and sugarcane fields, which are essentially human created habitats.

Why are leopards so successful? What traits and habits have allowed leopards to survive successfully? The answers to questions like these frame the narrative of this book. The book seeks to reveal why leopards thrive in their habitats, why they are so vital to the people and the ecosystems in which they live and what threats they face.

When I began working on leopards about a decade ago, I didn't know that one day I would write this book. The core of this book draws from these ten years of field-based research on this spotted cat that ranged from radio telemetry, camera trapping, distribution surveys, geographical information system (GIS) analyses, and human-leopard conflict.

I hope our work has helped enhance our understanding of one of the most flexible species of the natural world. But we need to be aware that once an answer to a scientific puzzle is resolved, new and often more intriguing questions pop up to further perplex us. Hence a sense of openness is very essential in wildlife science. Nothing remains carved in stone. Times change, society, economics, priorities also change, and along with it the genesis of many issues in wildlife conservation changes.

The leopard is the reigning rock star of the wildlife world. It's a species that is obscure and largely overshadowed by the tiger, especially in India. But it is also a species that is loved by some and hated by many others. Nearly buried in this cacophony of conflict lies the threat of this lonely, mysterious creature's remarkable story.

In the wild in India and Africa, leopards are perhaps one of the most photographed wild cats; yet most of their lives remain a secret to us, hidden, private events. We need to patiently prise out the secrets of these elusive cats. For instance, leopards have communication and networking methods that would leave Mark Zuckerberg open-mouthed. They are secretive and elusive predators that provoke conflicting emotions of terror and admiration from people who encounter them in the wild. But they have not mesmerised people throughout history like lions, tigers or cheetahs. For decades and even today, they were perceived as dangerous varmints and have suffered from habitat loss, death by road kills, illegal hunting, a depleted prey base and other catastrophes. In many areas where they have survived for ages, their habitat is getting limited, hemmed in as it is by human development.

Human beings are a storytelling species. Every practising naturalist has stories to tell. These are a few of mine. This book is as much about my transformation as it is about the leopards—from a full-time conservationist to a hybrid of researcher-conservationist-outreach professional.

When studying leopards, along the way, I encountered fascinating plants and animals as well as many people—from scientists and gardeners to merchants and chefs—whose stories were equally remarkable. So perhaps the artefacts of my work extend beyond observations on leopards, their prey, their habitats and what surrounds these habitats. For me wildlife is an ideal subject not just because I work on it, but because writing about it also provides a window through which we see several facets of society and many stories about animals, forests, people, rural India, urban India and the larger world can be told.

The chronicles in the book in different ways illustrate the power of the hidden secrets of the leopards' world, their conservation and the politics of working on large wild cats. To write this book, I went back to my diaries, field notebooks that had jerky jottings like that of an overexcited child, and e-mails. I tried to match press accounts of events to my personal memories and the recollections of my colleagues.

The structure of the book is roughly chronological. I begin with the evolution of the leopard and end with the current threats to the cat in the twenty-first century. I have written quite a bit from my field research on this spotted feline. This includes how these cats are distributed, how many leopards live in different parts of Karnataka, the conflict they have with humans and vice-versa. This book is an attempt to see the natural world, not just from our point of view, but also from the leopards' perspective. That to me is this book's principal reason to exist.

My research goal was to collect the best possible data on leopard ecology and to apply the data to leopard conservation. I decided to start my research even amidst the political difficulties of working on large carnivores functioning in a landscape where hegemony was already established. Leopards are territorial and so are those studying them.

My interest was not to master leopards but to slowly interpret their life to help contribute to their conservation, especially through conflict mitigation strategies. I have strongly felt that research should be more than a quest for facts. I don't want to merely leave records of the animals going extinct for our children to read. I am more interested in our children actually being able to see these animals. As George Schaller, an American large mammal biologist says, 'A researcher today also has a moral responsibility to help the species endure.' We can endlessly describe a species, but we need to help the species persist. Information is key but so is emotion.

The journey with the leopard was not intended to produce a guide to lead others and state how it is in the leopard world. This is not a manual on how to conserve leopards but a log of my journeys and observations. It records my experiences with the people I met, and the results of our study on this wonderful cat. We also have to recognise that there are things we cannot understand about leopards, or for that matter about any wild species. Leopards possess qualities and abilities well beyond the means of science to decipher. We have interpreted a little about this species. But nature knows a lot more. And we will never know many secrets of this spotted cat. Science has only been nibbling at the furtive biological facts of many wildlife species, and most of it remains to be understood. Our work added just another brick to this large world of ecology and conservation.

Wildlife biology, like all other sciences, has its own jargon, its own vocabulary with its own precise meanings that can be baffling and put off non-biologists. Therefore, I have avoided technical terms to the extent possible.

One final caveat about this book. I write this book fully conscious of the fact that there may well be facts of which I am unaware that undermine or disagree with some of my arguments and ecological perspectives. Still, the volume before you conveys in essence what I understand of this wonderful animal.

I hope this book does what little it can to shed light on the Indian leopard and the struggles it goes through to keep itself afloat. My offering here is merely a partial view of the leopards and science of leopards and a somewhat personal one which has grown from my modest studies on this enigmatic cat and travels through their habitat. It's also from a chance personal encounter that made me experience their force and strength.

# 1

# THE SPOTTED CAT

In popular vernacular, leopard, panther and black panther, all refer to the same large wild cat, scientifically known as the *Panthera pardus*. In Indonesia, this feline species is even referred to as the 'black tiger' and the 'spotted tiger'. The leopard—elusive, obscure and eclipsed in popularity by its larger cousins—is a stunning, high-performance predator. It is a marvel, worthy of our praise, wonder and any number of exclamations points.

The word 'leopard' comes from the Greek compound leon, meaning lion, and pardos, a male panther, reflecting that it was thought to be the hybrid of a lion and a panther during the Classical Era. The Greek word is also believed to be related to the Sanskrit word 'pradaku'. 'Dvipin' is another word for leopard in Sanskrit which means an animal having spots like islands. It is believed that the scientific name of the leopard, *Panthera pardus*, is derived from Latin. But there are alternative theories that argue that it is derived from Indo-Iranian words or Sanskrit.

Leopards are a mixture of several natural aspects—social but solitary, inconspicuous but significant in numbers, large but ubiquitous; they don't fit into any of the standard pigeonholes of large-cat conservation. In India, the leopard is a poster boy against extinction, but in many other areas around the world, its population has dwindled to the extent of either ecological or local extinction. Even then, it is certainly not a superstar of conservation initiatives, and is generally overshadowed by other larger felids such as tiger, lion, jaguar and snow leopard.

The leopard is currently categorised as 'vulnerable' in the International Union for Conservation of Nature's Red List, an inventory of the earth's endangered plant and animal species. Recognising the leopard as 'vulnerable' provides it a higher profile, affords it better protection and directs more attention towards this iconic species, a symbol of the vast scrub forest spaces that are on a perilous trajectory towards extinction in some parts of the world. However, this up-listing is not truly a matter to celebrate: leopards are not just important because they are beautiful carnivores, they also perhaps carry out important ecosystem services that have not been fully understood yet.

Though we don't yet fully know the consequences of their disappearance, some key aspects of the leopard's role in the ecosystem are worthy of understanding. This kingly mammal, a symbol of a healthy ecosystem, effectively helps in the conservation of smaller, lower-profile predators as well as other species that live in and make up its home range. In India, leopard conservation could effectively help the jungle cat, the rusty-spotted cat, civets, the four-horned antelope, chinkara, porcupines, the endangered pangolins and many other animals that the leopards eat.

Leopards might also help keep the circle of life turning. Since they consume small and large birds that feed on fruits, or seeds of fruits, and small fruit- and seed-eating mammals, such as primates, civets, porcupine, bandicoots and squirrels, leopards could be acting as important secondary seed dispersers, providing an important ecosystem service without which our landscapes and ecosystems wouldn't exist.

Carnivores like leopards have large gapes, and they swallow food without much chewing. They also have simple guts, so most seeds, those botanical marvels, pass through undamaged, a condition that is ideal for dispersal. Besides, leopards have large home ranges, so they carry seeds in their gut over larger distances than their prey, which mostly have small home ranges. For example, studies from southern India showed that a troop of langurs, the leaf-eating primates that are regularly consumed by leopards, had a home range of about a kilometre square (247 acres), while a leopard I had radio-collared had a home range of 141 sq kms (34,841 acres). This leopard certainly could disperse the seed over a wider area than its food source, the langur, could have. Leopards also eat graminivores, grass-eating animals such as hare, and hence, they could even be dispersing grass seeds and helping grow food for other herbivores. At some point, these herbivores will, again, become the leopard's food and so, in a way, leopards are helping their own food sources. This is the eternal paradox of nature—out of death comes life.

This process of seeds or fruits being transported in the gut of multiple animals has a complicated but meaningful term in ecology: diploendozoochory, where diplo means double, endo means inner, zoo means animal and chory means seed dispersal. Many other carnivore species, including the fox, the jackal, the hyena, the sloth bear, the jungle cat and the honey badger, perform this function of depositing seeds over a wider area through their faeces. This process of predator-assisted seed dispersal is important to colonise and recolonise plant life in the wild. In fact, some seeds need to pass through an animal gut to trigger their germination.

Leopards also potentially perform the role of controlling medium-sized carnivores, scientifically termed 'mesocarnivores', such as the golden jackal, the red fox, the Bengal fox, the golden cat, the clouded leopard and the marbled cat and others in Asia, or the caracal, the serval, the African wild cat, the black-footed cat and others in Africa, through intra-guild competition, thus maintaining a balance and strengthening the ecosystem functioning. The presence of apex predators like leopards suppresses mesocarnivores either by killing them or instilling fear, which motivates changes in behaviour and habitat use, that limit mesocarnivore distribution and abundance. If large carnivores like leopards were absent, the mesocarnivore population would explode and increase the predation of smaller prey. This would bring an unwanted imbalance in the ecosystem.

Top predators also have a role in protecting the plant world. A well-designed study conducted in Gorongosa National Park in Mozambique has demonstrated the negative impacts on vegetation when large carnivores like leopards are wiped out. The phrase 'trophic cascade' describes such a phenomenon, and it demonstrates the impact meat-eating predators can have on plants. Large meat-eaters in Gorongosa had effectively confined herbivores like bushbuck, a small forest antelope, to certain areas due to fear of predation. A sixteen-year-long civil war eliminated these carnivores, and thus changed the way in which and the geographical area over which the herbivores fed, affecting the food chain. The generally forest-dwelling bushbuck, which avoided savannahs and plains due to the risk of attack from predators, now started to expand into the treeless floodplains, adding new plant species into their diet. This started to affect a type of waterwort called *Bergia mossambicensis*, a plant species found in the floodplains.

The elimination of leopards 'had created a landscape of fearlessness', where herbivores browsed freely, impacting local vegetation. However, as soon as the large predators were reintroduced, the area began to regain its vegetation, as the carnivores controlled where the herbivores browsed, bringing back a balance in the entire ecosystem.

But the most sobering example of the large predators' role is the return of grey wolves to the Yellowstone National Park in the United States of America. Here, for nearly two decades, scientists William J. Ripple and Robert L. Beschta, from the Oregon State University, gathered evidence piece by piece that demonstrated the positive effects wolf reintroduction had on the entire ecosystem.

In the 1920s, wolves were killed off from Yellowstone as a part of an eradication programme. This led to an explosion in the elk deer population, the favoured food of wolves. As the elk grew in number, their consumption of aspen tree (*Populus tremuloides*) seedlings and other plants that grew along the stream banks increased. This started a decline in these plant species, which then led on to a rapid erosion of stream banks. The elk also affected other tree species in areas that had earlier been favoured by the wolves.

In 1995, wolves were reintroduced in Yellowstone National Park. Once these large predators were back, the elk population decreased from 15,000 individuals in the early 1990s to about 6,000 in 2010, which helped the vegetation along the stream banks to recover. Young aspen trees started to grow in the late 1990s. Once the aspen regenerated, there was less erosion. The river paths and stream banks stabilised and flourished, improving the overall health of the waterways. Insects, birds and amphibians that depended on stream bank vegetation rebounded. Fish population improved in the streams.

Due to the fear of wolves, the elk also kept away from the valleys that were preferred by wolves for hunting. Some of the stream banks were now completely avoided by the elk, as it would be difficult for them to detect or escape from predators nearby, due to the wood debris on the forest floor.

Willow trees (*Salix* spp.), which grow in wet areas along stream beds, also returned in good numbers along the stream banks. This, scientists believe, helped the beaver colonies to increase twelvefold, as beavers almost exclusively use willows in Yellowstone. With beavers building more dams and creating natural ponds, riparian hydrology and biodiversity improved. Now, the streams with beavers have seventy-five times more abundant waterfowl than those without them.

Pronghorn, America's antelope species, have also begun to recover in Yellowstone. When wolves were absent, coyotes, a medium-sized carnivore, preyed heavily on the pronghorns' young, leading to a decline of pronghorn population in the national park. With wolves back, the survival rates of the pronghorns' young ones increased, due to a control on coyote population and the coyotes' avoidance of certain areas because of the fear of wolves. Once the coyote population was under control, there were also more rabbits and mice, which, in turn, increased the number of hawks, weasels, foxes and badgers, bringing stability into the ecosystem.

More subtle but serious benefits also exist that demonstrate the role wolves played in the landscape. The herbivore kills made by wolves became a scavengers' banquet: coyotes and foxes, grizzly and black bears, bald eagles, vultures, magpies, ravens and crows, plus fifty-seven varieties of beetles, were all found feasting on the wolves' leftovers. The wolf as a predator was helping several other animals find food. The wolf kills also helped bring nutrients to the soil from the leftovers helping plant species.

The pivotal role that wolves played in Yellowstone after their reintroduction seventy years later proved that the damage caused to a terrestrial food web could be restored by the return of a single predator species. The central role of such top carnivores and their vital connections to ecosystem functioning have also been observed by the same scientists in other areas, including Zion National Park in Utah state. They found that in the Zion Valley area of the national park, cottonwood trees (*Poulus* spp.) were almost absent from sandbanks along streams in places that had a scarcity of cougars, the top predators of the national park. But in areas like North Creek, where cougars were common, a rich biodiversity flourished. Whether frogs, toads, lizards, amphibians, fishes, wildflowers or butterflies the contrast in numbers were astounding—there were forty-seven times more cottonwood trees, 200 times more frogs and toads, and five times more butterflies in the areas with cougars.

A recent study by Alex Braczkowski from the University of Queensland suggests that leopards might help prevent rabies, as they largely consume pye-dogs (stray dogs) when they live close to big cities. The researcher argues that leopards could be saving up to ninety human lives per year in Mumbai by consuming stray dogs. Another example of the ecological importance of leopards is their role in controlling wild pig populations, which use many of the same plant foods as humans, turning them into key crop raiders. Wild pig numbers and the damages they cause may be increasing wherever leopards have been exterminated. The consequence of this increase has been significant as communities turn more and more hostile towards wildlife. Another well-documented example exists in Ghana, where the reduction of lion and leopard populations have led to an explosion of olive baboons that wreak havoc around villages, attacking livestock, damaging crops and spreading intestinal parasites among the human population.

From the forests of the Deccan Plateau to the scrubs of southern and north-west India, each leopard is deeply linked to the ecosystem it survives in. Deep in the plains and rocky outcrops of India, the leopard is perhaps key to saving the dying dry forests. In most parts of the Deccan Plateau, the Aravallis, the Eastern Ghats, and the Vindhyas, where the tiger is absent, the leopard acts as the top predator, possibly affecting the health of the entire ecosystem, like the wolves in Yellowstone. There are still no definite answers if leopards hold the key to the stability of an ecosystem and to the maintenance of an extraordinary diversity of plants and animals where they survive. In fact, the same goes for tigers, but we need to take a precautionary approach.

Tiger-leopard, lion-leopard, wolf-leopard, dhole-leopard, hyena-leopard and even snow leopard-leopard: the leopard is a species that, amazingly, can co-exist with many other large carnivores. These permutations and combinations can be as varied as the variety of habitats the leopard survives in, and no other large carnivore can replace the space occupied by the leopards. How leopards interact and co-exist with other conspecific predators is important in determining leopard numbers in an area.

Leopards are the apex carnivores in the many areas they survive. They sit on the top of the Eltonian Pyramid, a concept floated by Charles Elton, an Oxford zoologist from the 1920s, where leopards are part of the population of predators that generally are not subjected to predation themselves. For instance, there are no super-monstrous predator species that eat lions, tigers or sharks. Of course, humans are super predators due to their ability to make and use tools that are used to eliminate large predators.

## *The origins of the spotted cat*

All modern-day cat species presumably evolved from Styriofelis, a subfamily of Felinae, the conical-toothed cats that evolved along with the sabre-toothed ones, which possessed dagger-like canines, around eleven million years ago. Analysis of genetic and felid fossil records suggests that the lion, the cheetah and the leopard shared the African landscape around a million years ago. The leopard first appears in fossil records of Europe from the late Pliocene or early Pleistocene, both part of the Cenozoic geological era. These leopards, attributed to the subspecies *Panthera pardus begoueni*, were replaced about 600,000 years ago by the subspecies *Panthera pardus sickenbergi*, which lived until the mid-Pleistocene in Europe. Leopards in these times were 25 per cent larger than they are today, and were possibly devouring our ancestors, the *Homo erectus* and *Homo sapiens*.

Around 300,000 years ago another subspecies, the *Panthera pardus antiqua*, replaced the *Panthera pardus sickenbergi*. At the beginning of the late Pleistocene, this subspecies gave rise to the late Pleistocene Ice Age leopard (*Panthera pardus spelaea*). Another Pleistocene form from Europe, *Panthera pardus vraonensis,* is now regarded as a junior synonym of *Panthera pardus spelaea*.

The Ice Age leopards that resembled the modern-day Persian leopard (*Panthera pardus ciscaucasica*) roamed Europe, including modern-day Great Britain, northern Germany and the Swiss Alps, during the late Pleistocene age. According to palaeontologist Cajus Diedrich of Paleo-Logic, an independent geological and paleontological service and consulting bureau, the most complete skeletons of the Ice Age leopards were found in the Vjetrenica caves, a 30,000-year-old burial site, in Dinarid mountains in what is now known as Bosnia and Herzegovina. Four adults—two male and two female leopard skeletons—were found about two kilometres deep inside these caves. The modern leopard is believed to have evolved in Africa 0.5 to 0.8 million years ago and to have radiated across Asia 0.2 to 0.3 million years ago.

Currently, science recognises thirty-eight living felid species, including the leopard. Today, the leopard is one of the most versatile and widespread large carnivores. It is the smallest of the four 'big cats' belonging to the *Panthera* lineage. Consisting of tigers, lions, jaguars and the leopard, these four share the ability to roar, a specific vocalisation not shared by other felids. This is due to the unique modifications in the larynx and the elastic hyoid structure. However, this genus cannot purr continually like snow leopards and clouded leopards both of which cannot roar.

Scientists today recognise nine leopard sub-species. Based on morphology and genetic analyses, they have put forth that there is one subspecies of leopard in the whole of Africa (*Panthera pardus pardus*) and eight other subspecies spread over Asia and parts of Europe. These include Arabian leopard (*P. p. nimr*), Persian leopard (*P. p. saxicolor*), Indian leopard (*P. p. fusca*), Sri Lankan leopard (*P. p. kotiya*), Indochinese leopard (*P. p. delacouri*), Javan leopard (*P. p. melas*), North Chinese leopard (*P. p. japonensis*), and the Amur leopard (*P. p. orientalis*).

However recent findings suggest that the *fusca*, *kotiya* and the western populations of *delacouri* perhaps represent the same subspecies, and the eastern *delacouri*, *japonensis* and *orientalis* represent one subspecies. This could reduce the number of Asian subspecies to five.

Carnivores and humans have a long relationship, and this extends to leopards as well. The link between leopards and humans goes back 35,000 years. In 1994, a group of three amateur spelunkers were delighted to find paintings of early humans in a cave along the Ardèche River in south-eastern France. The paintings included the figure of a leopard, painted in red ochre. This was the first-ever leopard figure encountered in any Paleolithic gallery, and it's the oldest known example of human art depicting a leopard. In addition, the group found figures of the cave bear, cave lion, mammoth, horses, bison, auroch, reindeer, giant deer, rhinoceros and many more animals in this cave art. The leopard painting stands under the shadow of a large hyena, and within the same panel as what is possibly a cave bear. The cave, which is now under government protection, was initially dated to be between 17,000 to 21,000 years old. But radiocarbon tests have found that some of the paintings in the cave are as old as 35,000 years, older than any other known rock art.

The New York Metropolitan Museum of Art, a 150-year-old museum that has art collections from around the world, has on display a jasper gaming piece carved in the shape of a leopard head. These pieces were used for playing senet and twenty squares, two board games popular amongst ancient Egyptians. Two more such leopard-head gaming pieces from the same set are on display at museums in Basel, Switzerland and Cairo, Egypt.

Leopards played a tremendous role in the iconography of ancient Egypt. They were a symbol of royal authority, symbolised strength and power, and were associated with gods. Mafdet, the goddess of justice, is primarily shown with the head of a cheetah, but often sported the head of a leopard. Seshat, the goddess of wisdom, knowledge and record keeping, wore leopard-print robes. Leopards appear as hieroglyphs and statues in many Egyptian artworks. Some pharaohs kept these felines as pets, and priests wore leopard-skin mantles during ceremonies. Archaeologists even found the remains of a leopard in the ancient cemetery of Hierakonpolis, an ancient Egyptian town that had the world's first zoo. It holds the mummified remains of animals from five thousand years ago, buried alongside elite members of the society.

As chronicled by Divyabhanusinh, the former vice president of Bombay Natural History Society, in his acclaimed book *The End of a Trail: The Cheetah in India*, paintings of leopards have also been found in cave shelters in the hilly and semi-hilly regions of central and southern India. He suggests that leopards may have been selected as a subject of paintings for religious or magical purposes, or to study the anatomy of the prey animals or those animals that posed a danger to humans. The *Arthasastra* of Kautilya, the chief minister of Chandragupta Maurya, who ruled from 324 to 300 BCE, regulated the hunting of leopards.

Leopards were the subjects of various art forms, especially miniature paintings, during Mughal rule. The rulers of Awadh (in current day Uttar Pradesh) used to have leopard fights as part of their lavish entertainment.

In many parts of Africa, leopards were supposed to be inhabited by the souls of humans, particularly those of chieftains. Hence these animals could be killed only in self-defence. Leopards were also believed to be guardian animals for humans. In the late nineteenth and early twentieth centuries, local chiefs in north-east Congo used 'anioto' or leopard-men to carry out killings to secure their authority over rainforest societies and resources and circumvent colonial rule. These aniotos used claw-like weapons to shift the blame of murders on real leopards.

We have also made peace with large carnivores by finding them roles in our emotional universe. In Isaiah 11, the Old Testament of the Christian Bible, the leopard that mingles with lambs finds a mention. Though, in India, the leopard does not enjoy the same reverence in religion or mythology as the tiger does, Lord Shiva, the destroyer, wraps himself in a leopard skin. In some parts of India, leopards are also believed to protect people from bandits when they walk through forests.

### Where are leopards found?

Leopards are considered biologically successful because of their evolutionary persistence and their widespread distribution. They are programmed for survival and do so in almost every earthly habitat. Cosmopolitan carnivores, they are found in scrub, deciduous forests, rainforests, and coniferous forests. They have the ability to exploit a variety of habitats—right from the sub-zero temperatures of the Russian Far East (-30° C) to the arid, mountainous areas of central Asia (50°C), the humid, triple-canopied rainforests of South-east

Asia and central Africa, the coniferous forests of Himalayas and the scrub forests of Africa and Asia. The only places they remain absent from are deserts and snow-capped mountains. Mostly found at sea level, their upper altitudinal limit is recorded to be 5,600 metres above sea level. Even this, however, has its exceptions. In his short story 'The Snows of Kilimanjaro', Ernest Hemingway, the Noble Prize-winning American novelist, wrote of a frozen leopard carcass found on the western peak of Mount Kilimanjaro, the rooftop of Africa, at a spot that is popularly referred to as the 'Leopard Point' among trekkers. No one knows if Hemingway's leopard actually existed or not. But in 1962, a Lutheran pastor named Richard Reusch discovered a freeze-dried leopard at roughly 5,639 metres, along the crater rim of Kilimanjaro's sub-peak, Kibo. In India, camera trap studies carried out on snow leopards by researchers from the Nature Conservation Foundation documented leopards at 4,132 metres in the picturesque Himalayan state of Himachal Pradesh.

In the Himalayas, the youngest and highest mountain chain in the world, leopards are fairly common even at 3,000 metres above sea level. This explains, in part, the cosmopolitan distribution of leopards. There are few other large mammal species that can survive in such varied habitats, including the tiger, the sloth bear and the elephant. The leopard's ability to survive in flat areas as well as hilly terrains and its capability to cross natural physical barriers such as rivers that restrict smaller species, or species such as the primates, is highly impressive. Its ability to thrive even in areas that have high habitat disturbance is another reason for its persistence.

Leopards are now documented as being present in sixty-three countries of the world. They are present in the Indonesian island of Java—their easternmost range, where they are extremely rare—and patchily exist in Turkey, their westernmost home. From the Russian Far East at the northern end to South Africa in the southern end, they are found everywhere. Though this range is vast, their numbers are dismal in many parts, and some regional populations have been virtually exterminated. They are thought to be extinct in seven countries and confirmed as such in thirteen other countries.

Leopards are widespread in the African continent, but their existence is highly restricted in North Africa, and has come down to a handful of disparate populations. The spotted cat is thought to be almost extinct in Algeria, Egypt and Morocco, areas where they were earlier recorded. They are reported in Senegal, Guinea and Liberia in West Africa, and all the way into Ethiopia and Somalia at the eastern end of the continent. Leopards exist as scattered relic populations in Djibouti, Eritrea and Sudan, where they tenuously survive. They are widely distributed in central and southern Africa, and even found in the Cape area in South Africa, where the habitat is very similar to the rocky outcrops they inhabit in southern India. In both areas, they reach some of the highest densities.

Unfortunately, the Arabian leopard has made it to the critically endangered list, highlighting that this subspecies is one of the continent's most at-risk carnivores, and drastic steps are required to conserve it. Its range spreads from Dhofar area in south-western Oman to north-eastern Yemen, where it precariously clings on. There are reports of isolated, relict populations in Saudi Arabia, thought to be numbering between sixty to four hundred and twenty-five. Some of the records of the spotted cat from these areas date back several years, with the last confirmed evidence of leopards being of two poisoned carcasses found in Al-Namas in 2007. The big cat is thought to be extinct in the United Arab Emirates (UAE), Jordan and Israel.

In south-west Asia and the Caucasus, a region between Europe and Asia that's one of the most linguistically and culturally diverse regions on the planet, the Persian leopard ranges through Turkey, Iran, Iraq, Armenia, Azerbaijan and Georgia. But there are only a handful in most of these areas, and are only found in a single area, threatening their survival locally. Today, the Persian leopard is estimated to be 800-1,000 individuals surviving in the dry mountains and is categorised as an endangered subspecies.

In central Asia, there are indications of leopard presence in the Babatag and Kugitang mountains of Uzbekistan and the Bamyan province in Afghanistan, but in very low numbers. They fare better in Pakistan, where they survive in the broken hilly or mountainous areas of Waziristan, Baluchistan, Sindh and parts of north-east Pakistan.

In Southeast and East Asia, they survive in the northern parts of China, Tibet, Myanmar, Thailand, Malaysia and other countries. Experts believe that a few leopards might even be living in South Korea. Finally, at the end of their eastern range, they are present in low numbers (350–500) in the beautiful island of Java in Indonesia. Leopards are likely to have migrated to the island of Java from mainland Asia during a prolonged period of low sea levels. It is thought that they crossed via a Malaya–Java land bridge approximately 600,000 years ago during the Middle Pleistocene period. However, they never crossed over to the other larger islands of Indonesia—Bali, Sumatra and Borneo (which partly belongs to Malaysia and Brunei as well).

The Indonesian island archipelago has disjunct distributions of wild cats despite being close to each other. For instance, despite tigers being present in Sumatra, Java and Bali (though now extinct in both Java and Bali), they were never recorded from Borneo, except during pre-historic times. Similarly, clouded leopards are absent from the islands of Java and Bali, but are present in Borneo and Sumatra. Fossil evidence suggests the presence of leopards in Sumatra only at the beginning of the late Pleistocene. They went extinct as a consequence of the Toba super volcanic eruption. Leopards were supposed to have been found in a tiny island archipelago called the Kangean Islands, close to Bali, till around 1980 but never on the main island of Bali.

The below freezing temperatures in the Manchurian mountains on the border of the Russian Far East and China have not deterred this elastic species from surviving the long, cold winters here. Evolution has helped these Amur leopards to adapt, but unfortunately, the world cannot be proud of their numbers in this part of the world. Fewer than ninety individuals survive, decimated largely due to poaching for their fur, which was once called 'soft gold', the extermination of their prey species, and the loss of the high-altitude forests known as the boreal forests, or the taiga, that they live in. This tiny relic subspecies population is now restricted to the mountains near Vladivostok and the Jilin province of China. The heart-stoppingly beautiful Amur leopards are today one of the world's rarest large cat subspecies. They weren't always so rare, and it's estimated that nearly 2,400 wild Amur leopards were surviving in the 1950s in the former Soviet Union.

Leopards become stars of conservation, especially outside protected areas, in Nepal, Bhutan, India and Sri Lanka. These four countries contribute to the global leopard populations substantially. Leopards are thought to have crossed to Sri Lanka from India, along with elephants and monkeys, through the 'Adam's Bridge', or the 'Ram Setu' as it is called in India. These agile cats arrived here even before Sapiens reached about 50,000 years ago. Today, the island nation of Sri Lanka hosts an estimated 750–900 leopards.

In India, as a species, the leopard fares well compared to the other large cats: tigers, lions and the snow leopard. Large rocks, perched on slopes with scrub, stunted trees and the occasional open grassy patch on the top of the hillock is the typical landscape one sees in the dry areas of southern, central and western India. This forms the ecological heartland of the region, and is the principal habitat of leopards in large parts of India. The totem of these rocky outcrops, these spotted felines survive here in great numbers. Although they are known to be living in close vicinity to human settlements, they are as elusive as a shadow—shy, solitary and nocturnal. It would not be a stretch to call India the mecca of leopards. India is also the likeliest long-term home for this cat. According to government estimates, based on camera trap-surveys carried out in tiger bearing forests, India hosts about 13,000 leopards across the country. I, however, believe that India has over 20,000 leopards as many parts of the country that hold leopards were not surveyed during the government's monitoring exercise. The diversity of habitats available within the country perhaps helps the numbers of this habitat generalist. However, we, from some of the African countries and India, forget just how rare these creatures are in some other parts of their distribution range. Albeit ubiquitous, it is now clear that humans are shaping leopards' lives, and are affecting their distribution and numbers in many ways. Their numerousness in India would be a matter of delight, ordinarily, but the conflict and biophobia people go through are a matter of concern for both people and the species. The leopard's future probably depends upon how much people are willing to tolerate this large felid.

# 2

# LEOPARD BIOLOGY

## *Physical characteristics*

A critical morphological trait of large carnivores is their physical appearance. It helps them hide, hunt, bring up young ones and survive in the harsh, natural world they need to endure in. This is no different for the leopard, and its coat, body structure and physical characteristics are all shaped to this end: it is an animal built for survival efficiency.

The leopard is one of the three 'visually stunning' wild cats of the world, as per Eric Dinerstein, an acclaimed carnivore biologist with several acclaimed books to his credit.

And, indeed, nature has crafted one of its best pieces of art in the form of a leopard. The colour of the leopard and the spots on its body give it the perfect camouflage. These dark spots, romantically called 'rosettes', and its yellowish-brown fur, with its irregular and complex patterns, camouflage the leopard even in bright sunlight by allowing it to blend into the background. The rosette pattern helps the leopard conceal itself amidst parched vegetation, dense habitat, low light levels and the rocks on which it often perches.

Sitting on tree branches, the leopard gets perfectly disguised and can merge into the tree bark and leaves, revealing itself only on careful observation and a little bit of luck. As Eric Dinerstein says, 'Evolution is an exquisite artist, even if an unconscious one.'

In physical appearance, the leopard is similar to the jaguar, the spotted cat of the Americas, but smaller and lighter: while it looks like a watered down version of the jaguar, the jaguar resembles a leopard on steroids. The jaguar and the leopard are two of the three big cats that sport spots on their body; the other is the cheetah. The rosettes on the leopard's body distinguish this cat. Though the rosette pattern on the leopard is similar to that of the jaguar, the leopard's rosettes are smaller, more densely packed and usually do not have the large, central black spots found within the jaguar's rosettes. Some individuals in southern India, where I have carried out extensive camera trap surveys, are found to have these central spots within the rosettes, but these are much smaller in size. The number of rosettes with such spots are also fewer in an individual, and do not range over ten. This pattern has also been observed in leopards in Gabon in central Africa, where the German, Philip Henschel, a carnivore biologist, has carried out camera trapping in the rainforests.

The leopard has been largely confused with the cheetah, and even to this day many people call the leopard the cheetah. Though similar looking to the uneducated eye, there are remarkable differences between these two large cats. The obvious visible difference are the spots on a leopard, which are irregular and grouped together to form rosettes, while the spots on a cheetah are rounded and solid. In addition, the cheetah has two clear black lines that streak from the inner corner of its eyes and down to its cheeks, called tear marks. These markings are missing on the leopard's face.

Less obviously visible, the tall and slender cheetah has a smaller head and a remarkably smaller waist in comparison to the leopard. The tail of the cheetah is much flatter in shape, while the leopard's tail is tubular and curled up at the end. The claws in a cheetah are non-retractable; on the other hand, the leopard has retractable claws, which it can bring it out when required to climb trees, pull down prey and fight with other carnivores. Leopard claws, therefore, are not visible in their paw prints. They also use the claws to mark their territories on trees in addition to keeping the claws sharp and clean.

The leopard's body size varies across its subspecies. This is probably related to climatic conditions and availability of prey. The ecological principle known as Bergmann's Rule states that body size among animals is larger in cold regions than in warm ones, and that races of warm-blooded vertebrates from cooler climates tend to be larger than races of the same species from warmer climates. Hence, though the Amur leopard's weight is similar to other leopard subspecies, the Amur leopard looks larger due to the thick fur it has to adapt to cold weather. While the fur of leopards in the tropics is thinner due to climatic conditions, they reach up to 90 kgs of weight. The largest leopards are recorded from the east and southern African woodlands. But their body mass is highly variable. The average body mass in Western Cape of South Africa is only about 31 kgs in males and 21 kgs in females, while the average weight of leopards from other areas is estimated to be 34 kgs in females and 54 kgs in males. The heaviest leopard I weighed in India was a male of 61 kgs. Leopards can reach heights of nearly a metre at the front shoulder, where their height is usually measured. The length of their body seems to be lesser in subspecies that range in the desert and semi-desert areas of central Asia and the Arabian Peninsula.

Leopards display sexual dimorphism. Sexual dimorphism is a condition where the two sexes of the same species exhibit different physical characteristics beyond the difference in their sexual organs. Wild adult males are significantly larger in size compared to their female counterparts, and are estimated to be about 30 to 50 per cent heavier than the females. Dimorphism is also observed in the head width and massive neck and upper shoulder muscles, which are extensively developed in adult males. I once measured a male leopard that charted 65 cms around its neck and had a head breadth of 32 cms. Most human adult male neck sizes range between 38–45 cms.

There is a noticeable throat dewlap, a hanging skin fold, in males by the time they reach the age of five. Sub-adults, animals that are independent of their parents but are not sexually mature, develop a secondary neck fold. These physical features are perhaps the prime weapons that help males in defending themselves during intraspecific combat.

The long tail of the leopard, which can reach nearly a metre in adult males, helps it stay balanced, especially while chasing or dragging prey on to trees. The total body length (from nose tip to tail tip) can reach over two metres, bigger than any average adult male human. There may not be much difference in the total body length of adult male and female leopards.

Leopards have a digitigrade foot structure—they stand and walk on their fingers or toes—with the forefeet having five toes and the hind feet having four. The first toe called as the dew claw is set on the inside of the foot, above the wrist, and is only used when bringing down prey.

The pugmarks of large cats, left when the animal walks on a soft surface, evoke a sense of excitement to anyone interested in wildlife. It feels wonderful to be hot on a trail, to tread where a leopard has trodden recently. An adult leopard has a paw width of 10–12 cms. The paw size can vary according to the age and health of the animal. Of course, the pugmarks they leave on the mud vary depending upon the condition of the soil: wet, hard or semi-solid. So, the gender or age of the animal can never be ascertained using a pugmark as indirect evidence. I once measured the pugmark of a leopard that had walked on both hard soil and wet substrate on the same path, and the size of the pugmark varied by 30 per cent. If you rested a baseball cap on it, the print would barely get covered, so large was the size.

## *Black panthers*

Like humans, there are some variants in the colour of leopards. The melanistic leopard, colloquially known as the black panther, is a normal leopard with black fur. Its rosettes are visible only under oblique light.

Melanism is the opposite of albinism. It occurs in individual animals due to a gene that causes a surplus of pigment in the skin or hair, making it appear black, so the animal's colouration is darker compared to the colouration in a normal individual of the same species. Melanism occurs in at least fourteen of the thirty-eight species of wild cats, and is not exclusive to leopards.

Black panthers are not a subspecies as often erroneously assumed. In older scientific literature by the Swedish zoologist Carl Linnaeus, who formalised binomial nomenclature, they even had a separate scientific name, *Felis nigra,* while the normal-coloured leopard was called the *Felis pardus* until the British zoologist Reginald Innes Pocock revised the system in 1917.

Mankind has been acquainted with black leopards for a while now, as a vast cultural legacy proves. It is believed that due to their rarity, they would have been high status, valued creatures in ancient Egypt. Archeologists have found a statue of Tutankhamun, an Egyptian pharaoh who died very young, standing atop a black leopard in the king's tomb. This is supposed to symbolise the king's triumph over death. There is also Bagheera of Rudyard Kipling's famed 1894 *Jungle Book.* The dark coat and greenish eyes of the black panther are the perfect colour combination, and are a sight to behold.

Black panthers are not a human artefact like the present day's white tiger, which does not exist in the wild anymore—white tigers are bred artificially in zoos for display. But a tiger with a pale skin color was spotted in July 2017 in the Nilgiris by a wildlife photographer arousing interest among the conservation community. However, it is yet to be ascertained if it is a true genetic mutant.

Melanistic leopards commonly occur in tropical southern Asian populations, especially in Malaysia, southern Thailand and Java. In Indonesia, indigenous names for the black leopards, 'harimau kumbang' and 'macan kombang', are separate from those for normally coloured leopards, 'harimau bintang' and 'macan tutul'. In the dense forests of Malaysia, rates of melanistic leopards climb to 50 per cent of the total leopard population. Initially, it was thought that melanistic leopards were found more in dense forests, as the colour provided additional camouflage against the shade of closed-canopy forests. But with their frequent occurrence in open forests that theory doesn't seem to hold good anymore. They have now been increasingly recorded in many parts of India, especially from the dry forests in the south. The famed Kabini tourism zone of the Nagarahole Tiger Reserve has become the black leopard-watching capital of the world. Photography aficionados come down from all over the world for their 'black-leopard moment'. A high number of black leopards have also been reported in camera trap studies of the forest department in Kali Tiger Reserve in northern Karnataka.

A coffee planter on the southern edge of Nagarahole Tiger Reserve has a trophy of a black leopard that was shot in 1970 for killing livestock. The carcass was immediately sent to the Van Ingen's of Mysuru, famous for curating wildlife trophies. The trophy is now slowly turning brown, possibly due to ageing. I have noticed the same happening with a black leopard trophy kept in the museum of the Kolhapur Maharaja's palace in Kolhapur, Maharashtra.

At present, black leopards have been documented in Karnataka, Tamil Nadu, Kerala, Goa, Maharashtra, Madhya Pradesh, Orissa, Chattisgarh, West Bengal, Assam and Arunachal Pradesh in India.

In Africa, melanistic leopards have been reported in and around Kenya for decades, but scientific confirmation of their existence remains quite rare. In 2018, researchers captured video evidence of black leopards from the Loisaba Conservancy in the Laikipia County of central Kenya: a young female black leopard was captured on camera traps with her normally coloured mother. The previous confirmed sighting from Africa was in 2007 from the

Ol Ari Nyiro Conservancy, located quite close to the 2018 spot. A photograph from 1909, taken near Addis Ababa, Ethiopia, is stored in the collections of the National Museum of Natural History in Washington, DC, providing evidence of previous sightings of the black leopard from Africa. There are also a few unconfirmed sightings of black leopards from the Mpumalanga and Gauteng provinces of South Africa. Overall, it is estimated that 11 per cent of all the leopards found in the world are black variants.

But there is another variant of the leopard coat that's similarly exciting.

## Strawberry leopards

In early November 2014, I was in South Africa for a meeting to exchange ideas with individuals working on leopards across the globe. While returning from the meeting, my van made a quick stop at a gas station in a small, beautiful village called Ohrigstad, in the Limpopo province. The hillocks around the village were all perfect leopard habitat. They looked very similar to what I would see in parts of Karnataka, Tamil Nadu and Andhra Pradesh.

To stretch myself and get the numbness out of my legs, I strolled into a small curio shop called the Fingerprint of Africa. Beautiful, handcrafted wooden furniture made out of weathered logs was neatly arranged throughout the shop. As I ambled across, the life-sized form of a leopard, mounted on a thick wooden base, caught my attention. It was one of the best taxidermist trophies I have ever seen. Even more interestingly, the colour looked a bit surprising. The animal didn't have a regular tawny coat but a pinkish one, and the spots were reddish-brown compared to the regular black spots. 'An odd colouration,' I thought. Something rang bells in my head. I suddenly remembered reading about 'strawberry leopards'. A male leopard that had a rare strawberry-coloured coat had been photographed by a safari guide in Madikwe Game Reserve here in South Africa in early 2012. The safari guide had the pictures sent to Luke Hunter, a leopard expert, to check about the odd colouration. Luke had suggested that 'the pale leopard had erythrism, a little-understood genetic condition that's thought to cause either an overproduction of red pigments or an underproduction of dark pigments.'

To my luck, Luke himself was present in the meeting and was also travelling back with my group. I quickly ran back to the gas station and got hold of him to check on the mounted specimen. Luke confirmed that it was, in fact, the same strawberry leopard. The shopkeeper told us that it was a trophy-hunted animal from a nearby area. The animal had been found over 550 kms to the east of Madikwe Game Reserve, where it was first reported in 2012. Pink Panther really exists!

In August 2019 another strawberry leopard appeared in the Limpopo province in Thabo Tholo Wilderness Reserve. Local wildlife lodge owners, Alan Watson and his wife, Lynsey, had set up a camera trap at the spot where they'd found a dead giraffe. To their surprise, a strawberry leopard turned up to feast on the giraffe carcass. It is said that strawberry leopards have been seen seven times in South Africa since their first documentation in 2012.

Records of such pale-coloured leopards have been documented even in India. Hunting records of five pale-coloured leopards, sandalwood in tone, have been reported from Bihar and Madhya Pradesh in central India. Interestingly, these records have emerged in areas that overlap with locations that have recorded white tigers and a white cheetah in the past. In January 2019, Sudhir, a Mysuru-based legal counsel who's very passionate about wildlife conservation, forwarded me two pictures that turned out to be of a strawberry leopard. The pictures, presumably from the coastal district of Udupi in Karnataka, were of a female leopard that had died after getting entangled in a spiky fence. However, forest authorities could not confirm if the images were from their area, so I am not sure of the existence of the strawberry leopard in India in recent times.

## *How do leopards use their space and communicate?*

All wild cats, either group living or solitary, need space of their own, which they use to find food, mate and rest—what is called a territory. Cat territories shape their social organisation, behaviour and, to an extent, their communication.

A leopard's land tenure is quite similar to that of other big, solitary cats like tigers, jaguars and pumas. Males have overlapping territories with several female home ranges. But, interestingly, even males seem to share habitat patches. Our research shows that the home range sizes of leopards living in small forest fragments or in a mosaic of forests and human-dominated landscapes are smaller compared to male leopards that live in areas that have larger natural habitat spaces. This suggests that the species could possibly survive in fairly high densities in smaller forest fragments, though, of course, with costs for both the animal and the people in the area because of livestock lifting.

An adult male leopard that I once collared had a home range of 141 sq kms, nearly the size of the historical city of Mysuru in southern India. No one would have perhaps believed this if it didn't have a radio collar on it. Another young male that lived amidst a human-dominated setting of agricultural fields and villages had a home range of only 10.5 sq kms, nearly fourteen times smaller than the former's. Of course, the former was older, about five to six years of age, while the latter was about two years old.

In India, in most places where leopards occur, their shy nature allows for only very brief observations in the wild, and conceals most parts of their life from scientific voyeurs. Directly finding these animals, especially in smaller forest patches, is very hard. Hence, naturalists and biologists rely on their signs and tracks to document their presence and to make initial assessments for further studies.

The important news of a forest is broadcast all over in tell-tale signs. To a trained naturalist's eye, these signs harbour the whole story. Finding all these, however, demands careful attention: the jungles are a world of sight, sound, smell and taste, but we are largely audio-visual while leopards and many other animals are chemical.

The trick to start 'seeing' these leopard signposts is to think like the animal we are following. How would a leopard squirt on a tree trunk? At what height would it do so? Which tree would it choose to squirt on so that the marks would be guaranteed the best visibility and other leopards would see them?

These signs act as a coded signature for each leopard, and are a way for leopards to advertise their presence and protect their valuable turf against invading animals of their own creed and ward off any potentially violent meetings. For these big cats, signs act as territory markers. These scent markings are designed to minimise fights between individual leopards so they can keep away from each other. It's a social system carefully designed to decrease conflict between males.

Leopards also like to keep in touch with each other, and they leave messages for each other. Like many other large cats, they post messages on rocks, against tree trunks, and bushes by squirting a mixture of urine and scent to announce their presence. This is an olfactory signal that reveals itself to other males or females in the area. At times, these signs announce that a female is in heat (a period when females are receptive to a male's affection). It is almost as if they're leaving a Facebook 'friend request' to announce their readiness to mate. The male who finds the 'request' goes in search of the female to 'accept' the request. They also update these markings regularly. The complex world of large cats works efficiently even without electronic social media. It has to, for it would be very difficult to find a receptive female—anyway in short supply—otherwise.

With tigers, it's easier to find these marks on surfaces, where one can easily see a moist-looking patch at the spot of the squirt. The glandular smell, too, is pungent and strong. But with leopards, this 'calling card' the animal leaves to exhibit its presence, is the hardest to see or smell. Even the pungent smell of urine on tree trunk is very rare, while it's a very common sign used by tigers. When it comes to tigers, we can sometimes see dark grey stains on the tree trunks from repeated squirting on the same spot. Even leopards, dholes and other animals seem to notice these urine marks on trees. In Nagarahole Tiger Reserve I once noticed a pack of dholes going hysterical and repeatedly smelling the spot where a tiger had urinated on a large teak tree (*Tectona grandis*) trunk. Two dholes even tried squirting at the same spot by rearing up on their hind legs like acrobats, as it was not possible for them to reach the height at which the tiger had sprayed. As they repeated the act, it looked almost as though the dholes were trying a side flip. This is perhaps how overwriting was invented.

In another incident, a leopard I had collared in Bandipur Tiger Reserve ran towards a tree when released but immediately halted about three to four feet away from it. He gave a flehmen, also known as a lip curl, a behaviour exhibited when smelling urine. His expression changed instantly, and in the darkness he ran away in the opposite direction of the tree. In the morning, when I returned to the same location to track the leopard's radio collar signals, I curiously checked the tree that had deflected the leopard last night. There was a large stain of tiger urine on the tree trunk that had possibly scared away the leopard. However, the flehmen behaviour in large cats and other species like the rhinos that display this behaviour is used to assess reproductive status through smelling urine.

Leopards also leave faeces and scrape marks on prominent locations as they leisurely patrol their territories. Patrolling their territories is an important component of their lives. Studies reveal that male African leopards expend 26 per cent of their daily caloric intake for territorial patrol activities, which is energetically a costly but a critical behaviour. Many a time I have observed that a small quantity of faeces is also left behind in their scrapes. If one bends down and carefully examines the tell-tale signs of leopards, the pungent smell in the scrape mark can be sniffed.

For me, the specialty of these signs are the footprints. I love footprints as they depict the fresh energy of live animals. They always leave me curious about the owner of the pugmarks. Even the thought that a leopard has been there earlier is fascinating.

One sign of a leopard that I have rarely come across is the long vertical engraving that wild cats make by digging and clawing down vertically on large tree trunks to demonstrate their presence. Some tigers can claw up to three metres high. Though leopards use this as a sign, they are hard to find, even in areas where they have the final word as apex predators.

Finally, the wood sawing-like calls of leopards is another mode through which they use to communicate and exhibit their presence. These calls are a delight to hear.

### How do they interact with other large predators?

In India, leopards continue to survive in areas with tigers, lions, dholes, hyenas and snow leopards. Leopards and tigers mutually avoid each other just for the sake of convenience. Occasionally, tigers have been documented to hunt leopards. In June 2016, footage of a deadly face-off between a tigress and leopard in Sariska Tiger Reserve in Rajasthan was widely circulated in social media.[1]

In another rare natural history observation, in January 2017, in the famed Nagarahole Tiger Reserve, a leopard was captured inadvertently walking alarmingly close to a resting tiger. The leopard, which seemed completely unaware of the larger cousin's presence, even squirted urine on a dead tree to mark its territory! As the lesser cat got closer to the striped cat, the tiger chased it. The video shows the leopard running up a tree and the tiger following it up for nearly twenty-five feet. The tiger failed to catch the leopard, which ended up, distressed, at the top end of the tree at a height of almost forty feet, balancing itself to save its life. In the background of the video, one can hear the guide excitedly explain to the tourists how rare the sequence is and request them to record the event. An immediate request comes from another tourist to share the video over email!

---

1. Tigress kills leopard in Sariska Tiger Reserve, Jaipur, 15 June 2016, https://www.youtube.com/watch?v=bZYXsCm0GmM

Another tourist video from the same area depicts the perilous scenario of this spotted cat and the threats it faces from competing with large predators. The video shows a large male leopard being harassed by a single dhole, its black tail curved up in a display of aggression, while the leopard is peacefully resting on the branch of a teak tree. The spotted cat expresses its displeasure by growling continuously. Taking a chance when the dhole is away for a moment, the cat runs down, only to scamper on to another large tree as the dhole reappears in a fraction of a second to continue its cat and dog game. After a while, another dhole joins the harassment team, and the first dhole even unsuccessfully tries to become a cat and attempts to climb the tree, managing only about a few feet. Meanwhile, the cat shifts to a higher branch on the nandi tree (*Lagerstroemia lanceolata*). When the dholes take a few seconds to move away from the tree, the leopard grabs the chance and frantically climbs down the tree and escapes into the bushes. The excited dholes run into the bushes, chasing the big cat. Audible in the backdrop is a Hanuman langur, continuously alerting the other forest dwellers about the presence of carnivores through its iconic guttural alarm call.[2]

On both occasions, the leopard's survival tactic was to climb a tree. This ability to climb trees, made possible due to its strong shoulder bones, makes the leopard an evolutionary success story amidst other competing large carnivores. Cats have the ability to survive free falls by acquiring angular momentum that helps them to land on their feet.

I am not sure how leopards in India respond to striped hyenas and snow leopards wherever they co-exist with the two, as there are no direct observations. However, one unprecedented event in Gir National Park in Gujarat, the only Asiatic lion habitat in the world, stunned wildcat enthusiasts. A lioness was seen caring for a leopard cub that was possibly six weeks old. The lioness also had

---

2. Kabini: Leopard vs Wild Dogs Standoff, 19 November 2010, https://www.youtube.com/watch?v=JKs5BPShLI4

two of her own three-month-old cubs. The lion cubs, twice the size of their spotted cousin, were seen suckling and playing along with the leopard cub.[3] Cross-species nursing from a wild cat, or other wildlife for that matter, is extremely unique. On the contrary, there are several amateur wildlife film footage on social media of lions sneaking and attacking leopards in the African bush. They are known to be mortal enemies.

Many scientific studies show that leopards mutually co-exist with their larger cousins by following three basic traits. They separate themselves spatially, avoiding areas where tigers or lions are more active. As a second survival tactic, leopards modify their activity patterns by being active at times when their larger cousins are inactive. Their last and most important strategy is to apportion and specialise on predation. Leopards adapt and favour smaller prey when prey species of different sizes are abundant. In areas where large- (gaur, nilgai, banteng) and medium-sized prey (sambar, chital, barking deer and others) are abundant, tigers will take the large prey, and the leopard will be satisfied with medium-sized game.

A study from Bandipur Tiger Reserve in southern India showed that gaur weighing nearly a tonne and sambar provided 73 per cent of the biomass consumed by the striped cat, while 65 per cent of the intake of the spotted cat consisted of chital and wild pig. In the neighbouring Mudumalai Tiger Reserve, where gaur numbers were lower on the à la carte compared to Bandipur, tigers took sambar as their ideal choice, with 56 per cent of their diet consisting of this large deer weighing nearly 270 kg. The leopard preferred to ambush the relatively smaller chital, with 67 per cent of the biomass consumed by it consisting of this graceful 80 kg deer.

It is generally understood that tigers, being larger, keep leopard numbers in check. I have also carried out work to understand if tiger numbers affect leopard populations. I needed a landscape

---

3. World's rare nature's phenomena in Gir forest | A mother lioness rearing leopard cub with her own!, 3 January 2019, https://www.youtube.com/watch?v=Rf9pYiII2mw

understanding of the populations of these two big cats to do so, and found that the BRT–Bannerghatta protected area complex, which consisted of Biligirirangaswamy Temple (BRT) Tiger Reserve, Malai Mahadeshwara Hills (MM Hills) and Cauvery Wildlife Sanctuaries and Bannerghatta National Park, was the idea area to test this. All of these protected areas are interconnected. Though Satyamangalam Tiger Reserve and Cauvery North Wildlife Sanctuary, as well a few other reserved forests in Tamil Nadu, are a part of this vast landscape, I decided to stick within the state of Karnataka due to lack of resources and the complicatedness of availing permission from the neighbouring state. The planned work was spread over 2,800 sq kms.

In November 2017, my team and I began a long saga of camera trapping that finally ended in March 2019 after sixteen months of continuous, backbreaking fieldwork. The sweep started in the enchanting BRT Tiger Reserve, a wildlife patch that's very unique and perhaps found nowhere else in Karnataka. When we completed this marathon exercise we had a nice spectrum of tiger and leopard numbers. In this landscape, BRT had the highest number of tigers. There were fifty tigers, with their spotted cousins numbering fifty-eight individuals. As we went west towards MM Hills, the tiger numbers plummeted to ten and the leopard numbers rose to seventy-one. Cauvery Wildlife Sanctuary, similar in size to MM Hills, had only four tigers but the spotted cat numbers were a staggering ninety-eight. Bannerghatta National Park, which is to the north of Cauvery, documented just one tiger but had forty leopards in an area that was one-fourth the size of Cauvery.

This gave a clear indication that the tiger had an impact on the leopard numbers. It is perhaps nature's way of keeping a balance in the ecosystem. If tiger numbers go up in MM Hills and Cauvery in the future, it would be wonderful to test if leopard numbers go down.

## What's on the leopards' menu?

Crows are the chatterboxes of the jungles. Once, on a drive near the backwaters of the famed Kabini reservoir on the southern part of Nagarahole Tiger Reserve, I heard a commotion of crows at a distance of about fifty metres. A group of crows causing commotion in the forests is music to our ears. It indicates something is happening, possibly a kill. Crows somehow get to know the presence of the carcass, and spread the news far and wide.

That day, I knew that in all probability the carcass would be of a prey killed by a large carnivore. Out of habit, I pressed my binoculars to my eyes and looked around at the trees. A tree fork in the distance became clearer and something stuck in it caught my eye. It was a chital carcass, its head and legs dangling down the fork on both sides of the crocodile bark tree (*Terminilia elliptica*). It was clear that a leopard had stashed its prized kill in a safe place about fifteen metres above the ground and would come back later to finish it. Leopards have powerful jaws and strong neck muscles that are a perfect combination for catching big prey but also for carrying prey up on tree branches. I decided to wait. Bahar Dutt, an environmental TV journalist, had come down to do a few stories on the Western Ghats and was accompanying me.

The jungles are usually far from silent. I liked this complete stillness in the forests. After nearly twenty minutes of calm and stillness, there was a commotion. All at once, the trees were alive with sound. *Caw, Caw, Caw.* The crows shrieked urgently. Bonnet macaques shouted *leopard, leopard* in their typical harsh *kirrr, kirrr, kirrr* call. Coughing and chattering, they darted around from branch to branch creating a cacophony and arousing other members of the group with their alarm. The tranquil jungle turned into a nerve centre of activity.

As I glued my eyes to the tree, I saw a spotted silhouette jump up the trunk. When the spotted cat reached the fork, it picked up the chital carcass and tried to balance it in its mouth, almost dropping it in the process. The leopard carefully moved the carcass in its mouth to ensure that the weight was well balanced and it was able to carry the weight of the half-eaten carcass. When the carcass felt safe in its mouth, the animal looked straight at us, as though saying, 'I know what I am doing.' Such eye-to-eye contact is rare, and the feeling is indescribable. Once the cat was convinced that we were no threat to it, it jumped down vertically, holding the carcass firmly in its mouth. In a fraction of a second it was gone. It had melted into the forests. For some reason, the leopard had become uncomfortable keeping the carcass up there. Perhaps the crows had informed too many, so it had decided to shift its treasure to another secret location. Bahar was one lucky woman. The same night we sighted another leopard along the highway in the neighbouring Bandipur Tiger Reserve.

Leopards stalk and kill their prey the same way a tiger would. They rely on seeing and not being seen, on acute hearing and smell. Leopards depend on these attributes because they are not pack animals that hunt cooperatively and expend energy in turns by chasing and wearing down the prey, like the wolf or the dhole. They can reach speeds of 60 kms per hour only in short bursts. They are not long-distance athletes but ambush predators. Hence, surprise is their main weapon. Their soft pads mute the sound of their movement to their advantage. As a solitary cat, they hunt by stalking and do not run down their prey as other cats like cheetahs or lion prides do.

To catch and bring down their prey, they need enormous power. They have to make the best use of their limited energy by expending it all at once on speed. After silently stalking their prey, they sprint out from cover like a train out of a tunnel and grab at the unsuspecting animal. Once the prey is in their grip, they strangle it by biting into its throat. They hold on until the animal is suffocated to death. When they get hold of their prey, their front paws convert from running pads to grappling hooks. The suffocating bite is generally applied on the underside of the throat or, on rare occasions, over the mouth and nostrils. For large carnivores such as lions, tigers, and leopards a dorsal neck bite is risky, as sometimes they kill prey much larger than their own size.

Since to hunt prey successfully, leopards have to get as close as possible to them, the survival of large carnivores like leopards always depends upon their constant efforts to outdo their prey. They are good climbers, and they patiently wait on tree branches to jump on any prey that inauspiciously happen to walk under the tree. For this, they minimise their body scent by licking and cleaning their fur regularly. Due to their keen hearing and excellent eyesight, they can see even under dim light, and are successful nighttime hunters.

Leopards haul their kills on trees in order to eat them without being harried by other predators like tigers, lions, hyenas or dholes. This phenomenon is called kleptoparasitism in biological jargon. It is a form of feeding in which one animal takes the prey or food that another has caught or stashed. This is a trick that has passed down generations—they do this exactly like their ancestral cousins, the hominin-eating leopards, did. These cousins preyed upon the *Australopithecus robustus*, a relative of modern-day humans who lived in South Africa and became a regular victim of several cat species. A leopard's prey can weigh three times its own weight, but its strong canines and powerful shoulders help it carry the meat up trees, a move that involves a climb almost perpendicular to the ground.

In the absence of large trees, leopards may prefer caves and rock crevices to hide themselves and their kills. Rock crevices also provide a cool place for them to rest during the day and provide a safe space to give birth and raise cubs. This is where the granite rocky outcrops in the Deccan Plateau, Satpuras, Vindhyas and the Aravalli ranges in northern India play such an important role in leopard conservation. The boreal forests in which the Amur leopard survives also provide the Amur leopards with the rocky ridges that are ideal denning sites for both adults and their cubs.

Leopards eat the meat of their victims from the rump or at the underbelly, but also cut the meat from the rib cage and even try eating the digestive tract. They disembowel the prey and eat parts of the viscera and the rib cage. This is very evident when we find livestock that a leopard has killed.

While a tiger normally eats from the rump and moves upwards of the victim's carcass, leopards devour almost everything. Bones, hooves, head, horns and antlers are the only parts of the carcass that the leopard may not eat because they know from experience that there's nothing to eat there.

Being a large, full-time carnivore entails the animal with high protein and fat but also carries its own set of risks. High failures of hunts, chances of being injured during the regular business of hunting, injuries caused even by small animals such as porcupines at times could be fatal. Many leopards die due to injuries caused by porcupines depicting the risk the animal goes through while accessing its food.

In this entire process of hunting and feeding, the teeth become an important tool for large carnivores. They are always a good way to determine the durability of mammalian evolutionary lines, including leopards. Large carnivores, in fact most modern mammals, are hetrodont, that is, 'different toothed': different teeth have different functions. A complex toolbox of a tactically arranged set of teeth of different shapes and sizes are found in leopards to perform dissimilar tasks. They are the carnivore's Swiss-army knife alternatives. The long, sharp canines help in catching, gripping, strangulating and tearing their prey. The scissor-like movement created by their carnassial teeth allows for efficient shearing, slicing and cutting of flesh, tendon and muscle. The premolars behind the carnassial teeth help in the crushing of bones. All these teeth together make leopards, perfect killing machines.

Unfortunately, if that all-important tool wears out with age or breaks due to other reasons, the functionality of the individual starts dipping. Unlike some other large carnivores such as the great white shark or the Komodo dragon, they do not get replacements when their old teeth are lost.

Leopards have a catholic diet, with different studies recording their prey as constituting 110 mammalian species that weigh more than a kilogram. If other vertebrates such as birds, herptiles (reptiles and amphibians), arthropods and fish are included, the spread exceeds two hundred species. In my research, I have leopards captured on camera traps carrying everything from gerbils to deer and poultry chicken to dog puppies. When available, they catch large deer, antelope, wild pig, the young ones of gaur or buffalo and even giraffes in Africa, a testament of their formidable strength. That's the à la carte spread of their menu. When they live in areas with abundant wild prey, 40 to 90 per cent of their diet consists of locally abundant large wild meat on hooves. Only in the Srepok Wildlife Sanctuary in Eastern Cambodia are they known to mostly feed on large prey—the banteng, which weighs more than 500 kilograms. The banteng is an endangered large wild cattle, currently found in small patches in six South-east Asian countries. It was once also found in northeast India, but has now gone extinct from the country. I have had the rare opportunity of a seeing a small herd of these bovines in Baluran National Park in east Java. They were chocolate-brown, with a strange white rump, and also possessed white stockings like that of a gaur.

Though the leopard will catch whatever is easiest and nothing seems to be safe from it, a two-kilogram black-naped hare, a jungle fowl or a gerbil provide a snack at most for these meat-eaters. The small 150g mouthful of gerbil wouldn't be much of a reward for all the effort it would have invested in catching it. Even an adult female leopard weighs as much as 35–45 kgs, and would require more than this appetiser. However, the leopard's variable body mass may enable it to exist on invertebrates or small prey species for short periods if large vertebrate prey are absent.

Though they may regularly feed on animals with lower body weight, leopards need high energy input per individual and so they also need large-sized animals for their survival. They cannot subsist on food sources below a certain body size alone, because it becomes impossible to catch a very large number of very small-sized animals in a short period of time to meet their dietary requirements. It's the simple principle of all wild animals—getting the maximum fuel for the least amount of energy. Hence, the popular theory that the leopard can sustain itself on small prey requires a lot more data.

Consequently, when adult leopards survive in human-dominated areas with little large wild prey available, they inevitably turn to livestock for their energy requirements and subsistence. No wonder they co-exist uneasily with farmers, shepherds and their livestock.

## How do we know what they eat?

Scats are like presents on a Christmas morning, and need to be opened carefully. The faecal matter of a leopard provides a mine of information about what it has eaten. Each deposit is a record of the animal's diet and a glimpse into the complex food web of the natural world. What goes in passes through within a day or two. Many of the inorganic components (hair, bones, hide, hooves and seeds of plants) in the faecal matter provide clues to leopard diets, allowing biologists to examine a lump of scat the way Sherlock Holmes would examine a clue. Learning what leopards have ingested has all the makings of an ecological detective story. Believe me, there is a mine of literature on turd biology, and people have made careers out of it.

Biologists collect these messy substances in the field and process them in their laboratories to understand the feeding ecology of leopards. But it needs trained eyes to uncover the secrets of these biological treasures. Scientists have even used specially trained German shepherd dogs to sniff out the scats of leopards in Russia, where the Amur leopard is very rare, so its faecal matter provides all the information.

## Reproduction and care of the young

Leopards are known to survive in the wild for fourteen (males) to nineteen years (females) and up to twenty-three years in captivity. During this period, an important duty this solitary cat needs to perform is to ensure that its genes are passed forward.

Like most cats, the leopard is often referred to as solitary except when a female has its cubs or when mating. However, they may be a bit more social than assumed. Though there is very little evidence for this, occasionally, males may tolerate familiar females and cubs they have sired.

In our camera trap work, which spanned over nine years, we got a total of 7,658 leopard pictures, and only on 84 (less than 1.1 per cent) occasions did we find two or more adult leopards walking together. On all occasions, they were a male and female, and in all likelihood, they were mating pairs. On 97 occasions, we got a mother walking with one to three small or grown up cubs. Often, the mother may avoid taking young ones on her hunting forays, which makes cubs less visible.

But one instance in Narasimhadevarabetta, about 50 kms north of Bengaluru city, surprised me. On a July 2019 morning, three leopards appeared in front of the cameras. They lazily strolled, checking the electronic equipment and marking their home ranges. From the images it was clear that one was a very large male, perhaps aged about six. There was an adult female, who was possibly three years old. The third leopard was also, in all possibility, an adult male. Older literature and field observations show that more than one adult male leopard can pursue a female in oestrus (heat), but they maintain a distance. But, astonishingly, in this case they were all hanging around together. Possibly both the males pursued the female, but tolerated each other. Nature has secrets and surprises at every corner.

## Sex strategies in the spotted world

As in some human cultures, both ancient and modern, female multiple mating appears to be common among large wild cats and has been documented in at least four species so far: tigers, lions, pumas and cheetahs.

On 10 April 2016, when summer temperatures hovered over 32° C even at night, MML-23, a young, graceful leopardess, aged about four years, walked past our camera traps set along the banks of the river Paalar. The river Paalar acts as the southern boundary of the MM Hills Wildlife Sanctuary, and is also the interstate boundary between Karnataka and the neighbouring state of Tamil Nadu. This area is one of my favourite locations, as the river flows through the valley and the hillocks on both sides are steep and offer gorgeous views. The seasonal Paalar flows through this narrow twenty-kilometre-long uninhabited valley before it merges into the larger, perennial Cauvery. During the summer, the still pools of water in the Paalar act as a magnet for all kinds of wildlife. Along the riverbank, the valley offers a small stretch of a flat area to which herbivores such as chital, sambar and wild pig are all attracted to graze and browse. This makes the valley a prime locale for large carnivores. It was a happy moment to see MML-23 again. She had been photo captured about 1.5 kms away from the current location about fifteen months earlier.

Within a minute, MML-20, a young, sturdy male of about five years crossed the same camera trap. It looked as though MML-20 was in hot pursuit of MML-23. It was again a happy coincidence, as MML-20 had been photo captured earlier in January 2015 but about 9 kms away from the current location. He lorded over an area of at least 56 sq kms, almost the size of 7,843 football fields. So we had a mating pair of leopards. But the story only started here.

Within five days, on 15 April, it looked like MML-20 had switched sides. He was now seen on a boulder-ridden trail with MML-18, a leopardess of similar age as his. To be with his new lady love, MML-20 had climbed up steep hillocks, into the valley and again up a hillock 9 kms away from where he was courting MML-23. My suspicion was proven right as the very next day, on 16 April, both MML-20 and MML-18 were captured together in another camera trap about 3 kms east from the previous night. But the saga continued.

Within five days, on the morning of 21 April, it was the turn of MML-18 to switch loyalty. She reappeared in our camera traps about 7 kms west of the location where she was previously captured with MML-20. Interestingly, she had a new boyfriend—MML-71, a slightly younger male of about four years of age. The same night, the lovers were caught again a couple of kilometres away on the ridge of the same hill where they were photographed that morning. The mating pair had spent the whole day together and continued their love walk.

To sum up, MML-20, a male, had possibly mated with two different females within five days; similarly, MML-18, the female had switched two boyfriends within a similar period. It looks like leopards do have complex sex and family lives. They are both polygamous (males having multiple female mates at the same time) and polyandrous (females having multiple male mates at one time). During the short period when the female leopards are receptive to males, they mate with different individuals.

Male wild cats kill young ones sired by other males. So it looks like females resort to multiple mating as a pre-emptive deterrent to avoid infanticide. This strategy may even be a way to avoid sexual harassment by multiple males, as seen with cheetahs. Polyandry may also result in multiple-sired litters, increasing genetic diversity, thereby increasing fitness in the offspring.

Leopards, then, may be following 'convenience polyandry'. So it does not appear, as popularly believed, that the females invariably prefer the victorious males. It looks like in leopards, female sexual behaviour occurs even in non-conceptive forms. These extra pairings for copulations have been demonstrated to be actively sought by leopard females as a sexual strategy suggestive of confused paternity among males. This female strategy has significant benefits on the very structure of wildcat society. Our data seems to be the first time that polyandry has been observed in leopards.

Of course, felids aren't the only class of animals where female dalliance strategy is common. It is observed in birds, arthropods, sharks, canids, reptiles and many others. The primate literature about polyandry and the potential strategies employed by our hominin ancestors is even more dramatic. Before I noticed polyandry in leopards, leopard sex was pretty dull stuff. When they did it, it seemed the act was quick, out of sight, and they usually kept to themselves. Now it looked like it was creative.

Leopards breed year-round and give birth after a gestation period of twelve to fifteen weeks. Female leopards probably breed when they are about three to four years old, though both sexes mature at two to two and half years. The litter mostly has one to three cubs, and very rarely, four cubs. In most instances, either through direct sightings, or in our camera traps, or reports of leopard cubs found in agricultural fields, I have noticed that it's generally two cubs.

A female leopard can be highly productive in her lifetime. A simple back-of-the-envelope estimate can explain a few facts. If we assume that a female leopard survives to the average age of six–eight years, and has an inter-birth interval of two years (considering that the young ones will wean from the mother at one and a half years), an adult female may contribute young ones three to four times in her life span. If an average of two cubs survive to adulthood, she will contribute at least six to eight new individuals to the population in her life span.

Cubs under the age of one year can be classified as juveniles, aged one to two years as sub-adults, and over two as adults. When they are one year old, their bones are strong enough for them to follow their mother around. Sub-adults are as big as an adult, but not completely independent and are not sexually active. They even have a childlike innocence on their faces.

The cubs weigh about half a kilogram at birth. They are born with their steel-grey eyes shut, and need to be nursed, often restricting the movement of the mother. As the cubs grow, their eyes become amber and look like honey. They continue to be under their mother's care for one to one and half years before they leave her security, venture out to establish their own homes and face a life in the forests alone. On some occasions we have had a fully-grown cub walking alongside the mother; it was probably the mother leopard's only offspring, brought up with care and love.

Mothers keep a vigilant watch on all the activities of their cubs. Their maternal instincts are on an overdrive when they have cubs. Cubs go through various levels of training from their mothers—from basic to intermediate to advanced course through theory, demonstration and practice, on the various topics a leopard would need to survive his or her own life. Only when they graduate successfully with high grades are they ready to move away from their mother. But, unfortunately, it is difficult even for a highly experienced mother to teach the many cunning ways humans destroy leopard habitat, hunt their prey and even poach the leopards themselves. Rapid and constantly changing, this isn't the sort of thing that their mother can teach them. More difficult is the fact that they have no skills to fight back.

There can be high levels of mortality in cubs before they reach adulthood. Records from South Africa show 50 to 62 per cent of cubs dying in the first year. If the cubs pass through the most vulnerable stage of their lives, which is zero to sixteen months, at which their natural mortality tends to be higher due to infanticide and other reasons, their chance of survival is higher. Infanticide is a common phenomenon in large cats: disease, starvation and competitors such as lions, tigers, dholes and hyenas all excluding young ones could all be taking a toll on the leopards. In India, since unnatural deaths of adult leopards due to road accidents and snares is increasing, starvation due to loss of the mother could also be an important reason for the mortality of cubs. Adult leopards also die of injuries inflicted by porcupines with many instances recorded from both Asia and Africa. We occasionally get pictures of leopards with the quills of porcupine hanging under their mouth or on the chest.

### Where do the cubs go?

My research has come up with very interesting results on the space use and dispersion of leopard young ones. I was once sitting at my office desk, which is not the most enjoyable thing I do, and we were identifying individual leopards from our camera trap pictures from the year 2016. Ashritha, who had joined us as an intern, and then went on to become a full-time colleague, excitedly walked into my room and said, 'Sir, I have found the cubs.'

We had captured three leopard cubs that were less than a year old along with their mother in our camera traps in January 2014. They were captured in the northern part of the Cauvery Wildlife Sanctuary, close to the seasonal stream Kesarakkihalla. We had christened the mother CU-12, depicting that she was from Cauvery and 12 was her unique identity number. It looked as though the cubs, with their mother were on a nocturnal wander. At that time I wondered what would happen to these cubs in the future. Would they survive? Would they see each other again?

Now, in January and February of 2016, all these cubs were back in our camera traps. Surprisingly, the leopard mother had achieved the daunting task of bringing up all the three cubs to maturity all on her own. She must have successfully taught them how to hunt and defend themselves from other large carnivores, including leopards, through a two-year, round-the-clock informal but rigorous education.

The cubs had grown considerably since the first time they were captured two years ago. They had moved far away from their natal home range, far away from their mother's watchful eyes.

The female young one (named CU-74 by us) had moved ten kilometres north-west of her original home, and had become a sleek, agile-looking hunting machine. She had crossed the deep gorges of the Shimsha River, and established a new home towards the north-western boundary of the wildlife sanctuary. I am not particularly sure if she moved to the edge of the protected area because of the higher density of leopards in the core of the forests, where the competition for home ranges is intense.

One male cub (CU-13), now looking big and slightly bulky, had moved south. He had crossed into a narrow arm of the forests, which stretched out into the heart of human habitations about twenty kilometres south. His coat had a mirror-like sheen, depicting him as a healthy individual. Though River Cauvery forms a natural barrier, blocking the dispersal of mammals, the male cub had found a way of crossing this barrier. Perhaps he had jumped over the boulders during the summer when the water is low and the large boulders provide an opportunity to cross the big river. Dispersal is an energy-consuming affair for leopards. Studies have shown that dispersing male leopards are known to expend 52 per cent more energy than their average daily energetic needs.

The third cub (CU-68) had taken the opposite direction to her other female sibling, and headed about 15 kms east of her natal home range. She had now taken shelter near the banks of the River Cauvery. She had established her area of operation in prime leopard habitat—a lot more wild prey such as chital linger along the river.

The dispersal of cubs to distant areas of forests is perhaps an ingenious biological strategy to spread their genes to newer expanses and also to avoid inbreeding. Our findings effectively showed the spacing mechanism employed by these cats if there is sufficient room available.

There is evidence from tigers in India, and leopards in Africa that once the female cubs become independent, their territories continue to overlap their mother's territory. There is a possibility of home range inheritance by female offspring, and females sharing part or full home range could be all related. But these two female cubs were not interested in their parent's real estate. They ventured out far and wide to develop their own properties. As adults, they had found their own place in the leopard world of the Cauvery. I was overjoyed to see all the cubs reaching adulthood. The female had successfully raised all her three cubs to adulthood. Such examples of cubs establishing their homes away from their mother and siblings are many from my field studies.

3

# UNDERSTANDING THE
# SPOTTED CAT

Lots of scientific information about leopards comes from South Africa. Their numbers, behaviour, home ranges and other subjects are extensively studied in this country, where these wild cats are also a tourist attraction. The magnitude of these studies is such that some researchers have even questioned the high levels of radio collaring of leopards that goes on in that country.

Information about leopards in India, on the other hand, has accumulated at a surprisingly slow pace, despite the country housing one of the largest populations of wild leopards in the world—India holds over 77 per cent of the extant range of the leopard subspecies *Panthera pardus fusca*. Andrew Jacobson, an American researcher, found that only 15 per cent of the scientific papers published on leopards in a span of fifteen years (2000–2015) were from India. This lack of knowledge becomes a matter of even more concern when seen in light of the fact that leopards are already extinct in Bangladesh, and though present in Bhutan, China, India, Myanmar, Nepal and Pakistan, they precariously hang on in four of these six countries. With this background and my interest in large cats, it was only natural that leopards occupied a spot on my shortlist when it was time to settle on my main research topic.

## Counting the rosettes—selfie-taking leopards

How big is a tiger's home range? How many tigers are there? These questions are easily answered when it comes to tigers. But replace 'tigers' with 'leopards' and the answers become scanty. Most often, we draw parallels with the tiger and give answers on the basis of what works for the striped cat. This lack of answers is what inspired my research on the spotted cat. It is important to study leopards because they symbolise the conservation challenges that are associated with a species that's spread beyond the safer boundaries of protected areas.

Thus began my peregrinations to understand a seemingly simple question: how many leopards live in different areas? Other than understanding the leopard population in different areas, I wanted to know how and where their numbers were distributed. Were leopards found more in forests and other natural habitats, or in human modified habitats such as agricultural landscapes? What were their numbers? What natural factors caused their numbers to vary? Did human activities affect leopard numbers and their distribution? If yes, what kind of activities caused the variation in numbers?

I also wanted to understand the issue of human-leopard conflict. Where does conflict occur? How do the authorities respond to conflict situations? What happens to leopards that are captured in conflict situations? Could I follow some of the leopards that are translocated by the authorities in response to human-leopard conflict?

The state of Karnataka has a good reputation for preserving its wildlife. It also hosts a variety of leopard habitats—evergreen, semi-evergreen, dry and moist deciduous forests, scrub jungles, rocky outcrops and man-made forests such as plantations. I knew I could expect a good leopard population here. Importantly, this is the state I knew the best and was closest to my heart.

And so, in 2011, I embarked on a quest to better understand the leopard in my home state of Karnataka in southern India, a pursuit that I continue till date. I have worked across a variety of leopard habitats, studying them in protected areas such as national parks, wildlife sanctuaries, tiger reserves and conservation reserves, as well as outside protected areas. The study has also taken me to interesting agricultural landscapes, some of which have had leopards. It has given me and my team the opportunity to explore new areas, unearth species that were not known to be present in the state, meet new people and have new experiences.

I began by attempting to understand leopard populations. To do so, my team and I relied on the age-old technique of placing automatic camera traps in the big cat's habitats—a process called camera trapping. This technique was first developed by the British forest officer F.W. Champion to photograph evasive mammals in the foothills of the Indian Himalayas. Camera trapping begins with identifying suitable locations to place the cameras. These locations are mostly on forest roads, and where such roads do not exist, slim trails made and used by wildlife or livestock grazers often provide good spots to place the camera. Our first job is to select locations that we think will fetch us the highest probability of photographing leopards in the camera traps. In such an exercise, leopard signs such as footprints, scrape marks and faecal matter, all provide vital clues in identifying suitable spots. Each location is then numerically coded to relate the location to the camera and the associated pictures.

The process of identifying locations is an intense one, and we treaded hundreds of kilometres in our recce operations on these trails. Many would start like a dirt forest road but then turn into nothing as we found ourselves amongst bushes choked with lantana or ambushed by the deadly Indian redwing, scientifically known as the *Pterolobium hexapetalum*. The recurved, wickedly sharp thorns of the Indian redwing pierced and tore our skin, to agonising pain. Though harmful to us, the pinkish-white, tiny flowers of these bushes are a major source of nectar, and are foraged on by many different species of the honeybee.

Later, we would discover that we had been exploited. When we took off our trousers, socks and shirts, we found we were carrying the seeds of one or the other plant species, attached by long hooks or recurved spines. Plants were trying to use us to distribute their seeds. I am sure they partially succeeded but not to the extent a wild animal would have helped them.

Making our way through these bushes was no less than an adventure; the narrow tracks were often overhung with sparkling cobwebs, filled with various kinds of spiders, and we occasionally disturbed one or two partridges that would fly from their cover, croaking harshly, almost scaring us to shivers. In some parts of our study area, the tracks were littered with elephant dung, both old and fresh, reminding us to be more alert.

Once we selected several such locations in our area of interest, we placed hundreds of weather resistant camera-traps. The name camera 'traps' is misleading—these are simple point-and-shoot cameras automatically triggered by infrared beams that get activated by any animal cutting across the invisible ray. So when a leopard, or any other animal walks past a camera, it will take its own picture. To put it simply, the leopards that appeared in front of our camera traps would be our 'captures', our count of them would be considered 'marking', and as they left the frame they would be 'released'. When any previously 'captured' animal came back in front of any of our camera traps, they were considered 'recaptured'.

As the rosette pattern on each leopard is unique, exactly like fingerprints, the tiny grooves that swirl around our fingertips and our known as dermatoglyphs, individual animals can be identified and counted to estimate their population size using statistical methodologies. Earlier developed for counting fish, this methodology has been used by biologists the world over to identify individuals in many animal groups—from zebras to giraffes and whales to small wild cats. Even to this day, camera trapping for counting animals with natural markings on their bodies continues to be the gold standard for estimating animal numbers in an area.

Though the leopards we capture on camera are a good indication of the minimum number of leopards in an area, are they all the leopards that are present in that area? Obviously not. In the 'mark' and 'recapture' process, not all leopards appear in the camera traps. This can be due to various reasons. The study period (which is called sampling period in biological terminology) might be too short, so some leopards might not get an opportunity to catwalk in front of the camera traps. Hence, it is likely that a few are missed out. This is called an 'observability' problem. Secondly, it isn't possible to place camera traps in every inch of the area being studied at the same time. This is called a 'spatial sampling' problem.

This is where statistical processes help us in calculating the true number of animals that are to be found in an area. After going through the complicated and fastidious process of sorting all the images, identifying when and where the leopards have been captured, and putting the data into a format the computer software understands, we are able to get to a number that is closer to the actual number of leopards in an area. This entire process— meticulous planning, initial recce of an area, disciplined field data collection, sorting, cleaning and curating of data, and finally carrying out the statistical analysis—can take anywhere between a few weeks to a few months depending upon the size of the study area and the number of images obtained from the field exercise.

### What did we find?

Once our traps were in place, we could move on to the daily process of collecting and analysing our data. When the day's data was downloaded and readied on pen drives, we would open each folder as eagerly as if it were a present on a Christmas morning, and sit entranced by the wide variety of animals that had ramp walked in front of the camera traps. This exercise also required a great deal of patience—to get a picture of a wild animal one has to first shuffle through endless boring pictures of livestock, pictures triggered by waving branches or grass blades, pictures of people casually walking past the cameras and hundreds of other such images. It was all worth it for the adrenaline that would suddenly rush up, like the fizz of a soda, when a leopard or some shy, nocturnal animal or a startling image of a common animal appeared. You never know what will turn up in a camera trap!

We got pictures of some rare wildlife behaviour. We found inquisitive creatures inspecting and sometimes trying to eat our cameras. Animals that were generally hard to spot always excited us. At times, we captured interesting images of humans—a small boy saluting the camera as though it was the national flag or a high school kid displaying his karate skills. Some images were not so innocent, and we often spotted poachers walking past our cameras. Several interesting stories have emanated out of such occurrences.

On Christmas day in 2015, in Cauvery Wildlife Sanctuary, at 8.40 p.m., two men in orange reflector vests were photographed carrying two large logs and a large, heavy metallic saw. To me, it was immediately apparent that they were carrying away sandalwood. The colour and texture of the bark, the girth of the log, the time at which these people were photographed, all made it very clear that this was an activity that didn't adhere to the law. We alerted the local forest officer immediately. After a few days the officer called me back and asked, 'What do you think those people were carrying?'

I emphatically said, 'Sir, those were sandalwood logs.'

His response threw me. 'No, no. We've taken a look at the pictures, and we feel they were just taking firewood.' The idea was laughable—someone taking the risk of going to the forests in the middle of the night, that too in an area teeming with wild elephants, just to fetch firewood was a bit farfetched. But different officers have different ways of responding to such situations.

About a year previously, in February 2014, at 11.05 p.m., a man was photographed in one of our camera traps located about ten kilometres away from Veerappan's village, Gopinatham, in Cauvery Wildlife Sanctuary. Veerappan was the legendary handlebar moustache-sporting bandit who had terrorised the area for nearly three decades, poaching elephants and sandalwood, kidnapping the rich and famous for ransom, and killing people. His moustache had become so synonymous with his name that people had expressed disappointment when he was found clean-shaven after being killed in an ambush by policemen in October 2004. His upper 'lipholstery' was so famous that in 2015 the popular cosmetic brand Lush even launched a 'Veerappan Moustache Wax'! This product triggered an online protest petition, demanding that the brand stop glorifying Veerappan.

The poacher captured in our camera trap was carrying a country-made, single-barrel, muzzle-loading gun. The gun looked well maintained, with three shining brass plates wound around the wooden forestock and the long, metallic barrel. A crude arm, but it had the capability of even bringing down a massive elephant. The camera trap couldn't capture the face of the person carrying the gun, but the picture till his neck was clear. The man wore maroon-coloured shorts and a khaki half-sleeved shirt. He was barefooted and had a small, brown cloth bag under his sweat-soaked armpit. From the bag, thin red and blue intertwined wires ran up his chest. They revealed that the small bag had a battery; the wires would be connected to a headlamp, a signature indicator of poachers.

The picture from the opposite camera (we place two cameras to capture both flanks of leopards, as the rosette patterns are different on the different flanks of the animal), which was tied to the bole of an acacia-like oil cake tree (*Albizzia amara*), gave a bit more detail. The man with the gun looked surprised and had turned his head towards the camera trap. The yellow beam from his headlamp fell on the camera trap, giving the picture an angelical glow. The picture from the opposite camera also revealed that he had two companions. One of them wore bright blue shorts and a black shirt and carried a machete in his right hand and a yellow flashlight in his left. The second man wore earthy-coloured clothing and carried a plastic sack in his left hand. Summer arrives early in this landscape, so these men had already shifted to attire suitable to the warmer temperatures. All of them seemed a bit startled by the camera. They would have been able to see the camera trap's small, red LED glow, which indicated that it had completed its work and was recharging itself for the next picture.

We immediately sent the pictures to Vasanth Reddy, a sociable Indian Forest Service officer and the manager of the Cauvery Wildlife Sanctuary at that time. He was in his early thirties but had enthusiasm fit to match a teenager's. He immediately got on to the task. Once Vasanth Reddy got the images from us, he gave Hanumanthappa, a young, plucky ranger, the responsibility to track down the person the cameras had spotted. From their intelligence sources, they soon found out that this person was from the neighbouring state of Tamil Nadu. They had identified him from the large mole he had on his right calf muscle as his face was not visible in the camera trap picture. He worked as an informant to the forest department in that state and regularly switched his role to that of a poacher in Karnataka.

A few days later, the man carrying the gun was apprehended. To everyone's surprise, he was identified as Ganesha—a notorious poacher and a sharp shooter from the area. Some even spoke of him as a mini Veerappan for his notoriety and his ability to kill elephants. It is an irony that he is named after the elephant god Ganesha.

Hanumanthappa tracked Ganesha down to where he was attending a marriage in Hanur, a small town not very far from where he was caught in the camera trap, but the accused got suspicious and escaped from the marriage hall. Ganesha returned after four days to his in-laws at Martalli, a large village nestled within the MM Hills Wildlife Sanctuary, from where he was arrested. During his interrogation Ganesha confirmed that on the night he was captured in our cameras, carrying the gun, he didn't hunt as the camera's flashlights had scared him and he had returned home. The camera traps had luckily averted the killing of some wildlife.

However, Ganesha was a prize catch as several other important poaching cases were unearthed due to his arrest.

We caught many other evidences of poaching on the camera traps. We spotted people carrying away wild animals—sometimes dead, sometimes alive. On several occasions, pye-dog dashed in front of our camera traps, chasing frantic sambar or chital deer, and people walked by with spears, most likely on the hunt for large herbivores. People walked by with hunting dogs; the men who carried dead hare or monitor lizards would have most likely poached them using snares or hunting dogs.

A picture that's forever crystallised in my mind is the gory scene of a female sambar walking past the camera trap with a long wire snare wrapped tightly across her head. The tightened metal noose had cut into her, and the wound had left a startling red gash. Fortunately, the snare had stopped at the base of her ears and had not slipped onto her neck—that would have instantly killed the animal. One end of the metal wire, which looked like the thick wire used in chain link mesh, hung long; it must have been tied to a weak tree or a bush that the animal had escaped from by pulling the wire free. Certainly, it was a painful ornament to walk around with. The sambar might have survived the noose, but it would be a long agonising process till the wound was infected with maggots and finally killed the otherwise healthy-looking animal. Similarly, in different areas, we found elephants, leopards, sloth bears, dholes and other wildlife walking around with snares caught around their necks.

All this data did not come cheaply. Camera traps were not a welcome tool for poachers, sandalwood smugglers, and those who harvested timber illegally. We lost several of these expensive electronic devices as people stole them, slicing the cables that were used to tether the cameras to the trees with machetes or merely smashing the entire contraption using large boulders.

At times, people just took the camera away as curios. In December 2014, as the year was coming to an end, we were shocked to see six camera traps missing from a road that led to Doddane village in the MM Hills Wildlife Sanctuary. Doddane is tucked away on a peak 1,088 metres above sea level. The gravel road leading to it, which is a steep, difficult climb even for a four-wheel drive, is hardly used, except by people walking to and from the village. The area has a nice growth of axelwood, the smooth, white-barked, highly fire-resistant tree. Obviously, our first suspicion was that someone from the village had taken away the black electronic boxes. But they would be of little use to anyone other than researchers or forest staff. The pictures had to be downloaded from the cameras using a jump drive and even then, they were password protected, so no one could see any of the images unless they were software hackers. I highly doubted that Doddane, which lacked basic drinking water facilities, had any such software geeks. We decided to immediately replace all six cameras but also placed an additional camera, stashing it away from view by piling a few rocks before it so that they camouflaged the hidden 'spy camera'. Now we were sure that if the culprit came back in search of more booty, the spy camera would reveal him.

We also inquired around without much positive result. The nearest police outpost was over 25 kms away, and no policeman would ever come to this remote place in search of a few cameras, worthless from his perspective. In addition, the entire exercise would take the policeman a full day. Even if the police took our written complaint, I had little hope that they would actually register the complaint in their official records, as they would then become accountable to show progress in the case.

We took the help of Deepak, who was the forester for the area. He was a good friend of our work, and had a decent rapport with the locals. Deepak enquired around through his network and zeroed in on a man from Doddane village.

The cameras were found tucked away in an attic, wrapped in plastic. When we brought the cameras back to our field station, they revealed interesting images. First, the man, who was in his early thirties and lanky, with a beard and long hair, had curiously checked the functioning of the cameras a few times and at a few locations.

A few days later a man with a light grey- and blue-checkered shirt and a checkered green lungi was captured in the camera traps, breaking the cables with a rock. Something seemed familiar about him, yet something was also different about this man compared to the one who was photographed three days earlier. Then it struck me. It was the same fellow. His clothes were the same but he had shaved off his beard and neatly trimmed his hair. Perhaps he had changed his appearance so that he would not be recognised as the same person who had walked in front of the cameras earlier!

The curio carriers were always not two-legged. At times, the four-legged ones were just as interested in using our equipment as takeaways, perhaps souvenirs to adorn their jungle houses. One large tusker was even caught being a habitual shoplifter. This amazing beast was at least nine feet tall at his shoulder and had liquid oozing out of his temporal glands, indicating that he was in musth—a tusker in his prime, perhaps aged somewhere between twenty-five to thirty years. In the pitch dark of a January night, he was photographed quietly carrying away a camera trap. He had carried and destroyed two cameras on the same night and smashed another two cameras to pieces. The same tusker had been photographed about a month earlier, too, over 15 kms away from this location, carrying away camera traps. At that time there had been no liquid oozing out of his temporal glands. Perhaps his musth phase hadn't begun.

Very interestingly, precisely thirty-five days later, a similar-looking tusker was photographed pulling down a camera trap and smashing it into pieces. The camera opposite had captured the tusker's rage against the innocuous electronic device. The tusker had first pulled the camera down from the wooden pole it was fastened to, and tried to break it, as the poor camera nestled underneath some green leaves. The leaves seem to protect the camera from the tusker's rage. So the pachyderm decided to go a step further.

Bringing the camera under its enormous front foot, it ground it like a massive pounder trying to smash a black peppercorn. When the camera slipped from under its rough sole, it placed the camera on a small rock and continued its onslaught till it got bored of the electronic device. But before the giant left, he made a final statement by pulling down even the small wooden pole to which the camera was tethered to.

For nearly nine minutes and twenty seconds, the tusker mercilessly bashed the camera. For reasons unknown, it did not show any interest in the opposite camera, which recorded his deed, taking seventy-two pictures of his act. All we found the next day were pieces of electronic chips and a bit of plastic. Our field team stitched all the images together to make an amazing video of the tusker going after the poor camera, a scene worthy of being in a Bollywood movie.

In another incident at the BRT Tiger Reserve, a tusker, possibly aged about twenty-five years, attempted to dislodge the camera from the *Chloroxylon swetenia*, commonly called the East Indian satinwood tree, to which it was fastened. The vinyl coating on the strong, braided steel cables was slippery, so the mammoth was unable to get a grip on the camera, which repeatedly slipped around the tree. With not much patience, the elephant, an individual with large holes in the right ear possibly caused by gunshots and lumps on its right leg again conceivably caused by pellet shots, simply brought down the small, approximately twelve-foot-tall tree, and with it the camera, and walked away, as though he wanted to make a statement.

In the heart of the MM Hills Wildlife Sanctuary, near Kalmatturdoddi, too, a young tusker, possibly aged about fifteen years, came inspecting one of our camera traps. While most pachyderms boldly came in front of the cameras, this naughty youngster came from behind the tree, standing about five feet away from it to stretch his trunk around the tree to 'quietly' check the camera. After sniffing the camera, he did not, for some reason, find the little device interesting and spared it.

Elephants exhibited curious behaviour when they noticed these strange objects in their homes. On occasion, small herds of these giant pachyderms circled around the puny cameras for several minutes, as though in discussion. On one instance, such a meeting lasted for over an hour. The females would gently touch the cameras and then withdraw their trunk for unknown reasons. In between the discussions, small snaky trunks poked through big legs to have a first 'hand' understanding of the strange object in front of them. At the end of the discussion, an adult female gently broke the cable with the trunk or the feet and removed the camera tied to the tree trunk. On most occasions, these herds decided to be merciful of the strange object and leave it on the ground. Once, even a captive camp elephant took away a camera in Bannerghatta National Park. Between 2014 and 2020 we had 204 instances where elephants showed curiosity towards our camera traps. Thirty-five camera traps have been destroyed by these pachyderms, costing us over half a million Indian rupees.

In Kukwadi-Ubrani and other adjoining forests in central Karnataka, where we were trapping in 2013, the culprits were completely different. Sloth bears—shaggy-coated creatures, with long curved claws that they use to excavate termites and ants—showed an inordinate inquisitiveness towards our cameras. They would often come inspecting the cameras, either solitary or in pairs, and bring down the devices. Fortunately, they wouldn't carry away their trophy. This strange behaviour of the bears didn't repeat in other areas, though they would come inspecting.

Besides wildlife, we also encountered images of the hardships people faced living in remote parts of forests. A picture that moved me was that of an old man being carried by two men in a makeshift cloth swing tied to a long wooden pole. Maybe the man was too unwell to walk and, hence, they had to make the tiring journey to reach the nearest medical help on the swing. This is unfortunately the scenario in many remote hamlets in the forests of the country.

## Local delicacies

Our camera-trapping work took us to several parts of the state, and we ate at a variety of local eateries. These were not fancy outlets but small places that more often than not had no menu cards; the menu here existed only in the hoteliers' minds. Yet, some of these eateries served us excellent food with lots of love. My favourite was the tiled, slope-roofed Veerabhadreshwara Bhavana in Halagur. Halagur, a large village along the main road connecting Bengaluru and Kollegal town, is quite close to the border of the Cauvery Wildlife Sanctuary and thus we got the opportunity to visit the eatery very often. It specialised in masala dosa, a south Indian breakfast dish with a history dating back to the sixth century.

One had to almost bend down three-fourths to go through the main door of the eatery. The door opened to a small hall crammed with things. A small, rustic, blue refrigerator, old newspapers, vessels and various other items were stacked in every possible corner. In between these were seven black, granite-top tables balanced on blocks of bricks and benches made of a similar material, all arranged in a U shape. The parrot-green walls of the eatery were decorated with photographs of Shiva, Ganesha and various other gods. More prominently displayed were the framed pictures of famous Kannada film stars, including that of Shiva Raajkumar, popularly known as 'Hattrick Hero'. Two other film stars, whom I couldn't recognise, adorned the wall, next to him. Suresh, the owner's young son, was the common factor in all the pictures, grinning widely at his good fortune at being photographed in his own eatery with celebrities. I am sure these images helped indirectly market his dosas.

Just at the entrance stood a large saucer-like open steel pan filled three-fourths with water on a table top. Small dollops of white butter that looked like a small compact mass of cotton floated in the water. Suresh's father, the owner, a spry, white-haired man, always draped in a lungi, mostly a patterned light blue, stood at the till right at the entrance of the hotel and shouted orders at the top of his voice into the kitchen, where Suresh made dosas on a hot, thick, cast-iron plate. Suresh said it took the better part of an hour to heat up the dosa plate before the dosa batter could be put to use. Slim in build, he mostly wore a white sleeveless vest that helped him keep cool in the hot, sweaty kitchen. A golden bracelet loosely dangled off his right hand, and showed that their handiwork with the dosas had paid off reasonably well.

Those golden-brown dosas, slightly smaller than the size of a palm, made for the most delectable of meals. Hot and crispy, they were served neatly folded in half with steamed spicy potato, onions, green chillies and spices filled in the middle. As the waiter served each customer a plate with four small masala dosas, he would utter one word—'Benne?' The Kannada word for butter. I do not remember a single time when I have answered no to that question. In a flash of a second he would fish out a dollop of butter from the steel pan and skilfully throw it on the topmost dosa in my plate, like a professional Frisbee player. Though the dosas were already loaded with enough oil to light up a hundred temple oil lamps for two days, the extra butter added to the taste. One had to let go of calorie consciousness at Veerabhadreshwara Bhavana.

A steel cup filled with slightly reddish chutney made of red chillies, coconut, gram and other ingredients was left on every table so that customers could liberally use the thick coconut chutney with the dosas they ate. Bright red plastic jugs, slightly dirtied with constant handling, filled with water would come to your rescue if the chutney was too hot to handle. Finally, a small square piece of week-old newspaper would be handed in place of a tissue, as it is in most small eateries across Karnataka.

Every time we passed through Halagur we planned to reach in time for breakfast. Harish, my laconic, sad-eyed colleague, especially liked the dosas and at times even overtook me with the number he shovelled down. The eatery always teemed with customers, many waiting around the occupied tables. If you ordered masala dosa, when the eatery was especially busy, the waiter would curtly respond that you should eat the 'set dosa'. These were another variety of dosa, not as crisp as masala dosa but soft and spongy with no potato filling and served in sets of three. If you still insisted on masala dosa, another sharp response would come: 'You will have to wait for twenty minutes.' It was only if you were made of tougher material and you stood rock solid with your decision that you would finally get your masala dosa.

Even our familiarity with the staff would only sporadically weaken this rigour. It was finally the event of me being bitten by a leopard, one which I shall discuss at length later, that brought me new privileges at the eatery. Suresh thought I had done something extraordinary, and thereafter ensured that we were never refused masala dosa. As soon as we entered the eatery the message would be relayed to Suresh and, even without ordering, in ten to fifteen minutes, piping hot dosas would arrive. Getting bitten by a leopard also has its advantages.

In the afternoons the eatery served rice and spinach leaf curry, and as we moved in for the kill, the waiter would generously pour ghee with curry leaves roasted in it. Before thoughts of cholesterol, obesity, cardiac arrest or artery blockage could enter, the thick liquid would be on the rice and one would have no choice but to gulp down the heavenly tasting, delightful lunch.

Suresh's grandfather Shivanna had started Veerabhadreshwara Bhavana sixty years ago. One day in August 2016 when I landed at Halagur on my way to the forests, the main road of the village looked devastated. Portions of most buildings along the road had been torn down. An old south Karnataka-style, tiled-roof villa that had a wood-columned portico, and which I had always admired, was razed down. It was a ghastly sight, and I was quick to realise that the road was being widened.

After one entered the village limits, it took less than a minute to get to Veerabhadreshwara Bhavana. As I reached the place, it was gone. All that was left of the eatery was the small kitchen, and the large metal plate on which Suresh poured the dosa batter lay there by itself. I inquired with a few people but got no convincing responses. Someone said the owners continued to serve dosa on a pushcart near the bus stand. I dashed there but could see no one who remotely looked like Suresh or his father. We tried to search for Suresh on several subsequent trips through Halagur but failed to locate him. Phone calls to him never yielded any response. Some marketed a few other places where I could eat my breakfast and said that they were as good as Veerabhadreshwara Bhavana, but for some reason, I refused to be convinced. I was finally able to reconnect with Suresh after six months and was relieved to learn that they would restart the eatery at a different location in a few weeks. The eatery was reopened after several months, but for some reason it didn't have the old flavour and taste to its dosas. Infrastructure projects, though important for development, have many direct and indirect impacts on various aspects of the society. Like the dosas of Veerabhadreshwara Bhavana, many of them slip by, unnoticed.

The village eateries also provided us the opportunity to understand people who came in there with no distinct agenda. Sometimes it seemed that they sat around endlessly, arguing about the latest political changes, discussing the market price of agricultural produce, smoking beedis, reading the free newspaper if the eatery had subscribed to it and if there was bus connectivity that would bring in the daily news from the world. Sitting there, a sample of the entire village would unfold in front of us. It was also a place where curiosity was generated about our work as a group. Rumours would soon spread that we were installing closed-circuit cameras, CCTVs, to catch people who went to forests to hunt, bring timber illegally and to monitor other forest-related offences. This was not the kind of publicity we needed, as some would steal our cameras, fearing being caught on it. But we also found friends in such locations, who were very helpful in finding us local guides and eateries, or explaining interesting local traditions to us.

### How many leopards?

Our research work has given me new insights into leopard population biology. It has helped reshape several old myths into new truths. But I am not sure if this animal can be reasonably understood in a lifetime.

Kukwadi-Ubrani in central Karnataka is a contiguous patch of 370 sq kms (about 91,500 acres), about the size of the island nation Saint Vincent in the Caribbean. With dry deciduous and scrub forests it is prime leopard habitat, and is where we first attempted our camera trapping work to understand how many leopards were there. Apart from getting leopards in camera traps it revealed other facets of Kukwadi-Ubrani.

Kukwadi-Ubrani was like the Wild West. The forests were pillaged by poachers and timber smugglers. But I was amazed by my own conclusions. Leopard densities were shockingly high in the area. Through our work, we estimated the area had forty-five individuals—a density of over eleven leopards per hundred sq kms. This is one of the highest densities of leopards anywhere in the world.

What started years ago when we first tried to understand the population of leopards in Kukwadi-Ubrani area has led to so much more. After the work at Kukwadi-Ubrani, we designed a new, scientifically robust research to select other areas in the state where we could study and understand leopard numbers. Thus began a long journey across the state of Karnataka. We worked in leopard habitats that varied in sizes from small patches as small as 3 sq kms (800 acres) to over 1,000 sq kms (over a quarter of a million acres). We walked in the sun, drove on rough forest roads, crossed rivers, carried heavy bags of camera traps over hillocks, enjoyed the cool streams, made new friends, all as part of the wonderful work of counting leopards.

We used primitively designed Mahindra jeeps that dropped us off at one location and picked us up as we walked on to another part of the forest or hill, marking locations for camera traps or setting up camera traps or downloading data from the traps. The jeeps were quite hardy but guzzled tyres like anything. Almost every 20,000 kms, we had to shell out a good chunk of cash for a new set of tires. The unpaved, boulder-strewn forest roads ate up tyres much as a pride of hungry lions would finish off a zebra. As these were not the popular protected areas, the forest roads were sparse and poorly maintained. Combined with the uneven terrain, the boulder-strewn roads tested the sturdiest of suspensions. We set up a kind of base camp in remote forest camps, using a rest house or forest quarter as a home and command centre for two-three weeks before we shifted base to another part of the forest or to a new area.

A couple of us acted as advance parties, recceing an area, identifying suitable locations for setting up our leopard counting machines, dealing with the officials, establishing contacts with local forest staff, scouting suitable accommodation facilities and completing other logistics. Then, we set up the cameras traps before moving on to other areas.

Each study site took us anywhere between twenty days to five months to complete the fieldwork. Once the field exercise is over, data curation and analysis would take a similar amount of time. Then, amidst the tens and hundreds of pictures of leopards, sorted by countless hours of labour and nested within a hierarchy of numbers, we compared our current data with that of previous years. This gave us a lot of valuable information, including information on which leopards had continued to survive and where the cubs had moved.

One by one, in a span of nine years we had completed work at twenty-four areas, each of them with their own ecology and leopard stories. The labour-intensive nature of counting leopards is arduous. But the effort was all worth it. All the walking, climbing, crawling and work in the office yielded some solid results.

Over the past nine years (2012-20) in Karnataka, our camera traps have captured 7,658 images of leopards from which we have identified 601 individuals. Though an estimate of leopard numbers was released in 2020 by the government, approximating 13,000

leopards in the country, no state could specifically list the number
of leopards in their state, and no reliable estimates of numbers
existed. There are hundreds and hundreds of square kilometres
of leopard habitat across the country. We will never know if the
leopard population has increased or decreased, due to the lack of
research, as we don't have a benchmark. Though no one will ever
be able to do a scientifically decent study over the entire area in
the country, our work has made a small dent in this gap. From
our study results and extrapolating the data from sampled areas, I
estimate that my home state of Karnataka might be host to about
2,500 leopards. This is an educated guess, one we have been able to
arrive at only after carrying out rigorous surveys for nearly a decade
across 4,500 sq kms. Even so, this study area perhaps represents
about 20 per cent of the state's possible leopard habitat. Based on
my work in Karnataka and the availability of leopard habitat across
the country, I would estimate that leopards in India number over
20,000 individuals.

Our study showed us that the numbers of the tawny-coated cat
did not vary based on the size of the natural habitat available. If
the Cauvery Wildlife Sanctuary, which is as big as 1,027 sq kms,
had about ninety leopards, Chamundi Hills abutting the historical
city of Mysuru had only five of these cats with an area of 8 sq
kms. Devarayanadurga, a boulder strewn hilly area with an area
of nearly 70 sq kms, an area slightly larger than Manhattan, had
thirteen leopards with a density of seventeen leopards per hundred
sq kms. Though Devarayanadurga was less than 7 per cent the
size of Cauvery, it had nearly 15 per cent of Cauvery's leopard
population. So the size of the area and leopard numbers were not
linearly related. If an area was larger, it did not automatically mean
more number of leopards.

The more I looked, the more I was enthralled by nature's
strange ways. So many leopards in some of the smaller areas!
Though leopards are found even in small forest patches, they lead
a life in the shadows, with hardly anyone aware of their presence.
Occasionally, when they pick up livestock, their existence is seen
in a negative light. This is inevitable—when leopards survive in

higher numbers in smaller patches, they survive due to the cost borne by people of a lower economic strata whose livelihood depends upon livestock.

The logical end point of our work was that leopards were not out there like the sky offers the stars—in millions in every corner of the sky. They had preferences where they were better-off ecologically and socially. After our extensive work at various sites, I even started to ponder on some of the popular scientific theories about leopards that say they survive 'happily' even in areas that have very high human populations.

Though camera-trapping gave us a good grasp of how many leopards were found in an area, it didn't help us much to understand the factors that shaped the leopard numbers in an area. We still had to find out why leopards survived in higher or lower numbers in some areas. What drove their existence? All this led to a new research area—understanding leopard distribution and the reasons behind it.

### Can we count the black leopard?

Some leopard researchers in South-East Asia faced a unique problem. In a few areas they found high proportions of black leopards in their camera traps. The way the rosettes are visible poses challenges to researchers wanting to count black leopards. Researchers in the north-eastern state of Terengganu in peninsular Malaysia had to face this unique leopard problem. Almost all the leopards in the area they worked are melanistic individuals. It is also possible that this is the only place on earth where an entire population of a wildlife species is almost completely composed of a melanistic form. Hence when they camera-trapped for leopards, the individuals appeared completely black in the pictures hiding their rosettes. This made it impossible for the researchers to estimate the black leopard population.

Challenged with this unique problem they came out with a simple but novel way of counting these ghosts of the jungles by adjusting the settings in their infrared camera traps. They forced the camera into night mode and allowed the researchers to consistently and clearly see the spots of a melanistic leopard. The rosettes would be seen when the light fell obliquely on its fur. This helped them to clearly see the rosettes, and ultimately count these leopards like they could do with normal leopards.

### Where were the leopards found?

We jotted down every leopard sign—pug marks, faecal matter, scrape marks, and similar traces of its prey and domestic livestock— we encountered as we doggedly trudged along under the scorching sun. We also noted any signs of poaching, mining, quarrying, or any other factors that threatened the survival of leopards. It was the start of our leopard occupancy survey.

Occupancy survey is a widely used method in ecological science to understand where an animal is present and where it isn't. The methodology is used on a wide variety of species, from frogs to birds to elephants, and uses the signs they leave to understand where they are found.

Where were leopards found and where were they not? If they were found, in what percentage of the study area (let's say a district or a few districts) did they occur? This methodology did not allow for calculating how many leopards were found in an area, like the camera traps, but using it, we could deduce what proportion of the area was used by leopards and then make inferences regarding the possible causes that drove higher or lower usage rates. It was a landscape view of leopards, their prey, and the threats they faced. To put it in lay terms, it was like conducting a market survey, say to understand the distribution of a specific type of restaurant in a city or in a state—what were the reasons such types of restaurants were higher in a particular city or within an area of a city?

Once we had such baseline information, we could go back to the same study area after a few years, repeat the surveys and check if the leopards now occupied more or less part of the study area. If it had increased or decreased, what were the possible causes? To continue with our earlier example of restaurants: we could study if a restaurant of a particular type had increased or decreased in a city. For instance, if there was an increase of south Indian restaurants in north Indian cities, we would need to find out the reason for the increase. Perhaps more people from north India now travel to the south and find the food delectable, so entrepreneurs have set up more south Indian restaurants in north Indian cities or other similar reasons.

It was the research Grand Prix of our work on leopards. No one else had tried this with leopards at such a geographical scale anywhere in the world. It took us nearly a year to complete the field component of this study, as we covered an area of 23,902 sq kms in southern Karnataka. All put together, it was over half the size of Denmark. Or to compare it to an Indian example: it was larger than Sikkim, Goa, Andaman and Nicobar, Delhi, Dadra and Nagar Haveli, Daman and Diu, Puducherry, Chandigarh and Lakshadweep, eight states and union territories put together.

Splitting up into teams of two, we would walk a minimum of ten kilometres every day. Volunteers from different professional backgrounds came from across the country to participate and help in the occupancy surveys, and for many who walked this vast geographical area, it was a learning experience. The study area had a mixture of forests, rocky outcrops, plantations and agricultural fields. We energetically bounced through the cool evergreen forests, deciduous forests and high-altitude grasslands. We footslogged through scrubland, where the bushes and trees didn't look like they crossed the height of Shaquille O'Neal, the famous American basketball player. We jumped from boulders and climbed rocky outcrops, crawled through thorny bushes and waded through swamps. Some of us encountered elephant, gaur, deer, antelopes and other large mammals, we enjoyed the birds, some saw large pythons coiled under the cool boulders, and a team even saw a leopard picking up a goat and running away as a livestock herder watched in despair.

During the course of the survey, we encountered forty-three kinds of crops being grown. There were various kinds of millets, pulses, lentils, groundnut, maize, paddy, cotton, jasmine, marigold, and numerous other kinds of flowers, vineyards, coconut, banana, sugarcane, mango, guava, sapota, papaya, pomegranate, jackfruit, areca nut, eucalyptus plantations, betel leaf farms, various kinds of vegetables, mulberry, tobacco, sweet potato, castor, lime, black pepper, and even coffee in this dry landscape. To some, it must have felt like an exposure trip to the state's agricultural practices.

By the end of the study, we had walked 2,768 kms, the distance from Bengaluru in southern India to Manali, the famed hill-station in the Himalayas. Many people who had met for the first time during the survey became close buddies and friends for life. Some even got married after meeting each other during this survey!

As we walked, some threats to leopards were very obvious. Our study area had a human population of 8.7 million. India, emerging from decades of socialism and underdevelopment, had changed its strategy to a free-market economy, optimistic in its growing fortunes. The countryside around Bengaluru, India's technology capital, had made way to an urban sprawl of gated communities, golf courses and housing layouts. This made our survey work extremely difficult around Bengaluru. Very often, we would hit huge walls of concrete that we had to manoeuvre around to continue our walks. I reckon that agriculturists had sold part of their land to housing developers and in the little land left with them they practised profitable irrigated agriculture such as wine grapes, floriculture, and vegetables. What were once large unbroken, landscapes of agricultural fields were now smaller pieces of real estate properties. The remaining farmland was dotted with yellow one-foot stones, denoting individual housing plots. It was India's gold rush, and in many areas, it had turned the countryside into second homes, a landscape dotted with villas. This was the scenario within a 40–50 km radius from Bengaluru city. As we moved beyond this development radius, normalcy would return, and agricultural landscapes were continuous, though they belonged to different landowners. There were no eight-foot compounds, no fences, no security guards, and no one questioned us when we entered their property. Rather, everyone evinced a keen interest in what we were doing. None of us experienced any hostility in rural areas; the fresh farm produce farmers often offered us were a welcome treat during those long walks. We always carried oranges and buttermilk to give us strength under the harsh sun.

We also methodically interviewed people to understand human-leopard conflict. Though the majority were farmers, we encountered people practising about twenty-five different kinds of occupations. Livestock herders formed the second-highest preferred occupation in addition to daily-wage earners, homemakers, poultry farmers, fisherfolk, blacksmiths, forest guards, minor forest produce collectors, those who worked in granite quarries, small-time shopkeepers, and many others. There were even elephant mahouts but no IT professionals, doctors, wildlife conservationists, artists, HR professionals, or animation experts. The only marketing personnel we met was a lone insurance agent.

Almost every farmer complained about wild pigs. Interestingly, in many areas, people complained about the peafowl, our national bird. Known for its beauty and symbolism, this bird would not be seen as a problem by most urban citizens. But farmers see it very differently, as a bird that creates problems for their livelihoods.

After nearly two years of data curation and analysis, our results showed some very interesting patterns. The occupancy survey results showed that leopards inhabited about 10,278 kms or 43 per cent of the total 23,902 sq kms we had surveyed.

Though leopards were found in a large area, their rate of occurrence was dependent on the availability of natural habitats like forests and rocky outcrops and the presence of large meaty prey such as the chital, sambar and the four-horned antelope. Within natural leopard habitats, we found leopard signs everywhere, but these signs started decreasing outside natural habitats and in human-dominated landscapes. This supported the idea that increasing the leopard population and promoting peaceful co-existence with people relies upon reducing the poaching of its prey and protecting its natural habitat.

It is likely that the occurrence of leopards in areas that are devoid of natural habitats is a fallout of their natural habitats disappearing and the species subsequently adapting to more sub-optimal habitats such as sugarcane plantations and maize fields and to a diet of livestock. Sugarcane is a crop that was introduced pretty recently when compared to the evolutionary time scales of forests and rocky outcrops. Though the first sugar mill was set up in India in the seventeenth century, sugarcane production took on industrial proportions only in the 1950s. Today, in India, over five million hectares of land is under sugarcane cultivation. Though leopards, through their evolving knowledge, have adapted to sugarcane fields, an interesting fact is that many of the areas where leopards have taken to sugarcane fields also have natural habitats such as forests and rocky outcrops peppered at the fields' borders. We would need areas where there are no natural habitats but only sugarcane fields to examine if leopards can survive in such habitats without conflict with humans. Even if they survive, I am not sure how long this would be sustainable, as the increased losses to people in the form of livestock will surely lead to high levels of intolerance, conflict and greater likelihood of local extinction.

At the core of what's been learned is one fact: natural habitats are extremely important for leopards. The theory that leopards can survive well in some man-made habitats such as sugarcane fields is true but it is not universal, and more dissection is required. Moreover, habitats such as sugarcane and maize fields are dynamic ones, that is, they are harvested on a rotational basis by farmers, and the entire country is not under such cultivation. Nevertheless, a conceptual fence has been built and it has become common practice to assume that leopards don't need natural habitats. Much like the emperor's new suit, this is nothing but empty air.

Humans adapt to changing situations. Some species take the responsibility to change and accept or adapt. Leopards are champions of extremes. They are resilient due to their flexibility and adaptability to various habitats, and there is hope due to this. But their co-existence in human-dominated areas presents a delicate balancing situation. Not everyone will tolerate these animals in their backyards.

# 4

# THE LEOPARD'S NEIGHBOURS

In many of the forests that were outside the protected areas where leopards survived, except for the occasional four-horned antelope or wild pig, we saw almost no large mammals during our forays. But in the nocturnal solitude, a world that didn't seem to exist opened up; the ghostly elusiveness of the animals prevented any of us from seeing them in the flesh, but our camera traps revealed fantastic photos—at times, even stunning near-postcard images—of leopards and other wildlife.

Camera trapping is an excellent tool to study secretive animals in their natural habitats, and over the course of our work, we got to see the hidden lives of many other animals apart from leopards. The images we downloaded from the camera traps yielded many surprises: a mother pangolin carrying her young on her long, scaly tail; a striped hyena running away with its dinner—a pet dog it had freshly killed—in its jaws; a pair of mating sloth bears and many more rare incidences. We also captured species rarely detected by human observers.

## *The sickle-nailed small carnivore: The honey badger*

One of our Eureka moments was when the honey badger, as elusive as final truth, appeared in our camera traps in Cauvery Wildlife Sanctuary. At that moment, I felt like I had won a mini biological lottery.

We recorded the honey badger for the first time in Karnataka in January 2014, and the camera traps unveiled many other facets of the species that astonished us. This aggressive species is active both during the day and the night in southern Africa, from where a lot of the studies about it emerge, but it seemed to be highly nocturnal in Karnataka. Only on two occasions, of the 392 times we captured it in our camera traps, did we get a daytime picture of the honey badger in our study areas. After our first recording of the species in Cauvery Wildlife Sanctuary, it revealed itself in the adjoining MM Hills Wildlife Sanctuary. We also recorded the honey badger in Bannerghatta National Park, and the Tamil Nadu forest department recorded it in Satyamangalam Tiger Reserve, where parts of the habitat are analogous. But, surprisingly, we never recorded it in the BRT Tiger Reserve, which abuts MM Hills, despite some parts of BRT and MM Hills having similar habitats. The animal's absence in BRT continues to puzzle me.

At times, we captured two honey badgers in the same frame. Though I am inclined to think they were a mating pair, literature suggests that they could even be mother and a male pup, as male pups outgrow their mother in size but stay with her. On one occasion, in the Hanur area of the Cauvery Wildlife Sanctuary, we got a shot of three honey badgers walking together. It looked as though it was a mother with her two pups. A very rare phenomenon, indeed, in the area in which we work.

The general public and the conservation community in Karnataka were very excited about the discovery of honey badgers in Cauvery. The forest department took the finding as a pride and even made the honey badger the logo of Cauvery Wildlife Sanctuary. No one had seen the honey badgers in the area, not even hunters, until a police constable saw a pair of these elusive mammals in the MM Hills Wildlife Sanctuary during the COVID-19 lockdown period in April 2020.

## The dainty antelope: Chinkara

My home district of Tumkur is a dry landscape with rocky outcrops, grasslands, scrub and dry deciduous forests. The woodland savannah forests found here are an endangered ecosystem with very few patches left. In Karnataka, they are spread out in Bellary, Davanagere, Tumkur, Ramanagara, Chitradurga, Bagalkote and a few other districts. These forests are dominated by dryland tree species such as Indian blackwood (*Hardwickia binata*), axelwood (*Anogeissus latifolia*), Dyer's oleander (*Wrightia tinctoria*), Indian redwood (*Soymida febrifuga*), Indian mulberry, as well as other species that can withstand low water availability and minimal soil fertility.

It had always been a dream of mine to carry out camera trapping in Tumkur. In the summer of 2015, this dream was realised, as we landed up in Bukkapatna Reserved Forest, a large, contiguous woodland savannah forest patch of nearly 200 sq kms, in Tumkur district. I had worked in this area in the mid-1990s on a community-based conservation project, but hadn't worked here from a wildlife conservation perspective.

As we started our initial recce work for camera trapping, we stayed at the British era forest bungalow in Bellara village, adjoining the forests. The old bungalow had remained the same since it was built in 1911. Its original triangular roof was intact, covered with the famous red Mangalore tiles made out of laterite clay, manufactured by German missionaries. The building stood elevated above ground level, at nearly two metres high, on a solid granite foundation. Large glass windows dominated the facade, and there was a separate kitchen constructed about fifty metres away from the main building. Most old forest bungalows are built in this fashion, possibly for the privacy for the British sahibs.

After the recce, we identified a hundred locations, where camera traps were placed. If jackals, blackbucks, four-horned antelopes and mongooses scurried in front of the cameras during the day, leopards, striped hyenas, sloth bears, rusty-spotted cats, civets, porcupines and many other species appeared in front of the cameras in the darkness of the night. We received a pleasant surprise on the very second day of our camera trapping. The goat-like, dainty antelope called the chinkara appeared in our camera traps. This went down as a new record and extended the limits of its distributional range. In India, Bukkapatna now became the southernmost limit where this antelope was found.

The Indian gazelle, or chinkara, as it is also known, is a beige-coloured antelope that leaps and likes open forests with grasslands. It survives in arid areas, and is one of the eighty-eight extant antelope species of the world, a group of animals that are widely hunted for meat across borders. The sandy brown colour and the white belly of the animal is perfectly in tune with its parched environment. This barrel-bodied antelope has ringed horns and a skull that has characteristics typical of a goat. The males have eye glands and pedal glands that they use to mark their area, like many other carnivores and antelopes.

The chinkara's pencil-thin legs are well-designed for bounding and leaping. The legs might look slender, even for an animal that barely exceeds 23 kgs, but they are made to absorb the shock of the impact of landing on the hard ground of dry areas. This black cocky-tailed antelope is also delicately structured so that it can flee fast when the need arises.

These swift animals are very patchily distributed in India, and their worldwide distribution includes Iran, Nepal and Pakistan. They have possibly become extinct in Afghanistan in the recent past. India is the chinkara's current stronghold.

I was overjoyed to find this small quadruped in my home district of Tumkur, which had not recorded any in the past. Except for Beelgi in northern Karnataka and the famed herpetologist Romulus Whittaker's confession to having hunted one near Thalamalai plateau in Tamil Nadu in the 1960s, there were no records of this animal in this part of the world. Now, it had been documented over 350 kms south of its current distributional range. The most unlikely places still harbour something, and I sometimes feel like a nineteenth-century biologist when I find something not previously documented in our state.

With my exhilaration came concern. The woodland savannah of Bukkapatna is one of the last remaining patches of this unique combination of light forests with grasslands. It is also one of the last remaining large, contiguous patches of forests in the drier zones of India. Even so, at the time, protected areas in the drier zones of Karnataka covered only 1,255 sq kms and formed only 11.8 per cent of the geographic area of the protected areas. Additionally, the mean size of a protected area in the drier zones of Karnataka was also small (66 sq kms). Enhancing the protected area spread in such drier zones would help bring better representation of these habitats under the protected area network.

The dry woodland savannah forests of Bukkapatna support an unusually diverse assemblage of antelopes not seen in many areas of the state or perhaps even in the country. Antelopes are a group of ruminant animals belonging to the family Bovidae, and both sexes possess hollow, unbranched horns that are permanently attached to the animal. Peninsular India is host to four species of antelopes: the blackbuck, the four-horned antelope or chousingha, the Indian gazelle or chinkara and the bluebull or the nilgai. Of these, except for the bluebull, the other three species of antelopes are found in Bukkapatna, a rare phenomenon at least for southern India. Apart from the antelopes, these forests are home to the striped hyena, which has a global population of less than 10,000 adult individuals, the world's smallest wild felid, the rusty-spotted cat, leopards, sloth bear and other lesser-known wildlife species.

When we started our survey in Bukkapatna, I was shocked at the number of poaching evidences we found in the forests. I found snares—nooses, traps, coils of wire—laid on most forest roads and trails. The poaching of wildlife was rampant. Not only did it look like the chinkara were threatened by the lust for sport but the hilltops had been taken over by windmills to generate electricity so that even during the peak of summer, the strong breezes there could keep the windmills turning. These forests and antelopes certainly needed better protection.

But my larger worry was the drilling rigs I noticed being operated inside the savannah forests during our camera trapping. Bukkapatna has historically had gold reserves. In the early 1900s, V.S. Sambasiva Iyer, an officer in the Mysore Geological Department and, later, R.H. Morris, the Scotsman who started coffee plantations in B.R. Hills, prospected for gold in Bukkapatna. A government-run gold company had, in the past, excavated the yellow metal in these forests, but had abandoned the enterprise due to financial non-viability. Though gold mining was started, it ceased to operate in 1905 as the content of gold in the ores was low. Gold mining was restarted in 1995 but shut down in 2002 for the same reason. Now, it looked as though the gold-mining company was looking for new reserves within the chinkara habitat, endangering it. Hence, it was of utmost importance that this area was notified as a wildlife sanctuary as soon as possible to save the habitat of chinkara, leopard, striped hyena and other dry-area wildlife species.

Based on these unique ecological reasons, in December 2016, I forwarded a proposal to the government to declare Bukkapatna and the adjoining forest areas of Suvarnamukhi, Muttagadahalli and Matthikere, covering nearly 200 sq kms, as the Chinkara Wildlife Sanctuary.

Very luckily, the local range forest officer, Mallikarjun, a lanky, young man, took interest in the initiative and got supportive letters from the local legislators, members of Parliament and the gram panchayats (locally elected bodies) of the area. Though these letters were not legally required, they would be an assurance to the chief minister, the forest minister and the forest department officials that the local political leaders were supportive of the proposal, and they would be more willing to support the move to notify of the area as a wildlife sanctuary.

In April 2017, armed with all the letters of support, Mallikarjun and I met the forest minister at his residence in Bengaluru. A bulky man, the minister looked relatively relaxed and jovial that morning. He had on a grey T-shirt with wildlife motifs, and was seated on a big sofa in the corner of a large living room. He was in a meeting with a retired forest official when we arrived. When our turn came, which didn't take too long, we explained about the chinkara, Bukkapatna's unique value and that all the elected representatives had already given their support. The minister was a straightforward man, and though not very supportive of conservation, as he thought it wasn't politically beneficial, he patiently went through all the six letters. Finally, he scribbled a brief note on one of them, directing the principal chief conservator of forests to send the proposal ahead. With his letter we met the big bosses of the forest department on the same day, and they agreed to send out the proposal to the government. We were on our way towards setting up a wildlife sanctuary at Bukkapatna. After we had a few meetings with the senior officers in the forest department, a supportive proposal was sent to the government to notify the areas as a wildlife sanctuary in August 2017.

As it is in the government, nothing moved much. The biggest problem lay with some of the senior-most officers in the government, who didn't believe in gazetting protected areas. I decided to test the waters by broaching the issue of adding a small area of 15 sq kms abutting Cauvery Wildlife Sanctuary. The officer responsible categorically told me that they could not keep adding forests to protected areas; the repercussions on development would be huge. This comment came from someone at the highest point of authority that was tasked to save forests and wildlife. After this experiment, I decided not to discuss Bukkapatna with him, or for that matter any other area to be notified as a protected area. It simply wouldn't work, and moreover, if he wrote anything negative in the file it would be enormously difficult to reverse the impact.

Hence, I did what I always did when my back was against the wall: I withdrew for a while. I knew these were issues that had no priority on anyone's list in the government, so the file would simply move to cold storage. I would wait, as long as it took, until an officer who was more positive about saving forests came to his position.

I tested my luck again in March 2018. Vandita Sharma, a tall, lanky lady who was known to be highly professional, had occupied the position of additional chief secretary of the Forests, Ecology and Environment Department for a few months by then. It is always best to allow a new officer to settle down in their position before approaching them. In our first, very brief meeting, which perhaps lasted for less than five minutes, as she was in a hurry to leave for another appointment, she said, 'This is a wonderful idea. Do bring all these proposals. We need to save as much forestland as possible.'

I walked out of her office almost floating on air. What perfect timing, I thought. It had been nearly five years since an officer who expressed anything positive about saving forests and wildlife had occupied this position.

But my joy didn't last long. In our next meeting, about three weeks later, the officer adopted a different tone. 'This matter has been pending here since the last one and half years, and you expect me to complete it in three weeks? Why didn't you follow up all these days?' she challenged.

I was pushed to the wall. I had to respond. Placatingly, I said, 'Madam, these kinds of things can be done only when officers who have an interest in doing something good for the society are here, hence I came now.' I had indirectly hinted to her that the previous officers were not interested in protecting wildlife habitats. I felt she was a bit nonplussed, and she saw me off saying, 'I will try and do my best.'

On-ground conservation work combines moments of excitement with long periods of monotonous repetition. If one is not like Vikram and Betaal, tasks do not get completed. Persistent, I appeared again in front of Vandita after two weeks. It was the last week of March 2018, and the state elections had been announced. In such scenarios, bureaucrats take all important decisions.

I gingerly said, 'Madam, declaration of Bukkapatna as a wildlife sanctuary.'

She immediately retorted, slightly angrily, 'It can be gazetted only after the elections.'

I responded, 'Madam, we have already got supportive letters from the members of the state assembly and the minister. In case the government changes, I am not sure who would be the minister and elected representatives. It would be a herculean task to get the letters again, so it would be great if you could gazette it now.'

'No, the matter has to be placed before the State Board for Wildlife before we proceed. Once we get approval from them we can notify it as a sanctuary,' said Vandita Sharma.

I tried to reason with her. 'Madam, it's not mandatory that it be placed before the board. So you could do it. There's previous history of it.'

She retorted, 'Does the law say that it shouldn't be placed before the State Board for Wildlife? Show me and I will notify it.'

I was taken aback. In our first meeting she had so enthusiastically said that we could notify all areas and now she had taken a U-turn. By then I had realised that it might be difficult to get support for wildlife conservation from her. She may have been well meaning and efficient, but she was inconsistent in her stand. I didn't want to get to the end of my rope by arguing with her about legalities, so I decided to change my tack and remain patient.

After this incident, the government, the forest minister, the local legislators, everyone changed in the May 2018 state elections. Bukkapatna was yet to find protection as a wildlife sanctuary and I kept waiting for the meeting of the State Wildlife Board, which hadn't been held since February 2017. We now faced the humongous task of convincing an entirely new set of officials. There was also political turmoil in the state due to coalition partnerships amongst the political parties, which could have jeopardised the notification of Bukkapatna as a wildlife sanctuary. I was doubtful if the meeting of the State Board for Wildlife would even take place due to the instability in the government: the chief minister was constantly engaged in pacifying his legislators and ministers.

Wildlife depends upon the goodwill of individuals who are in the echelons of power, and if we are unable to muster it, conservation takes a backseat. I kept waiting for the elusive meeting.

In February 2018, I had been diagnosed with Guillain-Barré syndrome, a rare neurological disorder that causes temporary paralysis, for which I was treated with some heavy doses of steroids. As a side effect of the steroid infusion, health issues haunted me again in January 2019. This time, I was diagnosed with avascular necrosis that was caused by loss of blood flow to the pelvic area due to the steroids. I was in severe pain in my legs and pelvic area and had to be hospitalised. As luck would have it, the meeting of the State Board for Wildlife was announced just then. They were to meet on 9 January 2019. I was flabbergasted. Why should this happen now, just when I was hospitalised?

There were a few important proposals, including that of Bukkapatna, that had to be debated in the board meeting. I couldn't miss the opportunity. My family wouldn't have permitted me to attend the meeting in the midst of this health crisis, hence, I kept them in the dark and took permission from the hospital to sneak away for a few hours. I organised for a set of fresh clothes and shoes, fit for the meeting, to be brought into the hospital. My colleague and a first lieutenant for conservation issues, the thirty-six-year-old, baby-faced Poornesha had prepared all the documents we would need, and agreed to accompany me to the meeting in case there was an emergency situation. He is a good man to have on your side on an emergency.

As we drove to the meeting venue, which was a two-hour drive from the hospital in Bengaluru's maddening traffic, I revised all the earlier documents so that I would be prepared to answer any questions from the chief minister or the forest minister or any other officials in the meeting. With a yellow marker, I highlighted certain important points in the documents, and put sticky notes to mark the important bits so I could find them quickly in the meeting.

I also made a few calls to the local forest officers to check for any new developments and to ensure that my understanding of a couple dates was correct. My final phone call was to G. Prabhu, the private secretary to the chief minister. In a previous meeting with the chief minister, regarding a different conservation issue, Prabhu had introduced himself to me, saying that he was a wildlife enthusiast and that he liked the articles I wrote in Kannada newspapers. Now, as he picked up my call, he greeted me warmly. 'Hello Mr Gubbi, how are you?'

I felt relieved and encouraged. Most officers who are at such influential positions are difficult to access, so a friendly response to my call eased my tension. I asked him if he was coming for the meeting that afternoon. 'No, I have some other engagements. Was there anything specific?' Prabhu asked.

'Yes, sir, two of my proposals are up for discussion, and I needed to explain the importance of them to the chief minister.'

Prabhu responded very favourably. 'I will talk to the chief minister and explain things to him. I'll also put in a word with the principal secretary to the chief minister. Don't worry. I know you mean the best for wildlife conservation.'

Nevertheless, I was a bit disappointed that Prabhu would not be there at the meeting, as the presence of a known official who was so close to the chief minister would have made a big difference. I was especially worried because there was to be a discussion in the same meeting about a proposal to develop a new railway track that would cut across the heart of tiger and elephant habitats in the Western Ghats, called the Hubbali-Ankola railway track. I had decided to oppose the railway proposal, and that stance could have a negative impact on notifying Bukkapatna as a wildlife sanctuary. The saving grace was that Bukkapatna was on top of the agenda list, so my position about the railway line, which would come up only later in the meeting, could not have an impact unless the chief minister or the forest minister took serious offence at my stand on the railway track proposal. The second cause of worry was that a gold mining company was toying with the idea of renewing its lease, to explore the yellow metal in newer areas of Bukkapatna forests. With the current gold prices it would be profitable for them to rework in the area. This could be a serious stumbling block for my cause.

The meeting hall was a large room that could accommodate over fifty people. A large chocolate-brown, rectangular table with cushiony chairs in the same colour dominated the room, giving it the feel of a larger space. A massive picture of the Vidhana Soudha, the historical stone building of the state government in central Bengaluru, and a picture of the national flag in a corner decorated one side of the wall, and a big projection screen covered the other. As I walked into the room with my pronounced limp, I found that the chief minister was already there, attending to other issues.

All the members of the board assembled, and—a rare thing in India—the meeting started on time. Jayaram C., the tall and picky chief wildlife warden and the big boss of the wildlife department, began the proceedings with his customary welcome note. Jayaram had been a classmate of the chief minister during his college days, so I was hopeful that their familiarity might help the chief minister respond more favourably. The chief minister's principal secretary asked us all to introduce ourselves so that everyone got to know each other. When it was my turn and I introduced myself, the principal secretary gave me an enthusiastic half smile, as though a flashbulb had jolted his memory, and at the same time raised his left palm just above the table as if he was acknowledging something. I wished him back with a smile and a traditional namaste. It looked as though Prabhu had been at work.

As the introductions ended and Jayaram started reading out the agenda points, I was on high alert. Nervously, I reorganised my papers one last time as he finished going over the previous meeting's proceedings that remained to be approved by the board. When Jayaram switched to the current meeting's topics, the chief minister and the forest minister were engrossed in reading the agenda list given to them by the forest department. I stood alert, papers held close to my chest, expecting a volley of questions from the people in power. I keenly watched the chief minister's face for any reactions or questions. But he didn't even lift his head from the agenda list before simply saying, 'Go ahead.' Jayaram went on to the next agenda point. And that was it. It was done without discussion, without arguments, and without any clarifications. Though my legs ached mercilessly, my heart swelled with happiness to see a new wildlife sanctuary approved by the government. Our other proposal—to add Muneshwarabetta and Sattegala forests to the adjoining Cauvery Wildlife Sanctuary—was also approved. To add to the celebrations, the proposal for the new railway line through the Western Ghats was not approved. On my way back to the hospital, it felt as though the air vibrated in victory. By sundown that evening we had over 45,700 acres of forests ready to be upgraded to wildlife sanctuaries. It was a small victory within the system. The science of wildlife conservation does not operate in a vacuum: though most armchair ecologists think conservation works in a straight line, conservation decisions are all connected to people, society, government, law and public policy.

Two and half years after I had written the proposal, 128 days after the meeting of the State Board for Wildlife, the notification declaring the Bukkapatna Chinkara Wildlife Sanctuary was issued by the government. That put an end to nearly four years of work, and hopefully, it will give a new life to the thirty-odd chinkaras in the wonderful woodland savannah forests of Bukkapatna.

However, while issuing the notification, the area of the sanctuary was reduced to 148 sq kms compared to our original proposal of 200 sq kms. Though some parts of the forests that we had proposed be notified as a wildlife sanctuary were left out, it was a good beginning. I intend to follow up on the remaining 60 sq kms for the Bukkapatna Chinkara Wildlife Sanctuary in the coming days. This inclusion was in addition to nearly 3,000 sq kms of forests that were earlier added to the protected area system due to our collaborative work with the forest department.

It is important now that Bukkapatna has been notified, it is protected in a manner suitable to its unique features; the area should not be managed in the fashion typical for protected areas in India. Normally, once an area is notified as a national park or a wildlife sanctuary, the general practice is to build structures such as water tanks, dig lots of trenches to artificially harvest rainwater to 'provide' water to wildlife, lay hundreds of kilometres of roads to every square inch of the forests and plant trees in areas where it is scientifically incorrect.

Antelope species like chinkara have unfolded through the evolutionary scale to evolve as a species that can survive in dry, arid environments where water is scarce. They do not need to be provided with supplementary water as their bodies are designed by nature to survive with very little of it. During the dry season they get their moisture requirement from eating vegetation, drinking dew and other similar sources. In addition, they need habitat with short grass to survive. Hence, any of the traditional protected-area management practices, such as planting trees and building water tanks, will harm rather than benefit the chinkara by eliminating their natural habitat. Developing water sources artificially will bring in heavy machinery that has the capability to modify the existing habitat, making it unsuitable for these antelopes. From my observations, whenever heavy machinery has worked in forest areas, monotonous repetitions of unpalatable weeds such as parthenium, eupatorium and lantana spring up automatically as soon as the first rains arrive. Once these weeds take root, they spread like cancer, altering natural wildlife habitats making them unsuitable for habitat specialist species like the chinkara. This would sound the death knell for chinkaras.

This is the chronicle of another positive output for a different species from our scientific work on leopards. Though the scientific evidence provided a base it was the larger focused outreach activity and perseverance that paid the price in favour of wildlife conservation.

## *The smallest wild cat in the world*

Besides the honey badger and the chinkara, another lesser-known wild mammal that surprised us during our work was the rusty-spotted cat. It is the smallest wild cat in the world, smaller even than domestic cats, and can weigh as little as 900g—30 per cent lighter than a MacBook Air! It is a secretive animal and mostly stays hidden, quickly disappearing into foliage, making it hard to study the species. During our studies, we found that it was highly nocturnal, with nearly 96 per cent of the sightings in our camera traps occurring between six in the evening and seven in the morning.

With global distribution restricted to India, Sri Lanka and Nepal, there is very little information available on the population of rusty-spotted cats. We found that they appeared in our camera traps in nineteen of the twenty-four sites we worked in, so we painstakingly used the same method we used on leopards to estimate the rusty-spotted cat numbers. It was the first-ever attempt to do so. We succeeded in only seven sites due to the low numbers of captures in the other twelve sites. Their numbers varied from fifteen individuals in Chamundi Hills to 460 individuals in Cauvery Wildlife Sanctuary. This is surprisingly not a large number for a species that is as small as a kitten and which possibly survives largely on rodents.

## *A brown mongoose that's not brown*

The habitat within the 574 sq kms BRT Tiger Reserve ranges from scrub to Shola forests amidst the glade of emerald-green grasslands, a representation of the variation in climatic conditions within this small area. When we camera trapped in this enchanting place in 2018, we were expecting to find not just leopards but tigers, dholes, brown palm civets, and a host of other species appearing in front of our camera traps. But one winter night of February, a small carnivore surprised us: a brown mongoose had its picture taken near the heritage Honnameti coffee estate planted in 1887.

What's so special about documenting a mongoose in a camera trap? And what is special about a mongoose being brown? Aren't all mongooses in India brown?

Not really. Unlike its cousin, the common grey mongoose, the brown mongoose, the *Urva fuscus*, has a dark brown coat, which looks almost black, with fine stripes and black legs. It also has a very bushy, conical, tapering tail that distinguishes it from other mongooses.

In Karnataka, this small carnivore had previously been recorded only in Virajpet taluk in the Kodagu district and nowhere else. Being endemic to the southern part of the Western Ghats and Sri Lanka, this curious animal has a restricted distribution range and is found in Tamil Nadu and Kerala apart from Karnataka. The brown mongoose is generally resident of evergreen forests, Shola forests and high-altitude grasslands at elevations of 450–2,000 metres above sea level. At BRT, it was recorded at 1,249 metres above sea level.

Insects, crabs, small reptiles, rodents, earthworms and birds comprise the diet of this nocturnal species. Not much else, however, is known about the cryptic brown mongoose, and there are no estimates about its population status. Our finding has added to the scarce information available about this species, another by-product of our leopard work.

## The lone wolf

In the first week of May 2020, with the world going through the COVID-19 pandemic crisis, a piece of positive news for wildlife emerged amidst the gloom and doom. A lone wolf crossed paths with us, appearing in front of the camera traps we had set up in the Kothnur range of the Cauvery Wildlife Sanctuary.

In India, both the cheetah (though now extinct in the country) and the wolf are species endemic to the dry grasslands. Though wolves are mostly a grassland species, they have been documented in the deciduous forests of Papikonda Wildlife Sanctuary in Andhra Pradesh and the Kanha and Pench Tiger Reserves in Madhya Pradesh. Yet, due to the expansion of agriculture, the habitat of both these species is very sparsely found in and around the Cauvery Wildlife Sanctuary. So we were in for another surprise when the canid (a mammal of the dog family) appeared in our traps in the woodland savannah at the foothills of Bandalli Gudda, the highest peak in the area. This inselberg (insel meaning island, berg meaning mountain, from German) is at a height of 1,286 metres above sea level. A ruined fort adorns the hillock and the area was once very much a part of Veerappan's domain.

In all probability, it was a male wolf that had trotted past the camera. I am not sure if it was a resident of the area or just transient, a visitor passing through on its way elsewhere. The last nine years of working intensively in the area had not revealed the animal, neither had we heard about its presence in the area. Nor was there any historical literature that mentioned the wolf's presence in the district of Chamarajanagara. The Manual of the Coimbatore District, published in 1887, and edited by the acting collector Nicholson, mentions the occurrence of the cheetah near Bandalli, but does not specifically mention if wolves were found near Bandalli or in the current Chamarajanagara district. This new record also extended the southern range of the grey wolf for the country by 170 kms.

Though our work was focused on leopards, it resulted in the detection of honey badger for the first time in Karnataka and range extension of three more species. I am surprised that despite being such a densely populated country we are still able to stumble on new findings.

### The plant from the dinosaur era

It was not always the mammals that enticed me in these lesser-known wildlife habitats. We documented the presence of an antique plant, one so vintage that the dinosaurs had fed on it—the cycad. Today, this species is found only in the rain shadow regions of Karnataka and nowhere else in the state. Cycads are old, very old. They have been around since the Mesozoic era, 230 million years ago, when they shared the planet with the dinosaurs.

With their stout, woody trunks and multiple fronds, cycads look a lot like a variation of the palm. Palms, however, are flowering plants, while—like pine trees and juniper bushes—cycads are gymnosperms, which means 'naked seed'. In other words, they make seeds, but they don't make flowers or fruit as a way of bringing those seeds into the world. Their male and female reproductive parts are located on separate plants. Cycads evolved on the earth as the first seeded plants. They might even be the first insect-pollinated plants.

We found cycads in the dry forests of Tumkur, Ramanagara and Mandya. One cycad plant, which we identified as *Cycas indica*, in the Devarahosahalli Reserved Forest in Ramanagara district towered, at over fifteen feet tall. These primeval survivors grow very slowly, adding only a few centimetres every year. Considering this growth rate, I assume the plant was over a hundred years old.

The presence of these primitive plants, after all these years, is surreal, making one feel like one is walking through the same forests that dinosaurs once trod upon. There are about three hundred species of cycads found in the world today, but recent scientific studies indicate that they are different from the ones the dinosaurs munched upon. Nevertheless, current-day cycads may be about twelve million years old. Most cycad species today are highly threatened by extinction due to habitat loss. Of the fourteen species of cycads reported from the wild in India, one is placed under the 'Critically Endangered' category of the International Union for Conservation of Nature (IUCN) Red List, two under 'Endangered', three under 'Vulnerable' and one under 'Data Deficient'. Seven species have not been evaluated.

In some parts of South-east Asia these plants play an important role in the cuisine, culture, and traditions of forest-dwelling communities. Starchy, small white balls called sago are made of cycads, and are eaten as porridge, either sweet or savoury. In India, too, sago or sabudana was made out of cycads until it began to be produced using cassava powder. Cycad fronds are also used for wedding decorations in India.

Cycads are also found in southern Africa, the landmass that was linked with India before the Gondwanaland split. The presence of cycads in both southern Africa and India is another example of resembling floral species in the two landmasses and proof that these two landscapes were once connected.

## Wildlife and history

Some of the leopard habitats where we worked were also sites of considerable archaeological importance—Nidgal, Devarayanadurga, Channarayanadurga and Madhugiri forests are all examples. Historical crumbling structures, probably built during the fifteenth and seventeenth centuries, are seen to this day in the midst of the dry scrub. Nature and wildlife have taken over the old ruins here, where kingdoms and local fiefdoms once thrived.

Walking through such areas, where scrub or dry deciduous forests currently flourish, gave us a fascinating overview of how history has made way for wildlife. It felt as though we had stepped back a couple of centuries.

We spotted telltale signs of leopards, sloth bears and other wildlife on the fort ruins and dilapidated temples that dotted the landscape. When pictures of spotted cats and shaggy sloths bears, imposed against the background of the crenelated walls of old temples, appeared in our camera traps, they provided photographic evidence of this co-existence of history and wildlife. The thorny dry forests held several secrets in their undergrowth. Once, while walking through the scrub forests of Nidgallu, my feet stumbled upon an old idol of Parshwanatha, the twenty-third Jain Tirthankara, who is said to have lived towards the beginning of the first millennium BCE. The idol had perhaps been lying there for a couple of centuries, as the area was ruled by several dynasties and was once a very prosperous area. One can only make intimate contact with these areas when one is on foot. This is what makes walking in the forests makes so magnetic and illuminating.

Camera trapping in various sites also exposed us to other interesting agro-ecological facets. During the peak mango season, when we worked in Tumkur district, sloth bear scats were full of large mango seeds and coat fragments of the fruit. It seemed they relished mangoes as much as we did.

Our work has also brought out a few hidden talents within our group. Harish has found his passion in wildlife science. He has gone from volunteering with us on outreach activities to being able to carry out museum-quality fieldwork. Aparna, our computer software engineer who wrote codes and analysed the data we collected from field research, has now completed her master's degree in wildlife biology. So has her coder husband, Santhosh, who earlier worked for a German company.

# 5

# DECCAN PLATEAU — THE GRAND HOME OF LEOPARDS

To understand how the grand leopard landscapes of the Deccan Plateau were formed, we must sidestep into the wholly unrelated subject of earth science for a short while. The Deccan Plateau is perhaps one of the most spectacular outcomes of the continental drift and tectonic plate movement of the Indian Plate. As the Indian Plate slid, it scraped over magmatic hotspots, releasing stupendous amounts of volcanic gases and lava. The process created layers of thick lava topped by granite boulders, which make up large parts of the Deccan Plateau as we see it today. This vast landform contains some of the oldest rock formations on earth; only Australia, Greenland and South Africa have rocks that are older than the ones found in southern India.

The rocky outcrops characteristic of the Deccan Plateau are made of Closepet granite, characteristically round-shaped, smooth and steep. These granite forms developed when the molten magma that had reached close to the surface of the earth began to cool slowly. The slow cooling hardened into rocks, and gave them their distinctive large crystals. The huge mounds, which look startlingly like gumdrops, rise above everything in the vicinity, hundreds of feet high.

According to Pranay Lal's classic book on India's geological history, *Indica: A Deep Natural History of the Indian Subcontinent*, these outcrops belong to a family of rocks called Dharwar Craton, after the eponymous town that is famous for the sweet Dharwar Peda, which, coincidentally, looks quite similar to these boulders. The Dharwar Craton is spread all over Karnataka, northern Tamil Nadu, Maharashtra, Andhra Pradesh, eastern Gujarat, western and central Madhya Pradesh, and was formed between 2.5 and 3 billion years ago. It provides some of the most stunning views in Karnataka and Maharashtra. Hampi—a combination of natural wonders, with boulders, history and wildlife—makes for an evocative example of the appeal of the Deccan Plateau. Thousands of people from around the globe have fallen in love with the grandeur of the rocks here. Anyone wanting a front-row seat for a lesson on Deccan Plateau needs nothing more than a visit to the historical place of Hampi and its environs in central Karnataka.

These rocky hillocks have also played host to some Bollywood blockbusters, including the 1975 subtle love story *Sholay* that gave birth to the iconic character Gabbar Singh, who lives on in Indian households to this day. Open Google Earth and type in the location 12.574904, 77.372470, and it will take you to Ramanagara, where *Sholay* was filmed. If you hover around the area, this technological marvel will give you a stunning perspective of these rocky outcrops. *Sholay* is not the only film to showcase the earthly appeal of these inselbergs. David Lean's *A Passage to India* also displays the grandeur of these rocky outcrops, and was filmed not far from where *Sholay* was, at Savandurga, one of the largest monoliths in Asia.

Despite these stunning features and history, rocky outcrops are one of the least-studied ecosystems, and there are no estimates of the total area they cover in the country. They continue to hold small secrets. Recently, a new species of the fan-throated lizard, the *Sitana dharwarensis,* was discovered by a group of three young researchers in Bagalkot district in northern Karnataka. Still, the rocky outcrops and open scrublands where the lizard was found are generally dismissed as wasteland as they are unfit for agriculture. Tree-planting drives are carried out in an effort to 'revive' the landscape but, in reality, these are at the cost of such lesser-known wildlife species. Many a time such species are gone even before they are known to the outside world.

These areas seem to have poor water-retention capacity, hence the streams that flow through these hilly tracts are seasonal. The Deccan holds streams only during the monsoon season and for a short period thereafter. But they still act as a key watershed for the scores of tanks and lakes in these dry landscapes. The vegetation in this habitat is largely scrub to dry deciduous forests, interspersed with small patches of dry savannah woodland. Small pockets of the Deccan Plateau host a special type of floral habitat called the tropical dry evergreen forests. These forests are predominantly composed of trees and shrubs that have thick dark green foliage throughout the year, unlike dry forests, where leaves are shed during periods when water is scarce. Hence the name dry evergreen forests.

The combination of rocky outcrops and forests provide ideal habitat for a host of species, both large and small, as they provide food and cover. Sloth bears, striped hyenas, golden jackals, Indian foxes, rusty-spotted cats, jungle cats, civets, mongooses, four horned-antelopes, wild pigs, porcupines, pangolins, langurs, bonnet macaques, slender loris and several other large and small fauna have found them an ideal home. A few patches of such forests continue to hold remnant populations of chital, sambar and four-horned antelopes. Many of these species make ideal food for leopards. This combination of cover and food availability has made these rocky outcrops a preferred natural habitat for leopards.

The rocky outcrops in many parts of Karnataka and Andhra Pradesh are disjointed in distribution. This has an effect on leopard distribution, as they tend to align themselves along the network of these rocky outcrops. Consequently, their home ranges may be larger, and leopards may be seen using the agricultural fields in between to move between the scrub forests present in the rocky outcrops. This could give the wrong impression, suggesting that they live in agricultural fields. Without long-term data it would be hard to assess their success of existence in human modified habitats. But for leopards to survive in these human-dominated areas, these rocky outcrops are a critical necessity.

However, the rocky outcrops of the Deccan have begun to yield, first to agriculturists, and then to merchants of granite, making them threatened in this modern day. In turn, the non-human inhabitants of these ancient rock forms also face the unnoticed threat of local extinction. Though some individuals may survive when their natural habitats are lost to wanton destruction, that's where the trouble starts. Left with no natural home and no natural prey, they turn to man's best friend, the dog, and one of human kind's oldest possessions: livestock. Thus begins a whole new aspect of the leopard and human relationship-conflict.

# 6

# THE CITY LEOPARDS

## *Leopards of the silicon city*

Over the years, globalisation has had a serious impact on Bengaluru's status as the 'garden city'. Yet, in 2013, less than ten kilometres from Bengaluru's international airport, the third busiest in India, we camera-trapped leopards, one picture taken as close as twenty metres from someone's backyard. To see these animals in the wild is not easy. To see one along the edge of someone's yard is both disconcerting and heartening. The leopard's ability to survive in human-dominated landscapes and to tolerate human contact is a testament to the robustness of this large wild cat, which of course comes at a cost to both the animal and people.

The world over, some cities do host large wild mammals in their neighbourhood. Of these, the most well-known is Nairobi, one of the busiest cities in Kenya. The city adjoins Nairobi National Park, and residents have large wildlife as their neighbours. Four of the African big five—(excluding elephants) lions, leopards, buffalos and rhinoceroses—in addition to giraffes, zebras, cheetahs, hyenas and several other of Africa's wild mammals have survived, over the years, in the neighbourhoods of this city.

In India, too, there are a few cities that host large mammals on their outskirts—Bengaluru, as we have just noted, as well as Jaipur, Delhi, Mumbai, Pune, Dehradun and Bhopal, to name a few. Amongst these, Bengaluru is perhaps unique as it hosts a variety of large wildlife—elephants, gaurs, sambars, leopards, sloth bears, dholes, and since July 2015 even a tiger has been reported—within a few kilometres of the city centre. A common feature of all these cities is that they have retained significant swathes of natural landscapes on their boundaries. Bengaluru, for instance, has patches of rocky outcrops and scrub forests that continue to exist on the city's fringes.

Where humans and potentially dangerous wildlife exist together, they are bound to come in conflict with people. Reports of leopards lifting livestock are not uncommon in parts of Bengaluru's outskirts where rural life continues to linger. Occasionally, the residents of apartment complexes and gated communities on the southern side of the city, near the NICE highway, report leopard sightings.

In June 2015, we got an emergency call from the residents of a gated community on the outskirts of Bengaluru. The security personnel had sighted a leopard during their nighttime rounds. We arrived at the location as soon as we could.

The complex was intended to accommodate a few families, in a parody of country-living. It abutted a beautiful dry deciduous forest, a part of which stretched into the housing complex. Owing to our interest in large cats and on the request of the community and the forest department, we initiated camera trapping in this gated community to understand how many leopards survived here and what their movement patterns were like. In addition, we initiated a study in other parts of the city's outskirts.

Around the same time, we got a request from a school, not very far from the gated community, for similar support. The large school campus, which was spread over nearly one hundred acres, hosted dry deciduous forests and was contiguous to other reserved forests, including BM Kaaval and UM Kaaval. These forests are nearly 1,700 acres in size and are connected to the Bannerghatta National Park through other forest patches that are under private ownership that are nearly twice the size of what is under government ownership. These forests made a good habitat for leopards. Our traps indicated that the school had three adult leopards, two males and a female, using its space besides the students, teachers and other staff. In the gated community, there were two sub-adults and a large male leopard. Though these animals were photographed by us within the school and the gated community, they were using the larger landscape.

Our study provided some wonderful insights into the lives of these spotted cats. Though we had a few leopards walk in front of our cameras, the sequence of images was more interesting. In the gated community, senior citizens walked past the camera traps for their end-of-the-day walks. A couple of kilometres away, young school children played, their playful performances captured on the cameras. A few minutes later leopards would trigger the camera traps, imperceptibly appearing in the same spots as the human activities drew to a close. At the school, one of the male leopards was frequently camera trapped near the art building. Perhaps it liked the artwork of the children! In some places, leopards revealed their presence in maize fields, but disappeared as soon as the crops were harvested. Tall standing crops, such as maize, perhaps acted as a good temporary cover for the felids.

Outreach activities by us at gated communities, schools, a space research organisation and research institutes have helped the residents deal with the leopard presence and learn other precautionary measures that needed to be taken. Our spatial information on the leopard's occurrence on the city's outskirts seemed to depict a trend but also confirmed what we had already started to piece together in other areas. Though they used agricultural areas such as maize fields, leopards mostly seemed to occur within natural habitats, such as rocky outcrops and forest patches, from the north-west to the southern side of the city, in a semi-circular form. The message was clear: leopards survive in areas where there is a mosaic of natural forests, rocky outcrops, and sub-optimal habitats that provide temporary cover. Importantly, natural habitats seem to be key for the leopard's survival.

My experience in Bengaluru indicates that leopards are not present 'inside' cities, but have adapted as the natural habitats around metropolises change. Solitary and nocturnal, they can slip by in the darkness without being noticed and, of course, their size helps them survive on medium-sized prey, like domestic dogs, that are found in high densities in urbanised environments. The leopard is increasingly making room for itself in an urbanised environment. But it is certainly not living amidst a sea of humans, residential and commercial buildings, and is not 'urban'.

During this exercise, apart from the secretive leopards, we found other interesting wildlife. Once, a smooth-coated otter, which survives in large lakes and rivers, suddenly appeared in the camera traps we had installed in the famed Svetoslav Roerich and Devika Rani Estate in southern Bengaluru. Often found traversing the estate were barking deer, chital and several other large mammals.

I wonder how long this feline population and other wildlife will survive on the borders of this ever-growing city?

Bengaluru's rise as a technological hub has made the city more affluent for some. As the city has become more prosperous and real estate has become more and more valuable, the city's outskirts have begun to change. Like an amoeba, the city is engulfing the villages within its boundaries to sustain itself. As Bengaluru's urban sprawl expands mile after mile, most rocky outcrops and the dry forests that provide refuge for the leopards are slowly disappearing, sucked into the needs of development. Overnight, habitats that once harboured a myriad variety of wildlife have been converted to a concrete swamp of industries, highways, malls, tall housing complexes and metro stations. As leopards and development compete for the same scarce real estate, it is the big cats and other wildlife that get caught in the relentless process of social and economic change.

Though the landscape surrounding the city has gone through a number of drastic changes over several millennia, the current modifications and the speed at which they are unfolding is unprecedented. The size of the city has increased over 300 per cent in the last twenty years. The city's greater metropolitan area has grown explosively from every side, doubling between 2001 and 2011 with the current area at 741 sq kms (183,105 acres). This has been accompanied by a colossal growth in population, unimagined in the city's past—Bengaluru's human population has grown by 47 per cent between 2001 and 2011, increasing from 6.5 to 9.6 million, currently matching the population of the New York metropolitan area.

The urban sprawl has rapidly become far less friendly as a neighbourhood for wildlife. As urban areas expand, not only do the natural habitats of leopards shrink, but so does the continuity to other natural habitats—the agricultural fields that leopards earlier used to move from one natural patch to another are now rapidly being converted to housing, commercial and industrial projects, isolating the leopards that live in the surrounding areas and decreasing their chances for survival. For instance, leopards that existed in the Turahalli forest have now disappeared, as this small reserved forest (2.5 sq kms) is now surrounded by housing complexes and its connectivity to the BM Kaaval Reserved Forest and to Bannerghatta National Park further south has been severed. Such local extinctions have been well documented in this country's history.

Leopards may still survive in the vicinity of large cities if there is sufficient cover and continuity to other natural habitats. To give an example, it is likely that leopards will continue to exist in the Bannerghatta National Park (260 sq kms), which adjoins the southern side of Bengaluru city. Luckily, Bannerghatta is connected to a few reserved forests in Tamil Nadu and, more importantly, to the Cauvery Wildlife Sanctuary to its south, through a very narrow corridor. Our previous conservation work had ensured that this corridor was brought under the protected area status. This should act as insurance for larger wildlife to survive in the long run in Bannerghatta. This hypothesis is backed by the situation in Nairobi National Park, across the globe. Part of the national park connects to other larger tracts of woodland savannahs, which continue for hundreds of square kilometres. Therefore, these natural habitats support the long-term subsistence of large mammals in this national park, and so should Bannerghatta.

The land around Bannerghatta, however, is getting highly urbanised. The northern and western edges of the national park are already ensconced in a sea of development. So the leopards that live inside Bannerghatta could venture into urbanised areas due to easy access to domestic food sources, including dogs, livestock and poultry. This is not an ideal situation, either for the leopard or for the people. Yet, if you eliminate the forests in Bannerghatta, there would perhaps be no leopards left in this area.

Most of the natural habitats of leopards on the city's outskirts may eventually vanish if concerted efforts are not made to protect them. In November 2017, after working in the outskirts of the city for nearly a decade, and documenting that this area has a lot of interesting wildlife apart from leopards, I initiated a proposal to notify BM Kaaval, UM Kaaval, Gollahalligudda and Devika Rani Estate areas as a 'conservation reserve', a legal category under the Indian Wildlife Protection Act that could help protect wildlife habitats, especially those that are outside the ambit of any protected forests. Though the proposal has not made big strides since, we continue to follow it up with the government and political leaders. The very high value of the real estate in the area is perhaps a big deterrent in notifying it as a conservation reserve.

Bengaluru is an emblematic case in point where the changing ecological, social and economic landscapes of the country demonstrate the altering fate of some of the wildlife species. Urban civilisation and industrialisation have invaded the city's environs and leopards have been losing ground. Many of the city's former leopard habitats—Kengeri, Hebbal, J.P. Nagar, Turahalli, Thathaguni, Doresanipalya, Kaadgudi—are now bustling residential, industrial or business hubs. Today, a Google search for 'J.P. Nagar' and 'leopard' lists out interesting results: Leopard Securities Services, Leopard Investments, Leopard Hi-heel Suppliers. Unfortunately, the formerly abundant true leopards have made way for these urban ones. These changes in leopard habitats adjoining cities are probably following a similar trajectory in other Indian cities as well; whether Mumbai, Jaipur, New Delhi or Hyderabad, with a few floral and geographic changes, the narrative could possibly be the same for all these cities.

## Leopards of the palace city

An old, picturesque palace stood atop the hillock. Two big brass padlocks secured the large entrance doors. When I peeped through a gap in them, the insides of the palace opened up. It looked as though some renovation work had been halted halfway. I could see a grand staircase of rosewood winding its way up to the first floor. Next to the steps, a large elephant trophy with enormous tusks hung from the butterscotch-coloured walls. The floors looked like they had once had fine floral designs worked on Athangudi tiles, which are made through a unique process using the local soil.

The palace had two Rajasthani-style, dome-shaped cupolas on each corner and a large central dome. Just outside it was a dilapidated garden, in the centre of which stood a two-stepped, marble fountain designed as the open petals of the lotus flower—a reminder of better times in the midst of the decaying, silent palace. Though the garden was small, it had traces of a tastefully designed park. It is fascinating to think that during the garden's heydays, the Maharaja of Mysuru and his family members leisurely strolled through it. Though it is said that the mansion was built in 1822 as a summer palace, the current building was completed in

1938-39. Situated on the top of Chamundi Hills, at about 1,000 metres above sea level and abutting the historic metropolis of Mysuru, the palace has commanding views of the city.

At the entrance of the mansion was a 1980s style large, neon signboard that read 'Rajendra Vilas Palace'. The high imposing iron gates were closed and remained closed until we could convince the caretakers of the honesty of our visit.

Chamundi Hills, where the Rajendra Vilas palace is built, is a small forest patch of approximately 2,000 acres, about twenty times the size of Vatican City, the smallest nation in the world. Chamundi Hills sits high on rocky outcrops, and is crowded with pilgrims and tourists who come here to worship the famous deity Cahmundeswari. A large statue of the demon Mahishasura, who can switch back and forth between human and buffalo form, and from whom Mysuru gets its name, stands atop Chamundi Hills. It is also on these slopes and dry deciduous scrub forests that lurk the leopards of the palace city.

Bengaluru is not the only city in Karnataka that hosts leopards on its outskirts. Mysuru, a city with great character and history and known for its quiet streets, hosts a few at its fringes. So, in 2015, we decided to study the leopard numbers in Chamundi Hills, and this is how I had landed that October day at the gates of the Rajendra Vilas Palace to do an initial recce. Gourishankaranagara, Chamundipura, Lalitadripura and other localities that lie on the foothills of the Chamundi Hills had witnessed a few cases of leopard conflict in the past. A study would also help provide ideas on how to deal with the conflict situation.

All around the palace were big bushes of the yellow trumpet flower plant (*Tecoma stans*). In the middle of the bushes was an old, dirt road through which a vehicle could pass, and at the edge of the road was the steep fall of the hillock. Since there were forests around the palace the possibility of leopards using this road was almost certain.

We continued our recce the next day. My task for that afternoon was to walk down the steep, narrow trail that started from the famous 4.9m high monolith of Nandi (big bull), towards Nanjangud Road, and identify suitable locations for installing our camera traps. I started the steep descent along with a staff member of the forest department. Though the distance was only two kilometres I assumed that it would take over two hours to cover it due to the steep gradient. My research assistant, Sandesha, was to pick me up at the base of the hillock. My other colleague Harish was doing a similar reconnaissance walk in another part of the Chamundi Hills.

I identified two locations for the camera traps without anything of note happening. As I walked down the slopes, I reached a cool spot with fairly large boulders. The boulders had been covered over with brown, dry leaves due to the dense tree cover that also helped keep the area cool. When I stepped on one of the boulders, it shifted, and before I knew it, I had rolled twice, like a large football. My head forcefully hit a medium-sized boulder, and everything spun. I don't recall much about the next couple of minutes. Then, to my surprise, I found myself sitting up cross-legged on one of the outcrops. There was something wet dripping down my nose. Blood. Dripping from the top of my head, over my forehead, and down my nose. From the back came the voice of my companion. 'Sir, tie your kerchief to your head; it's bleeding.'

I immediately took out my kerchief, poured water over it and held it against the injury. After resting for a few minutes, I tried getting up, but in vain, as I felt dizzy again. I was forced to sit down and relax for some more time before I could restart on my walk down. 'You are very lucky, sir. I was worried looking at the way your head crashed against the boulder, but you seem to have a strong skull,' said the forest department staff member.

We slowly descended towards Gourishankaranagara, marking the locations where we could install camera traps. We washed the sweat rolling down our foreheads, in a small puddle of clear water that we found on our way down; it had not evaporated due to the dense tree cover. As soon as I got to the vehicle, I headed to the hospital to be treated. Luckily, not much was needed.

In total, we identified fifty-four locations, of which we installed cameras at thirty-two. After sixteen days of camera trapping, our results showed that Chamundi Hills had about five–six leopards. Within 500m of the highway connecting Mysuru and Nanjungud town, a female leopard appeared every day in our camera traps. We spotted a lactating leopardess carrying away domestic piglet to eat it, and a large male leopard walking, the street lights of a sparsely populated area at a distance—empirical evidence of the leopard's ability to survive in human-dominated landscapes. Leopards also appeared in the camera traps that we had installed near the Rajendra Vilas Palace, giving a historical touch to our wildlife research. Despite the small area we surveyed, it was clear they survived in these forests. Slipping through the margins like spirits, they seemed to have mastered the art of melting away and appearing at the right time without being noticed by people.

Wild pigs, peafowls, rusty-spotted cats, common palm civets, small India civets, porcupines, all made their appearance in front of our camera traps. Interestingly, the Indian fox, a species belonging to the grasslands, showed up in these deciduous forests, surprising us.

### Tiger in the Chamundi Hills

Though this small patch of forests held pleasant surprises, history indicates it has also lost a few other species. The palace's erstwhile game preservation officer D.N. Neelakanta Rao mentions the presence of a tiger in his weekly inspection notes. On 23 October 1948, the Maharaja of Mysuru and his soldiers spotted a tiger near the Nandi statue on Chamundi Hills, writes Rao. Predicting that the tiger may have killed a cow near Rayanakere tank and walked past the Dalavayikere tank, Rao writes, 'It was not considered seriously when the locals started to complain that a large leopard with stripes had started to appear in Chamundi Hills, as even the oldest resident does not remember having seen a tiger here.' He ends his note saying, 'We have instructions to kill the tiger.'

Four days later, on 27 October, Rao wrote about a failed attempt to kill the tiger and that its pugmarks had been seen on a trail near Ashwathanarayankatte Bridge. Next day, the princess of Sananda, a small princely state in Gujarat, who was probably visiting, sighted the tiger at about seven in the evening but did not permit her soldier to shoot it as she was afraid that the large cat would jump on her small Austin car if he didn't get his aim right. Again, about half an hour later, the driver of a taxi belonging to the owner of Modern Café of Mysuru sighted the tiger, as noted by Rao.

Finally, on 5 November 1948, game preservation head M.K. Acchappa, watchers Putta and Bora, and soldiers Chengalaraju and Chamaraju killed the first tiger to be sighted in Chamundi Hills, with a twelve-bore gun. Such historical notes give enormous perspectives to our work on forests and wildlife. Perhaps the forests of Chamundi Hills were once connected to a larger forest area, which had possibly aided the tiger's move into Chamundi Hills. Now, Chamundi Hill is an isolated forest pocket surrounded by Mysuru city, and agricultural activities are fading further and further away from the city. Though isolated habitats will have some biodiversity, certain species like the tiger or the large-pied hornbill will need large swathes of habitat to continue surviving in the area, depicting the importance of connectivity and larger habitat conservation.

## *The big male CML-05*

We returned to Chamundi Hills in August 2017 to repeat our earlier study, but didn't find any change in the leopard numbers. A large male leopard that would regularly appear in our camera traps in 2015 reappeared in our cameras. The beautiful, healthy leopard was perhaps six years old and we had named it CML-05 (Chamundi Leopard-05). This leopard made big news in February 2018.

Someone driving to Chamundi Hills at night shot a video of a leopard walking on the road. The video went viral as soon as it was put on social media. As a result, there was a big demand that the leopard be captured. Out of curiosity, I compared the leopard with our database from Chamundi Hills, and we found that the video was of CML-05. It made no sense to capture a leopard that was resident in the area and had caused no harm to anyone. I immediately wrote a letter to the forest department with the details of CML-05's history and requested that it not be captured. A note was also circulated in the media, hoping that it would help bring in awareness against its capture.

I am not sure if it was our bad luck or CML-05's fate, but four days after I sent out the letter, CML-05 entered a banana trader's shop in Uttanahalli, at the foothills of Chamundi Hills. The leopard had probably been attracted by the dog in the shop and come in to eat it, when he was seen by the owner. The panic-stricken owner, who was sleeping in his shop, shut the door and informed the forest department, who promptly captured the animal.

But leopards preying upon dogs is not new for Uttanahalli, where CML-05 was captured. In February 1935, Neelakanta Rao had written, in his weekly report, of a dog being eaten by a leopard in the same place. The way we look at leopards has changed since then, and the matter has only become more complicated as human population increases and the leopard's natural habitat and prey decreases.

It was saddening to know that this leopard—one in its prime, and which we had monitored for nearly four years without incident—would have to live the rest of its life in captivity due to conflict. If the shopkeeper had not sighted the animal that night, CML-05 would have continued to range over Chamundi Hills. Though I understand the anxiety of the people, the leopard, forced to prey on domestic prey due to the loss of wild prey in Chamundi Hills, had to pay the price.

### The tragic end of CML-04

In December 2020, as the world was looking forward to ending what had been a most difficult year thanks to the COVID-19 pandemic, a leopardess was captured in Chamundi Hills. She had been found seriously injured by the roadside. Looking at the video footage, it was clear that the leopardess had been hit by some vehicle and her spine had been fractured. She was taken to a rescue centre. I knew her survival with this grave injury was doubtful.

I immediately checked our database and found that this was the same leopardess that was camera-trapped carrying away a domestic piglet in October 2015. The mammary glands under her belly, then, had indicated that she had cubs. She was a healthy individual and was aged about five years. We had christened her CML-04, and she was one of the two females camera trapped at Chamundi. In 2017, when we had returned to Chamundi, CML-04 was found to have a cub of about six months age. She had already weaned her previous cubs and had a new litter. CML-04 was active in the entire area of Chamundi Hills. To our surprise, she had reappeared in our camera traps in 2019. By then, her primordial pouch, the sagging layer of skin that hung along the length of her stomach, was much more pronounced.

In 2019, CML-04 was one of the only two leopards that our camera traps had photographed in Chamundi Hills. The other one was a younger male named CML-08, possibly four years of age. Leopard numbers in Chamundi Hills were certainly going down—mostly due to capture and translocation of these cats. Tragically, on the tenth day at the rescue centre, CML-04 died. Another of Chamundi's leopards had met a tragic, unnatural end.

Today, the leopards of Chamundi Hills walk a tight rope. The city of Mysuru is growing beyond the temple-town mystique of the 1970s and 1980s. It cocoons Chamundi Hills from all sides, and the conversion of the forests to buildings for housing and tourism is escalating. Will leopards survive on this historical hill?

A similar situation exists in several parts of Karnataka and elsewhere in India, where leopards exist on the fringes of cities and towns that have natural cover. Tumkur, Ramnagara, Bellary and Chitradurga in Karnataka, and Jaipur and Pune are a case in point. The future does not look very bright for leopards in these areas until steps are taken to ensure that the area leopards inhabit are large enough to allow them survive as an isolated population.

# 7

# FOLLOWING THE CATS

A man in his mid-twenties was delicately perched on a small wooden plank. It hung down by a frail rope from the tall areca nut palm tree, referred to as *Areca catechu* in scientific parlance. This was one of the tens of other trees of the same species in the plantation, interspersed with a few bushes. He had been posted as a sentry on the tree, and was keeping watch on the bush where a leopard was supposedly hiding. There were leopard spoors in the soft mud beneath the tree and in a few other spots. A small dash of blood in one area suggested that the leopard may have been wounded or it had killed some livestock. Forest department personnel were ready, with forked wooden poles and nets, to pin the animal down if it was cornered.

This is the scene that greeted us when we arrived at Hulikallu, a small village in Hassan district in Karnataka in October 2013. The landscape around the village consisted of a mix of dry farmlands and areca nut plantations, which provided shade and cool temperatures. A small hillock with natural tree growth, bushes and boulders was within sight of the areca nut plantation where the leopard was holed up. There were at least four to five hundred people gathered to watch the action. Some of them were armed with wooden poles, a few with machetes, and they continuously complained to us about the problems they faced due to leopards—livestock was being lifted on a regular basis, they were afraid to venture into their fields after sunset and, often, scared to walk through their plantations alone even during the day.

More and more, mostly men, arrived on motorbikes, auto rickshaws and by foot, eager not to miss out on any action. As some from the crowd spoke to us we could catch the occasional whiff of alcohol. Their one-point demand was that the leopard be captured and taken away. I tried convincing the leader, Srinivas, that if they would wait for a few more minutes, the animal would slip away in the darkness of dusk to the nearby hillock. Srinivas was categorical. 'We have been requesting the authorities to capture the leopard for several months now, and they haven't taken any action. Now we have the opportunity to do it and we will do so by sunset.' My efforts to tell him that it would be difficult to capture a wild cat and there were high chances of people getting injured in the melee didn't seem to have any effect on him or any of the others who had curiously gathered around us to listen to the conversation. No amount of convincing seemed to work, and the crowd's mood and decision seemed to be firm. The animal had to be captured at any cost.

By the time we wrapped up these discussions, daylight had started to fade, and we decided to call it a day, choosing to come back early morning. I didn't think it likely that they would ever be able to catch the cat, and in the morning we would be able to see its pugmarks and confirm where the animal had headed the previous night. We had turned to leave when I heard a big commotion, and I saw people running in all directions. I caught a glimpse of the spotted cat running between the areca nut trees, behind some of the panic-stricken people. The uproar followed the direction in which the cat ran, and I could track the commotion moving through the plantation for a while. Then the hue and cry stopped at one corner of the plantation. The trees and bushes completely blocked our view of the ongoing action. I decided not to add to the turmoil by walking into the disorder. In less than two minutes, the noise and the commotion seemed to die down and people began to disperse. I asked some of them about what had transpired, but none were willing to give a detailed or a straightforward response, and I didn't get any answers. All I understood was that the leopard had escaped and run away somewhere.

Leopards are amazing escape artists; they can slip away without being noticed from a place—even with an enormously large number of eyes trying to keep a watch on them. So we left the scene under the impression that the leopard had made its way through the crowd and safely returned to wherever it lived. The next morning, when we telephoned a local forest personnel in the hope of returning to the plantation, we were shocked to hear his news. A leopard had been found dead close to the plantation with severe lacerations on its body.

Revenge and expectation of protection is a natural reaction from communities affected by leopards. But what we witnessed at Hulikallu is increasingly becoming the norm. Tolerance in the country towards our wild denizens seems to be decreasing. Communities are becoming more recalcitrant, and demand the capture of any leopard that kills livestock, or even of any seen wandering close to human habitations.

In Karnataka, a spurt of conflicts, like the one explained above, led to 357 leopards being captured, and over 85 per cent of them being translocated by the authorities between the years 2009–2016. With nearly four leopards captured every month, it was almost as if they were being captured by the pound. Every time a leopard was caught it was dumped in a bigger forest patch. The favoured areas for leopard translocation were Cauvery Wildlife Sanctuary, the famed Nagarahole or Bandipur Tiger Reserves or the evergreen forests of Kemphole near Sakleshpur.

But there were no attempts to understand what happened to the animals that were released in new areas. There was no knowledge of how leopards fared when released into different areas with diverse management criteria. How would they respond if they were released into protected areas that supposedly had a higher prey density or if they were released into forests that were more disturbed? What would happen if they were released back into the same area where they were captured, or how would the different sexes respond to this management action?

Studying this gap was crucial, so I decided to work on the subject. One technique that could help understand the leopard's responses was to fit translocated animals with a radio collar. A radio collar would help us track the animal's movements and thus learn how they roamed as they move around their habitat during different periods of the day and night, and also to understand their seasonal movements. Little did I know that my radio collaring effort, which began as an initiative to understand the problem of leopard conflict, would end up as an expensive experience personally.

### What is a radio collar?

The radio collar device typically consists of an electronic transmitter, housed in a plastic casing mounted on leather belt, which sends out information about the animal's location. The casing also houses a battery to power the transmitter. A small antenna connected to the transmitter sends out radio signals that are then picked up by a mobile VHF antenna connected to a receiver. The researcher can pick up the signal using the receiver, and follow the bearer of the collar. This electronic tool is especially important when the animal you are studying is shy and secretive.

Radio collars that track purely using a VHF antenna get very limited data, as, though the animal can be followed in areas where there is vehicular access, it is arduous to get the data if the monitoring has to be done on foot in hostile and hilly terrain. An animal that's translocated from a different place, can initially move far and wide, so these days a satellite-linked GPS device, like the ones used in a smartphones, is embedded within the transmitter. Modern GPS-enabled radio collars can send locations a number of times each day, in batches, to a satellite which in turns relays

Leopards are one of the most beautiful wild cats in the world that are found in sixty-three countries. ©Sudhir Shivaram (top) and ©Shaaz Jung (left)

A leopard carries a flying squirrel it has just caught. Leopards eat a wide variety of prey. ©Vinay S. Kumar

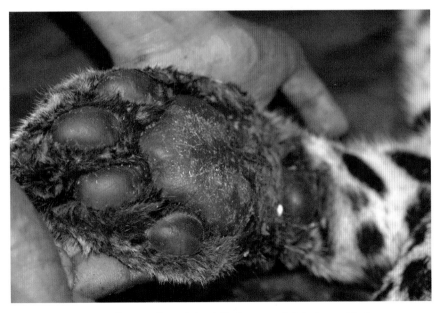

Leopard paws are extremely soft and their pawprints on mud help researchers find their presence in an area. ©Arun Simha

Leopards are extremely comfortable on trees, and haul heavy prey to keep them safe from other large predators. ©Phillip Ross

Black leopards get their colour due to a surplus of pigment in the skin or hair, making it appear black. This condition is called melanism. ©Shaaz Jung

Leopards have different kind of teeth that are varied in size and shape, and perform different functions such as strangulating prey, crushing of bones, shearing and slicing of meat. ©Shaaz Jung

Leopard and cub—A leopard normally gives birth to two to three cubs. ©Shaaz Jung

Strawberry leopards get their colour due to a genetic condition called erythrism. South Africa is the only country that seem to have strawberry leopards in the current day scenario. ©Deon deVilliers

Distinctive body patterns—A leopard (top), a cheetah (middle) and a jaguar (bottom) and their distinctive body markings.

Each leopard has a distinctive rosette pattern

Leopards face competition from other co-predators
such as the dhole. ©Ganesh Raghunathan

Large wild prey like the sambar are critical for reducing human-leopard conflict especially outside protected areas. ©Sudhir Shivaram

The Hanuman langur—In some areas, the Hanuman langur is one of the important prey species for leopards in the absence of large wild prey. ©Phillip Ross

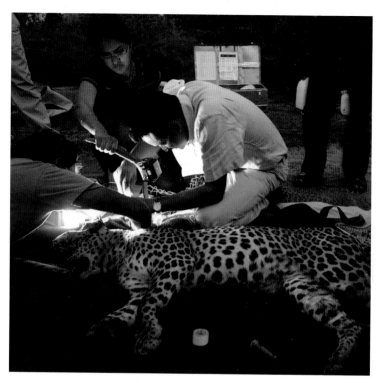
The author and his team placing a radio collar on a leopard.
©Arun Bastin

The author measures the body measurements of the
Chammanahalla male which was translocated into Bandipur Tiger
Reserve. ©Arun Simha

Quarrying and mining are the major causes of loss of leopard habitats in India. ©Shreyas Kumar Shenoy

Rocky outcrops that are part of the Deccan Plateau are important leopard habitats in southern India. ©Sanjay Gubbi

A leopard runs up a tree as the tiger chases it in Nagarahole Tiger Reserve, southern India. Its body size and tree climbing skills help the leopard protect itself against other competing large predators. ©Phillip Ross

Leopards are habitat generalists and can also survive on the outskirts of towns and cities. ©Ganesh Raghunathan

Leopards also occupy agricultural landscapes like tea gardens as seen in Valparai in Tamil Nadu. ©Ganesh Raghunathan

At an ancient ruin—Leopards are sometimes found amidst ancient ruins providing a unique perspective of human history and wildlife. ©Shaaz Jung

The black leopard in Nagarahole Tiger Reserve in southern India attracts a lot of tourists and wildlife photographers. ©Phillip Ross

The leopard flying out of the bathroom at a school in Bengaluru.
©Anantha Subramanyam

The author was injured by a leopard in a school in
Bengaluru during its rescue operations.
©Anantha Subramanyam

In areas that have a high abundance of large wild prey, leopards prefer chital and other large ungulates. ©Geetha Srinivasan

The strong shoulder muscles of the leopard help it to climb trees easily. ©Praveen Siddannanavar

The leopard squirts on a tree trunk to mark its territory that it defends against other male leopards. ©Praveen Siddannanavar

Leopards are found even on the outskirts of large cities like Mumbai, Bengaluru and other metros. ©Steve Winter

them to a computer server. This is finally downloaded on to the researcher's computer through an email in a coded format. The location of the wearer (leopard in our case) can be transmitted based on the researcher's requirement. It can be programmed to send locations over any pre-determined time period—whether every hour or every twelve hours and so on. However, the more number of locations we draw from the collar, the lower the life of the battery.

Most times, forest department officials capture leopards involved in conflict situations using a metallic cage. Luring leopards into cages is a fairly straightforward process. Dogs and goats are generally used as bait to attract the leopard in. Once the animal enters the cage it walks on a pressure pad that's connected to the trap door of the cage, shutting it automatically when the animal enters and imprisoning it. Then the animal is taken to the location intended for its release, and the trap door is opened for the animal to run out to freedom.

We received permissions from the forest department to fit radio collars on such captured animals before they were released. Thus began our journey.

### Benki the fire

In January 2014, 8 January to be precise, we got our first break. It was around eight in the morning when I received a telephone call from Vasanth Reddy, the head of the Cauvery Wildlife Sanctuary, informing me that there was a leopard that had been brought in and was to be released in Cauvery Wildlife Sanctuary. He told me that the head of the forest department had suggested that he contact me to put a collar around it, and asked me to discuss the matter with the forest officers from Tumkur and plan my collaring exercise. Chinnappa, the local range forest officer from Tumkur district, gave me a few more details. Due to pressure from villagers, the forest department had captured a leopard near Chalamasandra village on the border of Tumkur and Mandya districts. He told me they would wait for me at Halagur, and we could proceed together from there to the wildlife sanctuary.

Our office immediately bustled with activity. It was like an elite unit of the army had been mobilised. We had a list of seventy-four pieces of equipment that were required for the radio-collaring exercise. Our kit included everything from a portable stretcher to the rice grain-sized passive integrated transponder to be inserted into the animal. All the equipment were regularly checked for readiness. Even if we missed a small screw, the work could halt in the middle of the forests. Now, we checked once again that everything was in place.

Once we'd ticked off the essential items on our checklist, we loaded all the equipment. My colleague Rashmi, the erstwhile computer science engineer, directed the team to put all the gear in order: the large aluminium trunk that had all the measuring gear and our sample collection kit would be at the bottom of the four-wheel drive car's boot. The Stanley tool kit, which had the radio collar, antenna and other gear, would be placed above it. A large duffel bag with the weighing scale and a jerry can with water were fixed at the side of the vehicle, nets were fixed on top, and the wooden pole to hang the measuring scale to weigh the animal was attached to the rear. Everything else was stowed neatly so that we had space for the equipment but also for the entire team to sit. Things can get hectic during the actual collaring, so it was important that everyone know the equipment and where it was placed. The veterinary team would bring all the necessary veterinary equipment, including dart guns, jab sticks and drugs.

We left for Cauvery Wildlife Sanctuary within three hours of receiving the first telephone call. As we arrived in Halagur, which is about 80 kms away from Bengaluru, Chinnappa was waiting for us at the eatery at the entrance to the village. To my enthusiasm to leave immediately for the forests, he responded calmly, saying, 'Let's have a quick bite before we leave. You never know how long it will take once we enter the forests.' He was right. After a quick lunch, we headed off to the forests.

As we reached the forest edge, the officers from Tumkur had to stop to complete a few formalities. The mini-truck carrying the leopard was parked under a neem tree (*Azadirachta indica*) to ensure that the animal was kept under good shade. I was impressed when I first saw him peeping through the tarpaulin that his cage had been covered with to protect him from curious onlookers. He was a well-built, five- or six-year-old individual. But surprisingly, he had no scars from skirmishes with other suitors or challengers. This is a typical feature in large carnivores, especially when they are males who have to defend their turfs against intruders and challengers.

Energetic and angry, he was uncomfortable with anyone walking even too close to the vehicle. When someone's shade passed over his cage's blue tarpaulin, he reacted with a snarl. I soon realised that my wish to study leopards did not match his own desire to be left alone. But I knew I was doing the right thing for his species, even though he would not be very interested in my upcoming scientific arguments.

Formalities done, the animal was taken to the banks of River Cauvery adjacent to Kirumada, a deep pool in the river that was plush with the endangered mahseer fish. The river is rich with mugger-the armour-plated crocodiles, playful button-eyed otters, long-necked snake birds, grey-headed fish eagles that perch on branches at its edge, waiting for a catch, and many other wildlife. The valley was empty of people for nearly twenty kilometres with lots of natural prey, especially chital, that would visit the river often to quench their thirst. On both sides of the valley were rolling hills with savannah woodland forests and wide-spaced trees. The long grass of the forest floor helped grazers and browsing animals alike. Arjuna (*Terminilia arjuna*), tamarind (*Tamarindus indica*), sage-leaved alangium (*Alangium saviifolium*) and bastard sandal (*Erythroxylum monogynum*) trees grew luxuriously along the river banks, and this unique riverine habitat was always green due to the availability of water year-round. The setting could hardly have been more beautiful and serene.

We laid out our equipment under the shade of a large tamarind tree, as though a sumptuous picnic was being readied. A couple of thick cotton bed sheets were spread out over a tarpaulin. We had to clear the place of pebbles and any growth that could hurt the animal if it pressed on its blood vessels or nerves.

After inspecting all the other equipment, I checked and prepared the collar. The collar battery showed 6.678 volts. It was good to go. I had to remove the small magnet that's generally attached to GPS collars to keep them running on lowest current so the battery doesn't drain out when the collar is stored. Then, I went on to check for the three beeps: *beep … beep… beep,* sounded the collar in my earphones when it was motionless. I moved the collar around for a while, and the sound changed to *bip … bip … bip,* indicating that the collar was in motion. The collar was working fine.

The different beep patterns the VHF transmitter uses indicates if the animal is moving or resting, or even if the collar has gone into mortality mode. When the collar is not in motion it will give out a *beep* every two seconds, and when it is, it will send out one *bip* per second.

I connected the Wildlink module, a small white box with an antenna that enables the GPS collar to communicate with the computer and helps it to be programmed through the computer, to the laptop. I programmed the collar to provide GPS locations every two hours. The collar's battery life depends on the number of locations we demand from the collar in a day; the more the locations, the lesser the battery life. With the existing battery life and based on the number of locations we had programmed it for, this collar was supposed to last at least four and a half months. It was programmed to die on 17 March 2015 at 8 p.m. Even if the battery lasted that long, irrespective of the collar's remaining battery life, the collar would automatically drop off on that day through a release mechanism that's fitted into the collar.

To fit the radio collar, we needed to first tranquillise the leopard using a syringe or a dart to inject the drug. It was the job of the young but highly talented government veterinarian Sujay, in his light blue apron and rectangle-shaped eyeglasses, to do so, and he stood, preparing to fire a ten-inch-long dart loaded with a mix of

Ketamine and Xlyacine. He wanted to dart the large animal with the sleep-inducing drug through a blowpipe. This is a pipe-like equipment similar to the wooden ones normally used by forest-dwelling tribes to hunt wildlife in parts of India, Southeast Asia and Africa. But it didn't work, and Sujay decided to change his equipment. He then filled a syringe with the tranquilising drug and attached it to the end of a special six-foot-long aluminium jab stick.

Like a child protesting a vaccination jab, the leopard was uncooperative. He growled and moved to different corners of the cage, making it extremely difficult for Sujay to do the job. I tried to distract the leopard's attention so as to make it face me so that the dart could be jabbed into his rump. Sujay slowly climbed the vehicle and approaching the leopard from its back, he pushed the jab stick into the leopard's thigh. As it entered, Sujay calmly said, 'I got it.' I looked at the watch. It was 16.50 hours.

We all moved away and quietly waited for the drug to kick in. External stimulations like noise and people moving around the cage would only delay the drug's effect. Within the next ten minutes, the leopard was sitting in a sphinx position, dozing inside the cage. After a while, he was fast asleep, resting on one side of his body. I first poked the leopard with a small stick to check if the drug had taken effect. There was no response. Next, I guardedly slipped my hand between the iron railings of the cage and softly pressed his paw in search of a response. The paws and ears are good body parts to check to see if an animal is sleeping deeply and can be handled. The ears twitch if the animal is even slightly conscious of the happenings around it. Had the leopard been awake, he would have taken my hand off. But he was unresponsive to any stimuli. Once we were sure he was fast asleep, we pulled him out of the cage.

It was my team's turn to perform. We placed the leopard on a net, and the four of us carried him to the long pole with the weighing scale, held at two ends by the strongest men in the team. Our leopard tipped the scales at 60.9 kgs. The weighing process completed, he was placed on the bed sheet that had been laid out for him under the tamarind tree. His pulse and breathing were steady. We immediately ensured his eyelids were closed so that his eyes wouldn't become dry; this would also help keep him calm. I covered his eyes with a piece of cloth to protect them from the harmful ultraviolet rays of the sun and also to prevent any dirt and debris from entering. I extended his neck straight to ensure his breathing was smooth and pulled out his tongue so it didn't obstruct his breathing or accidentally asphyxiate him during the process of being anaesthetised.

Everyone had a task assigned to her or him. Poornesha was incharge of writing down all details on a data sheet. Rashmi provided all the equipment required while Harish helped me put the collar on. We fastened the 587g collar around the leopard's neck. A radio collar should typically weigh less than 3 per cent of the animal's body weight to ensure that the bulk of the external object does not become a burden on the wild animal. Here, it was less than 1 per cent of the body weight of this leopard.

The standard international practice is that the collar should be fitted such that there is space for two outstretched fingers to be vertically slipped between the collar and the animal's neck. It shouldn't be so tight that it hinders the animal's breathing, and it shouldn't be so lose that it slips over the animal's head. I cut the collar belt by a few centimetres to suit the 65 cm neck circumference of our leopard, checking multiple times to ensure it was well fitted. As I finished tightening all the four non-corrosive bracket plates and fasteners on to the collar, the time on my watch read 17.40 hours.

As a next step, Harish helped me take all the morphometric measurements of the leopard. The animal measured 2.2 metres from nose tip to tip of the tail at the last vertebra. He was over seven feet long, and over 41 per cent of his length was his tail. Our measuring tape put his height at 96 cms from shoulder to his front right paw. Older animals, especially males, have broader heads, but with a head breadth of 32 cms, he was a fairly large individual by Indian standards. He was a perfect anatomical specimen.

I always like to get my hands on the teeth, which are one of the most important body parts of a large carnivore, and hold a surprising amount of information. So my next move was to carefully examine the leopard's jaw. His canine and molars—broad, flat ones to rip, pull out meat—declared that this was an animal in his prime. The top right canine was slightly yellowish in colour with grains on it, and it measured 2.8 cms long on the vernier callipers. The small wear marks visible at the ends of the canine helped me estimate his age. The wear of the teeth and their colour confirmed he was about five to six years, as we had guessed earlier. As I had my hand inside his mouth, I could feel him purring, not fully asleep. The position of my hand and closeness of those large canines naturally made me a bit fidgety. Another small dose of the drug by Sujay quieted him and allowed us to complete our task.

All this while, a group of bonnet macaques sat on a tamarind tree, watching us at work under their world. Their loud alarm calls rent the air throughout the collaring exercise; they would only stop when the leopard was put back in the cage. Their short bark-like cough, much like a teenager after taking his first hesitant drag of a cigarette, is always a sign of the presence of a large carnivore. Some primates, in fact, have specific alarm calls for different predators. East African vervet monkeys warn their conspecifics against predators with different alarm calls for different predators and dangers, such as leopards, eagles or snakes.

As we went about our work fitting the collar and measuring the animal, Sujay was constantly checking in on the leopard's vitals. At one point, I realised the body temperature of the leopard seemed a bit high. When Sujay inserted the digital thermometer into the rectum of the leopard to check, the gauge displayed a temperature of 105.4°F which should be between 100 and 102°F. We covered the animal with a cotton bedspread soaked in water to bring down the temperature. It is normal for the temperature of an animal to increase or decrease when it is given a dose of tranquilising drugs. Hence, the temperature has to be carefully monitored or else it could lead to disastrous situations resulting in hyperthermia or hypothermia.

Two bottles of IV fluids were kept continuously flowing, to prevent any dehydration caused due to the sedative we had administered. Dexona, RL and NS drugs were also pushed through the IV to reduce the stress and shock to the animal.

It is an odd, exciting sensation to be so close to an unconscious wild animal, which if awake, would easily kill you. As I stroked his spotted flank, I felt a thrill of power run through me. I felt his tongue, which was pink and raspy, like sandpaper used to smoothen walls before coats of paint or varnish. This burred tongue and its hooklike, inward bent barbs would help him remove the fur on the body of his prey. His bulged, saucer-sized paws were softer than cotton and unexpectedly healthy with no wounds, despite the animal's journey over rough, hard surfaces and thorny terrains.

The leopard's whiskers, or vibrissae, were hard and stiff and firmly attached to the cat's body. Whiskers act as touch receptors for the animals to interpret the world around them, helping them to hunt and move in the darkness. This part of the leopard's body is the Swiss Army knife of the animal's sensory and communications tool kit, also acting as an emotional barometer. An individual leopard has up to thirty extremely sensitive whiskers on each side of the face that grow at a rate of approximately 0.65 mm a day. Some researchers from South Africa have even tried to estimate the dietary patterns of leopards using the growth rate and growth patterns of whiskers.

I couldn't, however, spend much time caressing the animal. We had about sixty minutes from the time the animal had been given the tranquilising drug, to fit the collar on him, give him a dose of revival drug and put him back into the cage. I barely realised how three-fourths of the hour passed. Except for checking in with Sujay about the animal's body temperature and breathing, I hardly noticed what was happening around me. I was aware of nothing except the yellow-brown, majestic creation of evolution in front of me in the form of this beautiful cat, the not-so-pleasant smell of the animal's breath, its safety and the job I had on my hand. I heard nothing. I noticed the guttural calls of the bonnet monkeys above me only if I forcefully lent my ear to it.

Finally, we checked for ectoparasites. I ran a large comb several times through the leopard's fur. We found ticks on his large ears, but he had no lice, eye worms or fleas. Meanwhile, Sujay also injected anti-parasitic and deworming medicines.

We were done by 18.05 hours, and as the sun started going down behind the hillocks, it threw long shadows. The simians were forced to call it a day and went noiseless as they went to their roosts. I stroked the warm, soft fur of the animal for one last time, as I knew I would never be able to touch this beautiful cat again. Sujay carefully injected Yohimbimine drug to revive the leopard, and we put him back into the cage.

In ten minutes, the leopard was wide-eyed and trying to sit up in the typical cat's sitting position. Twice he tried to stand up but staggered and sank back to the floor of the cage. With his paws, he checked the strange device around his neck a few times. In about thirty minutes he was fully awake and active, assisted by a few splashes of water from our side. He would growl in a low tone if anyone even walked close to the cage, making clear his displeasure with our actions. We waited for another twenty minutes before he was fully active.

Then, a couple of us climbed on top of the small carriage van where the cage was placed and the rest got into the vehicle that brought us here. Finally, we signalled to each other that it was time for the animal to be set free. As the trap door was opened, it took very little time for the animal to feel his freedom. At 19.05 hours, on the banks of the River Cauvery, nearly 80 kms south-east of the place of his capture, the mighty feline was set free. Within minutes, the leopard had jumped out of the cage and disappeared into the darkness and obscurity of the forests, puffs of dust exploding under his bounding paws. I immediately tuned the radio receiver to 150.043 mhz, the leopard's radio collar frequency. There was an answering *beep … beep … beep …* sound from the earphones.

Prakash Matada, who was assisting us in video documenting the entire collaring exercise, had placed the versatile GoPro camera on the floor, about 50m from the vehicle that had the cage. The beautiful video footage showed the dust flying in the air as the animal bounded away. He was poetry in motion; one of nature's most stunningly beautiful creations.

Thrilling and exciting days were ahead. Now on, we would get a peek into the private life of this big cat. I hoped to gain new insights into the leopard, especially in terms of its malleability—this was an animal highly acclaimed for its adaptability in various habitats and a greater tolerance to human presence, and I hoped to be able to study these claims more closely.

We woke up early next morning to the clucking of the grey jungle fowl. In the winter cold, we climbed up a tower on a nearby hillock. It had been built previously to watch for forest fires. The mist from the Cauvery emerged from the waters in the valley below. The soft early morning sun rose from behind the hardwickia trees dominating the hillock. Amidst this beautiful vista was the funny call of the laughing dove and the ascending *brain feever, brain feever, brain feever* call of the obscure common hawk-cuckoo.

It was time to get to work. I connected the VHF antenna to the receiver, plugged in the earphones, and wrapped them around my head. The small, box-like receiver had a knob to fine tune to the collar frequency and small black buttons to select the VHF channel number of the collar. I switched on the round receiver button, raised the antenna over my head, and slowly began rotating the antenna in a wide arc, a movement used by several biologists to locate their study animals.

As I slowly moved the antenna, I heard a feeble *beep ... beep ... beep* in the direction the animal had been released last evening. I fine-tuned the VHF frequency further, and the sound became louder and clearer. The sound confirmed that the collar was working perfectly, but that didn't comfort me much. If the animal were active and moving, the difference between each beep would have be shorter and I would have heard a *bip ... bip ... bip*. I tried for over an hour, but the pattern of the sound didn't change.

Finally, we returned to camp and headed to Halagur, the nearest village, where we could access internet to download the email that would give me the satellite location of the animal. The entire vehicle smelled of the leopard, but this smell would not last for very long if it was a healthy animal. From my experience, if an animal has any serious health issues, the smell lasts longer despite cleaning all the equipment with hospital surgical spirit.

We sat in a small eatery and ordered a rice dosa before checking on the email. When we finally did, I found I had received no e-mails from the from the satellite service provider. The satellite had still not received any locations even fourteen hours post collaring, though it was programmed to send a location every two hours. Disappointed, I headed back to the location where the animal had been released to once again manually check for signals using the hand-held antenna. The sound hadn't changed. The slowly paced signal indicated an inactive animal. I comforted myself with the idea that it must be resting somewhere, maybe under a boulder or near a ravine that would provide it a cooler temperature, and we returned to our base camp.

But even after twenty-four hours, we had neither received the location of the animal from the satellite nor had the inactive signal changed to an active one. These were very tense moments—there's nothing worse than when a radio collar does not move. I felt a twinge of apprehension in the pit of my belly. Could he have been asleep for such a long period? Could he have he pulled off the collar, like a female leopard we had earlier tried to collar near Hassan? Surely that couldn't be the case, because I was getting the slow, inactive signal and not the two consecutive short beeps followed by a long beep (*bip, bip, beep, bip, bip, beep*) that would show that the animal hadn't moved at least for an hour and would indicate a mortality mode.

I requested Harish to head back to the location of the release. He climbed up a few small peaks to check with the antenna, but the signals remained the same. My heart stopped and head prickled. How were we to find the leopard? It would be like trying to find a needle in the haystack. We could only wait and watch.

Finally, to our joy and relief, forty-eight hours after collaring the animal, we received the first GPS location through the satellite.

The leopard had finally moved from the release location, where it had rested for nearly forty-six hours. In the field, the signal was rapid, showing the animal was active. All was well.

When the satellite locations started coming in, I could see that after the release, the leopard had climbed up about hundred metres and settled down to rest very close to the location where we had freed him. At 4.30 a.m., on 10 January, when we received the first satellite location, he had walked straight to the Cauvery, possibly for a hearty gulp, and then walked east towards Hyra, where there is an anti-poaching outpost of the forest department. He rested and hung around in that area for another two days, coming down to the river a couple of times before heading north of it. This was the beginning of our entry into this male's otherwise secret life in Cauvery Wildlife Sanctuary. Then on, he would unknowingly send out his location every two hours, except in instances when he was resting under a boulder or in a deep valley where the collar was unable to communicate with the satellite.

When I returned home and showed the images and video to my four-year-old son, Ninaadha, he immediately named the leopard 'Benki', the Kannada word for fire. I was surprised at his choice. Ninaadha, whose own name in Kannada means the sound of the slow-moving water, had came up with a rather fiery name. But it was an apt name for this large male.

As a happenstance, at the time, we were camera trapping in the same area that Benki was released in, which helped us get some extra insights about the leopard. He walked in front of some of our camera traps within three days of his release, when he came down to the river near Galibore to have a drink, in the darkness of the night.

For the rest of that summer and beyond, we monitored Benki's choices through his radio collar as he walked by day, by night, inside the forest, up the hills and down the hills. Benki moved around, telling us, through his signals, that he was active both during night and day. But he was three times more active at night than during the daytime. He would also move twice the distance at night. He sometimes travelled no more than a few hundred metres in a day. But at other times he would do an amazing 16 kms in a day, patrolling his new home and finding the best on the à la carte menu the forests offered.

Benki moved quite a distance on a daily basis, with a mean distance of 7.8 kms per day as the crow flies. On ground, he may have done more than this distance, as he had to work his way through the hilly terrain. He meandered through the rough terrain of Cauvery Wildlife Sanctuary, climbing high hillocks, walking in valleys, resting alongside big boulders, and at times visiting the Cauvery. Some of the locations he visited surprised me greatly. He would venture onto steep cliffs or rocky boulders where even humans with expertise in rock climbing would have found it difficult to reach.

He regularly used the same routes, perhaps patrolling and marking his territory with warning signs to other males in the area. Though I went tracking Benki several times, using the handheld antenna, I never got an opportunity to see him again in the flesh. Radio collaring is all about hearing animals and not seeing them. The animals are almost always concealed from view by a wall of bushes or grass.

Benki lorded over an area of 141 sq kms, much of which was clothed with woodland savannah forests and rugged and mountainous. The area Benki called his home was as large as the city of Mysuru. It was an enormous area for a leopard to traverse and something I had not foreseen. Except for one time, Benki did not venture out of the forests despite the fact that he came from a human-dominated landscape. I wished he could tell me how he felt about his new home.

Every move and every trace of Benki made me feel alive. He became a sentimental favourite of the entire team, since he was the first leopard successfully collared and monitored by the project. Benki provided us with some rare understanding about the secretive lives of leopards, especially those that are brought in from other areas.

Another five adult male and five adult female leopards were photographed a few times within the area where Benki roamed. It looked like three of those males had their homes within Benki's area of operation, while the other two might have been floaters trying to find new home ranges. None of the other males that were operating within or in the areas adjoining Benki's territory looked physically large enough to challenge him, perhaps giving him an advantage over them. Benki had overlapping territory with at least two females (CU-03 and CU-07). Sadly, CU-07 died in a road accident in October 2015. Perhaps Benki lost one of his partners to someone's careless driving. These snippets of information came together to create a leopard eco-map, including information on how many males and females can survive within a large male's territory.

Benki's journey with us continued for twenty-one weeks. After tracking him for 146 days, the battery of the collar wore off and stopped sending signals on 2 June 2014. In that time, Benki walked 1,134 kms, a distance that would cover the journey from Amsterdam in Netherlands to Milan in Italy, spanning four European countries. I felt a sense of hollowness, as it had become part of my daily ritual to check Benki's location and understand his movement pattern. I didn't just see data and some leopard. I saw Benki and his story.

Unfortunately, I couldn't retrieve the collar as it had probably dropped off in some remote area of the forest, or so I thought. Since the battery was dead we couldn't even try to find it using the VHF antenna.

Late one morning in February 2015, Mohammed Mansoor, the slim, mettlesome range forest officer whose jurisdiction included part of Benki's territory, called and said, 'Sir, we have got a leopard in one of the camera traps we had placed near the Kolukote waterhole. It seems to have something strange around its neck. Can you check the images I've mailed to you?' Though the pictures were not a clear shot, I could see a large leopard walking around a drying waterhole. The 'something' around his neck turned out to be a radio collar. It was certainly Benki. Though the collar was not functioning, it must have still remained on his neck. A giddy thrill went through me. Two small bits of data had clicked together for a moment of epiphany.

As Benki walked at the water's edge that afternoon, he gave us some valuable information. Over thirteen months after the collar had been placed on him, Benki had remained close to the area of his release; he was camera-trapped only about nine kilometres from his initial release site. After this brief glimpse of him, he again disappeared from our radar.

In July 2015, again, to my joy, Vasanth Reddy called me and said his field staff had found the radio collar during their regular patrol duty. The location where the collar was found was well within the established home range of Benki. When I received the collar in my hands, it felt as though I had found a lost friend. Leopards can be tough on their collars: they tend to rub them on rocks and trees, take them inside water and slush, and do a lot of rough things during their daily routine. The collar needs to be sturdy enough to withstand the wear and tear of a large carnivore. The collar we got back was battered, with the leather belt worn off at several places and the metal antenna sticking out. There were a few leopard hair strands stuck in the nooks of the collar. I am sure they belonged to Benki. It reminded me of the last time I had stroked his smooth fur about eighteen months ago. Today, the collar cosily sits as a souvenir of a friend who helped us to understand a small part of his world.

At the end of the same year, we returned to Cauvery Wildlife Sanctuary with our entire camera trapping team for another round. As we swept through the forests, block after block, placing camera traps to understand the dynamics of leopard populations, we reached the last block—Sangama, north of the river Cauvery. On 4 January 2016, nearly two years after Benki was released in Cauvery Wildlife Sanctuary, he again ambled into sight. He was captured twenty times, on different days, in front of our camera traps near Nayakanakallubetta, Huliyammanagudda, Paadadaridoddi, Devarabetta and other areas. He radiated a wildness that could only come from fighting through life alone. The skin folds under his belly and neck were sagging, showing that he was ageing, but he otherwise looked as vibrant as the first time I had seen him. Of course, he posed in front our camera traps without his valuable jewellery: the radio collar. But his very unique, jaguar-like rosette patterns made him quickly identifiable. I felt as though I had run into an old friend, and every time I identified Benki in our camera traps, I was excited and jumped around in joy. It occurred to me that this is what species research is really about.

Benki now seemed to have a stable home range. He appeared well adapted and to be a tenant of a territory that spanned tens of square kilometres of excellent leopard habitat—rich in prey and rich in water. CU-03, the female that we had seen sauntering around in his territory earlier, continued to be in the same area as Benki. So she may have continued to be one of his partners. At the same time, another male, CU-01, who was also present in the area in 2014, seemed to have expanded his domain and had slightly overlapping territory with Benki. CU-01 was also a bit naughty. He was documented in camera traps as a livestock lifter.

After the stint in 2015, we returned to Cauvery Wildlife Sanctuary with our team and a host of camera traps in August 2018. By the time we arrived at Halagur and Sangama areas, where Benki had established his territory, it was mid-November. My excitement increased as we started our work north of the River Cauvery. Every time we got images of leopards from our camera traps, I eagerly went through them, check the size and rosettes of the leopards that had catwalked in front of our camera traps. I was looking for Benki's distinct rosette patterns. My hopes escalated every evening when there were pictures of large male leopards. But the disappointment continued; no Benki appeared in our pictures.

For nearly forty-five days my eagerness continued, until the camera trapping exercise ended in this area. Not having found my old friend, I was left with a hollow feeling. I am not sure if we just didn't detect Benki in our camera traps or if he had made way to a younger, more powerful male. In fact, we did capture two male leopards, who were about five years of age and big and hulky, in the area where Benki would operate. CU-63, a male leopard that had been photographed in camera traps on the edge of Benki's territory in 2016, was camera-trapped in the heart of the area where Benki was operating. He was now as muscular and as big as Benki was in 2014. In all probability, CU-63 might have been the new tenant of what was once Benki's home.

I finally had to concede the fact Benki had probably been replaced by a younger leopard, as is natural in the world of wild cats. The takeover might have been a rather brutal ritual, but that is the way of the jungle. Benki, after his youthful years at Cauvery, seemed to have vanished into oblivion. We repeated the exercise recently, in 2020, and Benki never reappeared in the camera traps.

I have made peace with myself that this wonderful individual will never come back into my life. I think of Benki often and have told his story to some. When I think of him, there is a feeling in me, one so deep I cannot name it. I believe Benki feels it too. That our purpose in life is to look out for each other. Our tribes hardly meet, let alone become part of each other's life. But fate brought us together.

In India, it had been the trend to claim that leopard translocation is a total failure. But these conclusions were based on very small sample sizes with no variations in age range, sex of the translocated individual, translocation site or any other factors being considered. Benki defied this theory. He pulled another veil away from our view of leopards. Apart from the tremendous joy he gave us by allowing us to peek a little bit into his mysterious world, Benki provided new understanding about leopards. Finally, he showed that life is a magnificent cycle of birth and death.

Another experiment in Sariska Tiger Reserve, Rajasthan also demonstrated that some translocated leopards would settle down at the release location.

## *The young male of Hulkudibetta*

Two hours after being tranquilised, the young leopard stumbled off, still a bit unsteady on his feet as he wobbled around the vehicles for a few minutes. He even tried digging his sharp canines into the front tyre of a jeep belonging to the forest department. Luckily the rubber tyre survived as he withdrew the canines before much damage was done. We waited until the young male was steady and walked away in the darkness. This was to ensure that any other larger male leopard in the area would not have easy picking of this young male if it ventured nearby. Now that the male was steady, we could breathe easy.

Just over a month after we had collared Benki we were again asked to collar another leopard closer to Bengaluru. This time, the phone call came from someone I had known for an over a decade and a half—Nizamuddin. He was a young, tough forester with large eyeglasses, who had fought many poachers and timber smugglers in Bhadra Tiger Reserve. Nizamuddin had now become the range forest officer and was working in Doddaballapur, an area that had little forest cover, unlike Bhadra.

His team had captured a leopard in Hulkudibetta, about two hundred metres from Maadeshwara, a small hamlet that had about ten dwellings. When we landed there, before the sun had even risen overhead, a few hundred villagers had gathered in the eucalyptus plantation, wanting to take a look at the cat. Many told us how relieved they were and of the difficulties they had been facing—losing their livestock and living in fear when their small children walked back from school as the leopard sat on a boulder and watched them intently. Nizamuddin and his team had the cage well covered to reduce the duress to the animal, and the crowd was kept away from getting to the cage. This was good management practice, for in its absence, the animal would have charged at the cage, resulting in broken canines or claws or injuries to its forehead. If an animal loses its canines, it makes it harder for it to hunt its natural prey, and can possibly lead to more conflict as the cat might then prefer animals that are easier to catch, like livestock.

We avoided peeking at the animal as others would have also demanded the same privilege. Soon, the forest department personnel loaded the cage into a mini-truck and left the location, asking us to follow them. We simply did as we were asked to and followed the mini-truck on the dusty roads through a few other villages. I had no clue where we were being led. In less than thirty minutes, the mini-truck took a right turn off the main road and led us into a scrubby area. After driving for a few more minutes into the scrub, the mini-truck halted, and we were told that the leopard would be released here. We weren't too far from the location where it was captured, but the decision of capture and release was in the hands of the forest department authorities. Our role was to fit the animal with the radio collar and report our research findings.

As earlier, Sujay, the veterinarian, got on with the job of tranquilising, using a blowpipe that yielded the required results. Unlike Benki, this was a smaller animal, and required a lower dosage of the immobilising drug. As the animal stopped responding to physical stimuli, we brought him on to the portable stretcher and hooked it to the weighing scale. He was but half the weight of Benki; this young male tipped the scale at 32 kgs while Benki was almost 61 kgs.

Once the collar was fitted on his lean neck it was time to measure him. His one-inch pearly canines, essential machinery for strangulating and killing his prey, were clean and had no signs of wear. They had fully developed dentition. This indicated that the animal was young, perhaps about two years old.

He had a total body length of 208 cms from nose tip to the end of the tail and a shoulder height of 72 cms, and would be another half a foot taller when he would grow older. His neck was of a circumference of 52 cms, more than half a foot smaller than that of Benki's neck. All his morphometric measurements were proportionately smaller than that of Benki's, underlining the fact that he was a young animal.

At exactly 19.00 hours in the evening, when the winter sun had set, the leopard jumped out of his cage and walked away, carrying with him our hopes to understand a bit more about the young male.

Apart from the scrub, the area had a lot of commercial eucalyptus plantations on private land. Within forty-five hours, the leopard had returned to his adobe in Hulkudibetta. He initially walked north from the location he was released and then south and finally west to reach his home. On his journey back, he took refuge in the eucalyptus plantations.

This young male revealed many secrets as I tracked him for 123 days. He was largely a nocturnal animal, and as the sun set, he would become active, descending from the hillock and heading straight towards the villages. Though he wandered off every single night, for some strange, unknown reason, he completely avoided going west of the hillock. He had a few favourite locations as well.

His daily travel distances varied from 2.9–9.7 kms at night. A few times he wandered off to places that he had not visited earlier, and did not return to those locations again during the study period. He once wandered off about 4.3 kms from Hulkudibetta, almost hitting the highway connecting the Bengaluru International Airport to Dobbaspete, a small industrial town on the Bengaluru–Mumbai highway. During the day he was inactive and spent all his time on the hillock, probably resting for about twelve hours.

To understand where his nightly sojourns took him, we went back to the locations he visited. Interestingly, many of his night-time visits were to chicken farms that had proliferated in the area in the last couple of years.

Today, India ranks seventh in the world in chicken consumption, and sixth in production, which has boomed since the early 2000s. This seems to correlate with economic growth. As the economy grows linearly, access to more expensive protein seems to be growing phenomenally, with nearly 3,820 metric tonnes of annual chicken consumption (nearly 120 kgs per second) in the country. The space to set up the messy and often fetid farms required for this production has to be carved far from human habitation.

Often, lands adjoining forests are found to be the most convenient locations for these since there is little human habitation and social opposition is less. This, however, also makes it convenient for a leopard to pick up a few chicken from these farms and has perhaps led to an increase in leopard conflict.

In addition, the disposal of dead chicken and chicken waste in open pits make them a magnet for carnivores such as leopards. Many of these waste-disposal sites are near villages, and when a leopard arrives at these sites at night, their chances of encountering farmers, many of whom may be in the fields to water their crops, are high. Since three-phase electric power, which can run motor pumps to lift water from boreholes or open wells, is supplied largely during the night, farmers are forced to venture out after dark to water their crops. Large wildlife species such as leopards and sloth bears, that are conflict-prone, are also active during this time period. Eventually, the chance encounters lead to fear and, at times, fatal encounters.

Hence, an increase in chicken consumption and production has become one of the reasons for higher human-leopard conflict. Our camera traps occasionally capture leopards carrying away broilers; a clear indication of demand-induced conflict. Human-wildlife conflict is not merely ecological, it also occurs due to social and economic reasons.

On 18 June 2014, the young male's collar stopped sending out signals. I waited for a couple of days in the hope that the collar would restart sending out the locations but in vain. I finally went to Hulkudibetta with the VHF antenna to track down the animal. My first port of call was the hillock there, where I knew he usually rested all day. When I reached there and switched on the receiver, I was shocked by what I heard. The receiver was emitting *bip, bip-bip, bip, bip-bip, bip, bip-bip* signals—a worrying sound for a researcher. More cause for worry was that the signals did not come from the area where this young male regularly rested but from the direction of a village. I started tracking the sound. The antenna took me south-east of Hulkudibetta, past a few chicken farms and eucalyptus plantations.

About four hundred metres from the Basavanapura village, the signal became very strong and led me to a eucalyptus plantation. This made me very nervous. Had something gone wrong with the animal? The area was too close to the village. My doubts were many, and in my anxiety to find the animal, I forced myself heedlessly through lantana bushes, their small sharp thorns piercing deeply into my skin. As I followed the antenna, the signal grew stronger and stronger. I disconnected the cable that connected the antenna to the receiver and the beeps continued on the receiver. It no longer needed an antenna to receive the signals, which indicated the collar was very close.

Adrenaline pumping high, I started intently searching for the animal. I looked under the bushes, in the small ravine that ran at the edge of the plantation, on the branches of the few non-eucalyptus trees that were around. I was certain it was somewhere very close. Finally, I found the radio collar lying amidst the dry eucalyptus leaves and a few white chicken feathers. It was only the collar and not the stationary animal that had led to the *bip, bip-bip* signal. The collar must have dropped off him after its battery had run out. I picked it up, extremely relieved.

About twenty metres away, at the confluence of the eucalyptus plantation and an areca nut plantation was an open pit half filled with chicken waste. Perhaps the young animal had been scavenging on the disposed chicken. He must have started taking part as one of the cleaning crew of the waste dump—not an ideal job for a young leopard. He probably made his living from the chicken dumping ground and the livestock near the villages. From our observations, he seemed to largely use the eucalyptus plantations that were on private lands for concealing himself and his movements.

These two male leopards I radio collared provided very insightful information. One was a large male in a wildlife sanctuary, who moved around both during the day and the night. Another was a young male that was in a highly human-dominated landscape, and stayed put in a small hillock the entire day and moved into villages almost every night. His home range was only about

10.5 sq kms. Astonishingly, it was fourteen times smaller than Benki's 141 sq kms. He sourced his food from a much smaller area, while Benki, who was in near natural settings, had to walk, climb, and struggle a lot more to survive.

It was clear that their daily movement patterns and home ranges varied depending upon where they survived: in a large forest or in small forests, surrounded by human habitations. There were some indicators, such as the number of instances of conflict, that leopards are better off when they are in near natural settings than in largely human dense areas.

Our radio collaring efforts and the concomitant opportunities to handle a few leopards also gave me an insight into how these animals respond. Individual animals do have their own temperaments like humans. While the Antharasanthe female, as we shall see next, was imperturbable and cooperative, Benki was sullen and petulant; he didn't tolerate even the shade that would fall on the cover on his cage.

## The Antharasanthe female

Two and half months after we had collared Benki, the forest department informed me of a female leopard that had been captured in a human-dominated area south of Mysuru, and requested that I fit the animal with a radio collar. It was a long drive from Bengaluru to the location where she was to be released, but we had to reach there at the earliest. When we arrived at the Anechowkooru forests north of the famed Nagarahole Tiger Reserve, it was beyond noon. The March afternoon sun was unsympathetic. The forests were a mix of eucalyptus plantations and a dense growth of bamboo.

The entire team had landed with all our equipment and gear. The only change in the team was with the veterinarian. Sanath had replaced Sujay, who had other commitments to deal with.

The leopard hadn't arrived yet. The tractor carrying the leopard finally arrived at five in the evening. There were a few people accompanying the tractor, including a couple of villagers from the area where the leopard had been captured, possibly trying to ensure that the animal was not released too close to the location of capture. The cage with the leopard was placed in a small, open trailer towed by the tractor. We immediately requested that the black plastic cover that had been put over the cage to protect the animal from the sun be removed so that she could get some fresh air. Everyone was kept away from her to allow her to calm down a bit.

We wanted to get an initial assessment of the animal—her body condition, her status and other external features. As Sanath and I walked close to the cage, I was surprised to find that the animal completely disregarded us, unlike Benki or most other wild leopards that were caged. She did not growl or charge towards us or engage in any other aggressive, unrestful behaviour. When we continued our visual examination, peeping between the iron bars of the cage, the leopard merely turned her head towards us for a few seconds and gave us a disinterested glance. She was composed and phlegmatic. Rarely had I seen any caged leopard that was not agitated at the sight and gaze of people. She remained calm despite the noise of the preparations that were going on around her.

Sanath tried twice with a blowpipe to tranquilise her without success, but the third time the dart hit its target and the animal slept off. As soon as we were confident that the leopard was under the effect of the drugs, we brought out the animal. We followed our usual steps and first weighed her, then carried out the medical and official checks prior to fitting the radio collar. She weighed about 33 kgs, which was normal for a leopardess of her age and condition.

My immediate priority with the leopardess was to check her mammary glands. I pressed her teats, and was relieved to see that she was not lactating. Had she been, I would have immediately requested the forest officials to take her back and release her at the capture site. Any lactating leopardess shouldn't be captured or translocated, as her cubs will be left without a mother and this could lead to serious consequences for the cubs. Once this critical factor was confirmed, I took up the task of fitting the radio collar.

Sanath, and his guru Dr Chettiappa's trusted assistant Ramesh worked carefully to complete medical formalities. Ramesh had no formal veterinary qualifications but was an excellent assistant to any veterinarian, and had a sound knowledge of various aspects of wildlife. He had assisted veterinarians on several operations to capture leopards, sloth bears and deer, and helped to treat both wild and captive animals. Working in the Bannerghatta Zoo for several years had provided him a great opportunity to pick up wildlife rescue and treatment skills.

When I tried to fit the collar around the leopard's neck, I realised that I would have to alter the collar length to a great extent, as her slender neck was only 53 cms. Her neck was nearly 20 per cent smaller than that of Benki, and 40 per cent larger than the average neck circumference of an adult female. Her yellowish canines and other features on the teeth indicted her age to be about four years.

The punching tool used to make holes on the leather belt of the radio collar, however, would not cooperate. The punch slipped off every time I applied the slightest pressure to puncture the leather belt. At long last, I had to change over to the standby punch, thanking my stars for having the backup equipment ready. It would have been extremely hard if we didn't have the standby tool, as the nearest place where we could have bought a replacement was 30 kms away, and the diversion would have halted our work for at least two hours.

It was getting dark. By now the birds had quietened down, and the wailing of the peacocks had ceased. I could now hear the empty *chuk-chukurrrr-chuk-chukurrrr* sound of the nightjars. We were in the middle of elephant country, and so had requested some of the forest personnel to stand guard for any elephant movement. If any elephant or a herd came in without our notice, it could prove disastrous and hence we had to exercise extreme caution.

After the collar was fitted and morphometric measurements were taken, it was time to say goodbye to this leopardess. Exactly sixty-one minutes after injecting the sedative, Sanath gave her a jab of the revival drug. Once the leopardess was put back into the cage, it took ninety minutes before she could walk free. She didn't look groggy and was back in full consciousness. She was firm on her feet and sauntered off into the jungle. At that time, little did I realise the political angle this collaring exercise would take.

Next morning, I returned to the location to track the leopardess using the VHF antenna. She had only moved a few hundred metres, but it was no surprise that we found the animal close to the release site. Satisfied that she had recovered from the sedation effect, we headed back.

The initial weeks after the radio collaring exercise were very tense days for me, spent hoping that the animal would recover well from the anaesthesia. I would endlessly wait for the emails from the satellite, always expecting a tsunami.

Two days after the leopardess was released into Anechowkooru, on 24 March 2014, she interestingly started to move out of the forests and headed west. She entered a large eucalyptus plantation where she halted for a day. When she started moving again, it was in human-dense areas. She walked through agricultural fields during the night and rested in scrub patches and the thick growth near tank beds during the day. In exactly eight days from her release, the leopardess had reached the southern outskirts of Mysuru. She had covered about 60 kms from the location of the release.

Based on the geolocation we received from the satellite, I reached the site where the leopardess was supposed to be hiding. It was a deserted area close to the Outer Ring Road that circled around the perimeter of the city, with some patches of scrub. A few liquor bottles were strewn around, indicating people used the area as an open-air bar—a typical scene in quiet, deserted areas close to human habitations. A thirty-foot-tall white babul tree (*Acacia leucophloea*), possibly where she had rested, was raked with claw marks. But I couldn't locate her.

After a brief two-day stint in the outskirts of the palace city, she started moving south. In another day, she had reached south-west of the Mysuru airport, which was about 5 kms from the edge of the city suburbs.

Eleven days after collaring, I was once again at the spot where she was supposed to be. The place looked desolate, dry and deserted. There was a large, abandoned stone-quarry pit, with some water, at least three-fourth of a kilometre long. All around the quarry pit was eucalyptus and thorny scrub growth. The signals from my antenna showed that she was somewhere close by. I walked around the deep quarry pit to locate her but in vain. When I suddenly spotted the scat of a leopard, I was, somehow, sure that it belonged to the collared leopardess. After walking around for a couple of hours, I decided to return the next day. The next morning, the signal had moved into the adjoining sugarcane fields. I was certain that she was inside the long sugarcane growth, but didn't want to disturb her or make anyone in the area panicky by moving around with the strange antenna and receiver.

She hung around the quarry and the sugarcane fields for nineteen days and again decided to move south. Within 2 kms she had reached the edge of Kabini River, also called the Kapila, a tributary of Cauvery but smaller in width and force. The riverside and the adjoining sugarcane fields were perfect hiding ground for the leopardess. During the day, she would move into the cover of the white babul trees that were linearly spread out along the water canals. The trees provided shade and were surrounded by thorny bushes, which discouraged anyone from venturing too far in. She could quietly slip in to drink water if she felt thirsty, as the area was desolate but for the occasional farmer walking to his fields.

Soon, I had to break my monitoring of the leopardess and go to Bandipur on work-related issues. When I returned after five days, along with me was Ganesh Ramani, a staunch supporter of our work and a serious wildlife conservationist. Ganesh was also keen to understand the tracking of wildlife using radio collars. The antenna beep signal was very strong. 'She's very close,' Ganesh whispered with the headphones wrapped around his ears. She was somewhere in the large bushes within a few metres of us, but we could not locate her. She must have been watching us and moving around to escape from our view. Then she started to move along the river and headed north-west. She had eluded us again.

Thirty-nine days after she was released in Anechowkooru, the leopardess reached Chikkanahalli Reserved Forests. With 23 sq kms (5,600 acres) of dry deciduous and thorny scrub and another 4 sq kms (1,000 acres) of forests in the adjoining hillocks, it is wonderful leopard habitat. The terrain is mostly flat, but Malleshappanagudda, a small 600-acre hillock with a small temple on the top, lies to the west of Chikkanahalli forests. It is an ideal spot to climb up for a bird's eye view of the entire landscape, and also served us well to catch the signal from the leopardess's collar.

By now, the leopardess had walked nearly 90 kms from her release location and was 85 kms from her capture site. I wondered if she was headed back to her home. On an average, she had moved a distance of 3.6 kms daily, travelling largely during the night and completely avoiding any kind of long-distance movement during the day. On one particular day, she had walked 22.6 kms. This was the longest a leopard had trekked amongst the ones I had radio collared.

At this time, interestingly, the forest department was bombarded with applications asking for data on the collared leopard from individuals who otherwise had no interest in wildlife. This sudden interest in leopards, especially animals that were fitted with radio collars, from individuals who were in no way connected to wildlife was strange.

Ninety days after collaring the leopardess, the electronic device started malfunctioning. The collar went silent, and I was not sure what had gone wrong. I immediately brought the issue to the notice of the authorities. Strangely, nine days after the collar first malfunctioned, on 1 July 2014, it transmitted a single location. The leopardess was still around in the same forests, but after that no information was available. I regularly climbed up the Malleshappagudda to find out if she was around.

There wasn't much I could do without the collar. It should have worked for at least another four months, but no one can guarantee the reliability of any electronic device. Even the best equipment one brings from the market can stop working on any day.

Tragedy stuck on 12 September 2014. I was in the middle of heavy traffic in Bengaluru, at about ten in the morning, when I received a telephone call from Karikaalan, the head of the forests of the Mysuru area. He said, 'Mr Gubbi, we've found a dead leopard near S. Kallahalli, and it has a collar around its neck. I think it's one of the animals you have collared. Can you please come immediately?'

Shocked, I headed straight to Mysuru. On my way, I called a couple of acquaintances within the forest department. I was told that early that morning, villagers had noticed a leopard hanging down from a tamarind tree, with its hind paw stuck in between the fork of a large branch. The animal was brought down from the tree with the help of a thick white cotton rope. There was not much detailed information available. As I reached the forest department campus in Mysuru, I was asked to go the back of the large building.

For the first time after she was released, I met her. Plucked too early from her life, she was lying on her side on a large granite stone slab. Just a few months earlier, I had appreciated her calm and composed character. I remember the fierce speck of light in her eyes, as she had looked straight into mine for a moment. Now, her eyes were hollow—I did not want this memory. I could not bear to look and felt crushed. But duty called, and I summoned the strength from somewhere deep inside.

The radio collar was still there around her neck. I immediately checked the fur surrounding it to see if there were any marks of struggle. I have seen several wildlife that have died of strangulation largely by wire snares. If an animal has been strangulated by something like a collar, it will have marks on the neck area—small pieces of fur will be pulled out, leaving patches of bare skin; at times there are even marks of laceration caused by the animal's struggle to free itself. There were no signs of any such struggle. The fur was intact.

I slipped my fingers between the neck and the collar to check if the space was adequate and hadn't obstructed her breathing or any other normal activity. It looked fine. At that instance, the collar didn't seem to have obstructed the animal in any way.

Her body was not bloated. A few drops of blood dripped from her tongue on to the granite slab. The colour of the tongue looked purplish, resembling that of the inner pulp of a black plum fruit. There were no other injuries on the leopardess. I wondered what had gone wrong.

Karikalan and the senior veterinarian Nagaraj arrived and took a thorough look at the carcass. The veterinarian and the forest officer, too, meticulously checked the radio collar and the space between the collar and the animal's neck and for any signs of injuries due to the collar. Once they were satisfied with their examination, they ordered for the post-mortem.

I watched with dismay as the thorax area of the animal was first cut open. The lung had turned blackish blue. As the veterinarian moved from the thorax to the abdomen, he collected pieces of various body parts and dropped them into small bottles filled with absolute alcohol. These samples would be examined in the laboratory to ascertain the cause of death. When the veterinarian opened the intestine, it was clear that they were not in a normal state of health: body parts that were normally pinkish were now purple. As the veterinarian started removing the contents in the intestine, large pieces of undigested goat meat were found. Small chunks of black hide along with the flesh of the goat were still intact. On seeing her purplish tongue and the similarly coloured intestine parts, I knew something was not right. Though I had a vague idea of what could have gone wrong, I still had to wait for the laboratory reports to come for my guess to be confirmed.

It was five in the evening when the post-mortem was completed, and the animal was placed on pieces of wood to burn the carcass as per official procedures. More wooden pieces were placed over the remains of the leopardess, light blue paraffin was sprayed over the woodpile to help the fire catch faster, and then the fire was lit. As the fire engulfed the wood, more semi-dry, small logs from a banyan tree were arranged like a small teepee. From the other corner, two hind paws—paws that I had carefully measured a few months earlier—jutted out of the fire. I moved away from the fire unable to take my eyes off those paws.

By the time the carcass was burnt and all the official formalities were completed, it was past six in the evening. With a heavy heart I returned to my vehicle to head back to Bengaluru. The death of that leopard is one of the most painful pictures of wildlife for me. As the vehicle slowly meandered through the city before hitting the highway, my mobile phone started buzzing. It was the media, wanting to know my response to the leopard's death. One reporter said that 'he had credible information from experts that the leopard had died of radio collaring.' I responded that I didn't think that was the case, and it was best to wait for the post-mortem report to come out. He immediately retorted, 'Sir, do you want more credible information than the experts who have given me their opinion?' I had no answer to that but just reiterated that it was best to wait for the lab results to come out. My telephone buzzed many more times with similar questions and opinions. A judgment had been made in the media circles that the leopard had died due to the radio collar. Without any test reports, which would take at least ten days to arrive, I had little defence.

The next morning, the news were all over the place. One of the country's leading newspapers put a picture of the leopard being lowered from the tree using a rope and captioned it 'Grim end: A radio collared leopardess was found hanging from a tree at S. Kallahalli near Mysuru on Friday.' Another newspaper printed the same image with a note that read 'Gory end: A radio collared leopard was found dead on a tree in S. Kallahalli village, Mysuru taluk, on Friday. There were rumours that the feline was thrashed to death and hung atop a tree by locals. Forest officials, however, said that the leopard died of natural causes. The picture shows the carcass being lowered from the tree.'

A leading local language newspaper, which was known to be seriously followed by the state's forest minister, announced that the death of the leopard was due to the radio collar. It further went on to claim that no one knew who had collared this leopard and an investigation was being undertaken. The statement was strangely attributed to the local forest officer. This misleading information was published despite the reporter of this newspaper having spoken to me the previous day.

Social media, too, was abuzz with expert opinions about the leopard's death. One discussion that caught my attention went this way:

A 'wildlife expert' who was sitting in Hyderabad, nearly 600 kms away from where the incident had happened, had posted a picture of the leopard being brought down using the rope and written: 'Does every morning have to (sic) start this way!!! What's the story?'

A freelance journalist sitting 320 kms away near Chennai had responded: 'It apparently naturally hung itself from a tree.'

Another 'wildlife expert': 'With hind legs entangled?'

'Wildlife expert' from Hyderabad: 'all rubbish…!!'

A leopard expert who was 850 kms away: 'actually it died of starvation. Good chance the post mortem will say that.'

The freelance journalist from Chennai: 'And then went and hung itself?'

Leopard expert: 'by its back legs?'

The 'experts' were having a field day with their taunts. They were neither witness to the issue nor did they know what was going on, but simply sat in the comforts of their living rooms several hundred kilometres away, passing judgement. I was stunned. This was a horrific situation—not just because of the accusation that the animal had died because of the radio collar but because it came from a leopard scientist of 'repute', one whom people would believe without even blinking.

But the next day, after kicking up the dust and instigating many to make lewd comments, without even knowing the facts, the leopard expert and scientist, who was based out of Pune, made a statement on social media saying, 'Everyone, relax, the leopard was found dead on a tree and the FD has put a rope around it to get it down. The picture title is wrong—it was not hanging from a tree. Shows how important it is what the media says....' And with that this leopard expert had completely washed off his hands, and conveniently shifted the blame on the media. It was this very expert who had given inputs to the media that the leopardess had died due to the radio collar.

Social media 'expert' opinions clearly had a political angle to them, though most of the public missed these undertones. Leopards are territorial. So are those who work on them. Though it all seemed high-minded and innocent on the surface, deeper down it was a plot of hatred, wonderfully masked. Two large cat biologists were especially vindictive in the campaign against our work. They had always looked at any work of mine through jaundiced eyes. With such ill-intentioned rumours, stories were circulated to build anxiety amongst communities, people, officials, conservation enthusiasts and the media. Anger and shock hung like a storm cloud over me, but I could do little about it.

But never had I realised that the lines had been drawn even before I had started my work. I learnt that one of the decorated wildlife biologists who had instigated the attack on social media had previously written to the organisation supporting my work, arguing that the work I wanted to undertake had all been 'studied', and there was no need to support new studies on the issue. This, despite the fact that I had been consulting the same biologist in all earnestness to get her opinion and suggestions on my work. I hadn't realised that there was an agenda out there in the research community. Why didn't I think of that? The community will use any excuse to harm others.

The wait until the laboratory reports came out was agonising. Finally, exactly ten days after the leopardess's tragic death, the laboratory report from the Animal Disease Diagnostic Laboratory and Information Centre, Mysuru, was given. The report clearly stated that the cause of death was the zinc phosphide poison that was found in the leopard's liver and stomach. Zinc phosphide is a commercially available super-toxic rodenticide that causes lingering disability and finally death. The telltale signs noticed on the leopards tongue, liver, and the presence of goat meat in the stomach had all pointed in the right direction.

I started to piece together the possibilities. Humans have long killed certain types of creatures that are unwelcome in their vicinity. This female leopard may have been poisoned by irate villagers. It's very likely that the leopard had caught a goat, and when it was not around, people may have laced the carcass with zinc phosphide in their anger at having lost prized livestock. Once the leopard returned to its kill it would have consumed the meat and climbed the tamarind tree to rest. There the poison must have taken effect, and it died of respiratory failure. It had tipped over and its hind leg had got stuck into the branches.

I like to think that if the leopard could tell its tale, here is what it would perhaps say:

> I had settled in this area only in the last few days, and found that it had some wild pig, porcupine and peafowl with which I could feed myself. But, like in my original home, this place also had a lot of goat and sheep that were easier to catch as a meal than the wild pigs, which are powerful, especially the big males. I was able to hunt the livestock more efficiently and regularly, as they had less natural instincts against us predators. They didn't smell me even when I was a few metres away from them. Imagine the same with a deer or a wild pig—they would have panicked and created chaos with their loud calls, and would have alerted their entire herd and every animal in the vicinity. Plus, I hated those monkeys—they sat on the tree branches and barked loudly at me all the time, ruining all my plans. They could see me better than the deer and the pigs from their perches, and they would follow me through the forest, until I had moved several hundred metres away from them. By then, of course, the entire forest would be alerted that I was on the hunt. This had become such a common experience when I entered the forest that I developed a preference for hunting the goat, sheep, small calves and chicken that ventured into the sugarcane fields nearby. It made much more sense to make those sugarcane fields my home, and pick up a goat

or two as and when possible. A goat or a sheep would suffice me for two to three days and then I would kill another. I was very happy with my meal plan.

That day, I had been following a goatherd since morning. A black goat had caught my attention as it always straggled behind the herd. The shepherd moved ahead of the herd, guiding it to areas he thought had better forage. I carefully put one paw ahead of the other and followed the last goat. At times I crouched when it occasionally looked in my direction. This didn't last long. I was able to get very close to him without him detecting me at all. Normally, with wild pig or deer I couldn't get closer than about a hundred feet and then I would have to pounce at a high speed, with all my energy before I could get the prey. Even then, catching something was not guaranteed. But here was this goat, just a few feet away. I pounced and directly landed on it. I killed it in an astonishingly short time. I didn't have to strangulate it long like with wild animals; its neck broke with one swipe and the animal lay dead. I was proud of myself—I had made the kill without any sound that would have alerted the shepherd who was now over a couple of hundred metres away.

I dragged the carcass to a nearby bush under a tall tamarind tree. Though it had rained a couple of times in the last few days, it was still reasonably hot here. It was good to be under the shade of the tree. I immediately started licking up the fur off the meat. I was in a hurry to get to the meat before the shepherd returned to look for the straggler. I had managed to finish off a substantial portion of the goat when I saw the shepherd headed in my direction. I immediately left the sheep and ran away to hide in the bushes.

As he approached the dead goat, I quietly observed the shepherd from the bush. He inspected the carcass of the goat and shouted something, looking towards the hillock. Then he left, taking all his goats with him. I was relieved that I hadn't been detected. I had also eaten enough for the day, so I decided to nap in the bushes. I don't know how much time had passed when the loud talking of humans disturbed me. When I opened my eyes, I recognised one of the shapes. It was the shepherd with another human being. Both walked straight towards the carcass of the goat, and squatted in front of it for a couple of minutes. I don't know what they did there, but they left soon after. I went back to my nap.

On waking, I decided to finish off the goat before the maggots got to it. Something tasted a bit fishy and bad when I ripped into the meat, but I thought it was probably the hot weather that had turned the meat's taste bad, and I continued eating.

It wasn't too long after my meal that my stomach began to churn. I hastened towards the tamarind tree I regularly used to rest on. It was large and hardly anyone one came under the tree. I hurriedly climbed up the tree and lay down on a large branch. Suddenly, my throat started drying up. I felt very thirsty, but I didn't have the energy to climb down and walk to the large water tank that was quite a distance away. My stomach also began to hurt a lot and I was soon in agonising pain. It started to become harder to breath, and I began to choke. I didn't know what to do. My breathing didn't improve.

I was so dizzy, I rolled over. My hind paw got caught in the fork of the branch, and I hung with my head down for a while. The blood rushed into my head. Finally, my eyes rolled. I felt the last breath I took in.

This, of course, is conjecture. It never became clear if the leopard was poisoned through livestock (remains of which were found inside the intestine when the post-mortem was carried out) or if it had died due to secondary toxicity.

The chances of secondary toxicity to mammalian predators from zinc phosphide are rather low, primarily because the compound does not significantly accumulate in the muscles of the target species that a large predator like the leopard would like to feed on. When toxic effects are seen in predators it has been due to the ingestion of zinc phosphide that was in the digestive tract of the target organism (the prey). Though most predators will not eat the digestive tract, leopards sometimes may.

Till the laboratory report came out, the storytelling by the large cat biologists continued. They continued to plant factually incorrect press stories, complained to officials and donors, and did all they could do to stop our work and defame me personally. This political intrigue could have damaged the credibility of various persons and institutions. But our long-drawn work with the government and media turned out to be our biggest support.

After the laboratory report came out, I spoke to one of the news reporters who had conclusively stated that the leopard had died of radio collaring. He apologised and said that he had been misled by a person who works on tribal development issues in Nagarahole, and is one of the staff of an international conservation organisation led by a leading tiger biologist.

I licked my wounds for some weeks and waited for my confidence to return. One has to be made of tougher material when it comes to the wild. I could treat each new challenge as a source of worry and defeat or as a new adventure. This was not my first and far from last experience of territoriality among biologists, especially cat biologists. No sooner would one predicament be solved than another would materialise.

Putting radio collars on large cats in India is like walking on a tightrope between two skyscrapers. You are always heart-stoppingly close to the edges because of the political angles and attention the activity attracts from other researchers, some misdirected conservation enthusiasts and the media. Getting government permissions for radio collaring of wildlife is also a tedious and incredibly difficult task. Anyone who manages to get permits is closely watched by other researchers, who, at times, try to create controversies.

There are a lot of misconceptions about radio collaring. One prevalent notion is that the radio-collared animal can be followed in real time, so both conflict with people and any dangers to the animal can be avoided. However, this is not true—not every second of the animal's movement can be monitored. The location of the animal can be lost for lengthy durations if it moves into highly undulating terrain or if it comes to rest in a place (for instance, under a boulder) where the satellite is unable to communicate with the collar. Yet, if something out of the ordinary happens during such situations, the researcher is blamed.

One of the times we faced this situation was in April 2014, when an approximately three-year-old male leopard was translocated to Chammanahalla in Bandipur Tiger Reserve from its outskirts. He was collared by us on the request of the authorities. Our job was to monitor the movements of the leopard and keep the authorities informed. Seventeen days after his release, the leopard left the environs of the tiger reserve and ventured into the surrounding agricultural fields and small scrub forests. Unfortunately, twenty-eight days after he was released into Bandipur, the leopard entered a house in a small village called Mantipura, 19 kms away from his release location. Luckily, no untoward incident took place as the cat hid under a cot inside the house, and he was recaptured by the authorities.

We had shared the location of the animal with the authorities a few hours before it had entered the house. But two large cat biologists took advantage of the opportunity to spread rumours among the public and in the media that we had put people under risk by not alerting the authorities about the leopard entering the house. The radio collar was programmed to send information once in twelve hours (twice a day), and between these twelve-hour intervals, we did not know the location of the animal. Though the biologists were themselves aware of these technical details, they purposefully took advantage of the situation. The same large cat biologists had also previously misled the media during a tiger radio-collaring exercise in Maharashtra.

Complicating the human and political angle to radio-collaring, are the technical aspects of hardware and environmental conditions. The risk of failure of radio collars, as with any electronic device, is high. Some common problems encountered with radio collars are equipment failure and curtailment of battery life due to extreme weather conditions. Between 1983 to 2013, in studies covering 330 radio collars in India, researchers of the Wildlife Institute of

India found that nearly 50 per cent of the collars had failed during their usage.

Even if everything goes well, the risk of animal mortality due to other reasons such as road accidents, injuries caused by snares and poisoning is always omnipresent. Yet even these incidents get attributed to the researcher. An insufficient understanding about radio collaring, overenthusiastic animal rights activists, and the media have all play a role in making radio-collaring, especially of large cats, such a controversial subject in India.

Scientific work has now become a business of conquest; small armies of personnel are employed to spread hate against other researchers. With the two large cat biologists creating enough controversy, I decided to stop the radio collaring work. But leopards continue to be captured and translocated. Who knows what happens to them? They all either leak away into oblivion or, as luck and wit bless a few of them, find ways to survive.

One roll of the dice proves nothing about what's likely to emerge. Our data, with its small sample size of only five animals, is difficult to interpret and use to make larger observations, as the animals responded differently. It is only by carrying out more fieldwork in this vein and broadening our sample size that we will be able to understand the patterns better.

Wildlife biologists, however, are very resistant to anyone thinking in a new direction. They forget that even the theories of the most revered biologists have been reworked and corrected over time. Natural history is a bottomless rucksack of knowledge, and requires space for everyone to express and carry out experiments. Unfortunately, pursuing research on large cat biology is very difficult in India, largely due to the hindrances biologists erect against each other.

# 8

# THE UNCOMFORTABLE REALITY
# OF LEOPARD CONSERVATION

### *Why do leopards turn man-eaters?*

Elephants, hippos, snakes, wild pigs, hyenas, sloth bears, piranhas and scorpions are all responsible for the death of thousands of people across the globe. Malaria-causing mosquitoes might be some of the deadliest wildlife for humans. Yet, it is a group of large predators that evokes the most dramatic response with respect to human killings. Tigers, lions, leopards, great white sharks, crocodiles, and a few other species have gained infamy and are seen from a very different lens of fear when they, on occasion, consume the meat of people. At times, their attacks are even deliberate.

Termed 'man-eaters', some of these species have been the epicentre of Hollywood blockbusters. Movies such as Steven Spielberg's *Jaws*, its three sequels, and *The Ghost and the Darkness*, a fictionalised account of the Tsavo man-eating lions that killed workers in Kenya during the building of the Lake Victoria–Mombasa railway line in 1898, have shaped popular perceptions, injecting fear about large carnivores into the hearts of people. But there has never been a film or a book about human-trampling elephants, which possibly kill nearly 600 people a year in India which is possibly five times higher than the number of people killed by all large carnivores.

Though leopards have a bad reputation of being man-eaters in India, the same does not apply to them in some of the other regions where they occur. In the Indonesian island of Java, leopards hardly ever kill humans, and attacks on humans mostly date back to the 1920s. Peter Boomgaard, a professor of environmental history and the author of the book *Frontiers of Fear: Tigers and People in the Malay World, 1600-1950*, documents that between 1882 and 1904, 317 people were killed by leopards in India and none in Indonesia. The most common explanation given for the difference between lethality to humans in the Indian leopard, where man-eating seems to be more prevalent, and the Javan leopard is that the Indian leopard is bigger than its Javan counterpart. It is also believed that the Javanese killed, with their daggers, any leopard that attacked them, while Indian villagers did not defend themselves against leopards, which might have reinforced the inclination that humans were fair game. Indonesia, however, witnessed a high number of human killings by tigers, in what were often referred to as the 'tiger plagues' or 'tiger epidemics'.

In India, Col. James Edward Corbett, popularly known as Jim Corbett, became a legend by ridding local people of the menace of large predators—tigers and leopards—that were killing people. Corbett was an Indian-born, British hunter-turned-conservationist, author, naturalist and possibly the man who coined the term 'man-eater'. A similar, larger-than-life figure existed in southern India: Kenneth Douglas Stewart Anderson, Kenneth Anderson in short. While Jim Corbett hunted mostly in the north and was associated with tigers and leopards, Kenneth Anderson, the celebrated, licensed hunter from southern India, was associated with the killing of tigers, leopards, sloth bears and elephants. Though many have questioned Anderson's credentials, he remains one of the most acclaimed hunter-naturalists from his era. Both these men from the

Raj period shot to prominence due to their ability to reduce the incidence of human deaths at the hands of large cats, something we today know as human-wildlife conflict.

Both the hunters' stories gave birth to a kind of thrilling 'shikaar' literature that finds readers even to this day in India. David Quammen, the acclaimed science and nature writer, calls such genre of literature as 'marketing of zoological melodrama' and 'predator pornography' in his book *Monster of God*.

In his books, Jim Corbett attributes man-eating to a variety of reasons, including traditional rituals where human bodies were disposed of without burying or burning. When epidemics swept villages in the Kumaon and Garhwal hills in present-day Uttarakhand, the casualties were high and frequent. At such times, villagers were forced to keep rituals simple and often carried the bodies to the edge of a hill, put embers in the mouth, and cast the dead bodies into the valley below, rather than carry it to the riverbank for cremation. In areas where natural food was scarce, leopards scavenged on these bodies and acquired a taste for human flesh. According to Corbett, once the disease died down and normal conditions were re-established, this food supply for the leopards was cut off, and they took to killing humans. He writes that during the reign of two of the man-eating leopards in Kumaon and Garhwal, which killed 525 people between them, one man-eating spree followed on the heels of a very severe outbreak of cholera, and the other followed a mysterious disease called 'war fever', which swept through India in 1918 and cost over a million human lives.

The man-eating leopard from Garhwal came to be known as the man-eater of Rudraprayag, since it began its man-eating career at a small village near the town of Rudraprayag. It was one of the most publicised animals, and was mentioned in the press in the UK, USA, Canada, South Africa, Kenya, Malaysia, Hong Kong, Australia, New Zealand and, of course, in many dailies and weeklies in India. Its reign of terror went on for nearly nine years, and it killed 125 people before Corbett eliminated it on 2 May 1926. The mango tree on which Corbett was sitting when he eliminated the Rudraprayag leopard continues to stand as a witness to the incident, and a concrete stele stands at the location where the leopard is supposed to have been killed.

In the year 1907, another notorious renegade that came to be known as the Panar man-eater, named after the river in the area, is said to have killed four hundred people. After a futile attempt in April 1910, Corbett was able to rid people of this man-eater during his second attempt in September of the same year. There were several other leopards that carried names, such as the man-eater of Basim, the Nanda man-eater, the Gunsore man-eater, the Khandesh man-eater and the killer of Jalahalli. They were all killed by white colonial hunters who were part of a kind of boy's adventure club, with members including Kenneth Anderson, J.D. Inverarity, W.A. Conduitt, L.S. Osmaston and T.R.D. Bell.

R.G. Burton, a British military officer and a hunter, suspected that leopards turned to man-eating partly due to 'circumstantial temptations'. If, say, a mother left her young child unattended and a leopard was skulking around the village outskirts, it would be tempted to carry off the child if no one was watching. Another popular theory is of injured leopards that take to human killings, as natural prey have good anti-predatory instincts and skills. This makes it difficult for an ailing leopard to get close to the prey, capture and strangulate it. Large carnivore behaviour is shaped by acculturation, where they learn from their surroundings, from mothers, and possibly their siblings. So if a mother is attacking humans, it is likely that the cubs will learn from it. However, there is no corroborative evidence for any of these theories about why leopards consider humans fair game.

In India, human killings by leopards have not just taken place in the distant past. In the district of Bhagalpur, on the southern banks of the Ganges in the state of Bihar, leopards reportedly killed 350 people between 1959 and 1962. In recent years, in Rajaji National Park, in the state of Uttarakhand, twenty-two human deaths and twelve injuries have been attributed to leopards between 2013 and 2018. One theory with respect to this is that during the devastating floods of 2013, which killed scores of people in this Himalayan state, human bodies accumulated in a barrage near Motichur, and leopards fed on them. The leopards seem to have figured out that humans could be prey, and this triggered the human killings that continued till July 2018. In the melee, eleven leopards were captured and one was shot down. The man-eating episodes finally ended in the middle of 2018, but no one knows why they started and ended. And the question of why the leopards developed a taste for human flesh has remained a subject of much speculation.

In the Pithoragarh district, again in Uttarakhand, a man-eating leopard is attributed to have killed twelve people over a period of two years between 2012 and 2014. It seems that the majority of people who were killed were drunk and walking back home after dark.

During 1994-95, near a small town called Kadur in southern Karnataka, leopards killed eight people before twenty-two adult leopards were shot dead. Eleven cubs also died in the process. Here, it is assumed that the unclaimed, dead bodies of migrant labourers, working on the conversion of a railway line to broad-gauge had been discarded, and some leopards may have picked up the habit of feeding on human bodies.

Most of these incidents are related to leopards scavenging on discarded human bodies, which is then followed by a series of human killings. But scavenging is a different phenomena compared to stalking, killing and eating humans as prey.

For most leopards, humans are typically far from their first choice of prey. And rather than viewing people as potential meals, leopards tend to go out of their way to avoid humans entirely. Though leopards occasionally prey upon people, habitual man-eaters are very rare, and for this reason, very little is known about them. Man-eating is an exception, not the rule. Humans normally do not fall under the mental rubric of prey for leopards. They hurt or kill humans only after some unfortunate convergence of factors. There's a lot of science and speculation one can build on, but there is no way to resolve this question easily. For instance, the reason why the two massive, man-eating lions of Tsavo hunted humans was only resolved 120 years after the man-eaters' lives were ended by the railway engineer Col. John Henry Patterson. Latest research indicates that their preserved skulls shows evidence of dental disease. The pressure on the abscess would have caused unbearable pain and hindered their ability to catch bigger and stronger prey, possibly causing them to go after punier humans.

## Human killing at the mining town

Waving his hand in the direction from where he thought the leopard had appeared, the young man explained to us that his uncle had been squatting and harvesting maize when he was killed. The landscape around was a mixture of agricultural land and dry deciduous forests. The hills were partially ravaged by both legal and illegal mining for iron ore in Sandur in the district of Bellary in central Karnataka.

No man-eating leopards had previously been recorded in the Sandur area, where the young man was explaining to us about the death of his uncle. The man-eating record started in October 2015 when a farmer harvesting maize near the village of Sushilanagara was killed by a leopard. The farmer had not committed any notable provocation, but part of the problem was possibly the posture. A standing person's head and neck are in the wrong place for a predator. Most adult human beings are taller than many large prey species so they do not make for good prey. Someone squatting, on the other hand, can be construed as prey by a leopard. A man harvesting maize is obviously squatting with his neck bent down, as he concentrates on aiming his sickle at the base of the maize plant.

The killings continued near Sandur, and within a span of three weeks, leopards had killed three people. Two of the three victims were killed in maize fields, close to the forests when they were harvesting maize in a squatting position.

In November 2015, we were summoned to help the forest department. We set up camera traps in the dry deciduous forests and the adjoining agricultural fields to understand the number of leopards in the area and their movement. We also wanted to see if we could pinpoint the animal that was causing human deaths. After two weeks, we began to see a pattern of leopard movement. From our research, we analysed that there were about seventeen leopards in the area. One leopard had been shot before we arrived, and when the large male, aged about five or six years, who we had labelled SU-06, was captured, we found he was blind in his severely damaged right eye and his lower right canine was missing. Surprisingly, the human killings stopped after this leopard was captured. So we wondered if this injured animal had been responsible for the killings.

Unfortunately, the human killings returned to the district in 2018. This time around, the reports were from Kampli, about 30 kms north of Sandur. Three people were killed between July and December 2018. In response, twelve leopards were captured and translocated from the area. In November and December 2020, a repeat of these unfortunate incidents resulted in the death of two more people from adjoining areas.

The reasons for the man-eating were never ascertained, but the time period of the killing matched with that of Sandur: all the killings took place during the harvest season of crops, especially maize. We suggested that the forest department should actively help farmers during the harvest season by continuously patrolling when the farmers harvested their crops and that farmers stop their fieldwork by late afternoon.

### Leopards of the areca nut plantations

In my home district of Tumkur, a sudden spurt of human killings occurred in and around the little-known village of Hebbur in 2019. In October, a sixty-year-old lady was killed and dragged into the bushes by a leopard. The incident came as a big shock. Though there were past records of wolves killing children in the district in the late 1970s, human killing by leopards had not been recorded.

The following month saw the death of another victim, a sixty-year-old man. He had been picked up from the edge of a eucalyptus plantation overlooking a mango orchard. The leopard had crept in from the bushes in the eucalyptus plantation while the man sat tending his sheep. A checkered, lavender-coloured cotton bath towel and a white plastic cover with small pieces of dried areca nut and slacked lime that belonged to the deceased man mutely lay at the location as a grisly reminder of the incident.

What followed then was the most tragic. In January 2020, a young boy of five years was killed, followed by a toddler of three years on the last day of February 2020. The toddler was supposedly picked up right from the porch of the house as her grandparents watched in extreme shock.

We were requested by the authorities to help with the monitoring of leopard movement in the area after the second human death took place. The landscape was peppered with areca nut, coconut and banana plantations, mango and sapota orchards, and maize, ragi and vegetable crop fields. Two small plantations of about hundred acres of eucalyptus and earpod wattle (*Acacia auriculiformis*) were perhaps the only thickly wooded refuge. Dry nullahs, overgrown with bamboo (*Dendrocalamus strictus*), Dyer's oleander, soapnut (*Sapindus emarginatus*) and other vegetation, snaked through the entire landscape, connecting it to nearby tanks. These perhaps acted as a highway for the leopards to move and rest, as the nullahs were cool, provided sufficient cover, and contained puddles of water.

We put out camera traps amidst the various plantations, in nullahs and in agricultural fields. Within a period of a hundred days, a staggering number of leopards were captured in our cameras in an area of 117 sq kms. We spotted eleven adult leopards, two sub-adults and four young cubs of about six months. But a male and a female and two sub-adults were the ones that intensively used the area where all the four human deaths had taken place. We suspected that the culprits were these two adults.

The morning after the fourth ill-fated death, I was asked to accompany the forest minister and senior officials of the forest department to the village where the unfortunate incident had taken place. When we arrived at the house, set amidst banana, areca nut and coconut plantations, the scene was agonising. The bereaved parents of the toddler wailed in pain. Hundreds of people gheraoed the minister. Villagers and the local legislators yelled at the forest department for being insensitive to the serious problem people faced. The minister agreed to put down the leopard to put an end to the misery of the people.

An environmentalist from the nearby city of Tumkur watched the incident unfold from under the shade of an adjacent tree without involving himself in the melee. But the very next day his name appeared prominently in the media, condemning the decision of the minister. He had not offered a solution nor had he tried to talk to the aggrieved villagers, but he was active in castigating the decision of the authorities. This is the unfortunate gap between armchair environmentalism and conservation problems.

In response to the problem, the authorities captured twelve leopards, most of them away from the location where the human deaths had occurred. Despite their efforts, the male and the female leopard that extensively used the area where the killings had taken place were not captured. We stayed there for over five months and were asked to end our camera trapping as things seemed to settle down in May 2020. However, five days after we stopped our camera trapping work, terror stuck again, this time about 30 kms away from the location where the previous human killings had taken place. A five-year-old child was dragged out of his house, and his half-eaten body was found in a bush nearby in a village near the historical town of Magadi.

Exactly a week later, a sixty-eight year old lady sitting in the open portico of her house was killed by a leopard, 3 kms away from the previous incidence. We were asked to go to this area to provide similar support like we had at Hebbur. Magadi is also the place where Kenneth Anderson shot a potential man-eater several decades ago.

The landscape around Magadi is different from that of Hebbur. There are a lot of rocky outcrops in this landscape and many of them have been gouged out for granite. It looks as though leopards have lost their natural habitat and their natural prey, which has diminished with the loss of habitat and poaching, in the area.

Nearly two months after the killing of the sixty-eight-year-old lady near Magadi, a four-year-old boy was killed nearly 27 kms away. Again, twelve leopards were captured and translocated from the Magadi area with no scientific monitoring of the released animals.

Finally, in Hebbur, the male leopard we had suspected to be one of the man-eaters was captured in December 2020. The authorities, especially H.C. Girish, the young district forest officer, who had put in an enormous amount of effort to solve the problem of human killings, were a bit relieved. But within a week of the capture, another six-year-old boy was injured by a big cat. We continue to believe that the leopardess that was the other suspect might be involved, and the authorities continue their efforts to capture her.

In Karnataka, since 2009, encounters between the two species have increased. Though some of these have had tragic consequences, most have ended peacefully. During a eleven-year period between 2009 and 2020, our records show that thirty-six people have been killed and 283 injured by leopards in Karnataka. During the same time, over 120,000 people have died in road accidents in the state. But traffic fatality does not impinge on public consciousness as sharply as a leopard kill. It's one thing to be dead. It's another thing to be meat.

Large carnivores or apex predators are inseparable from stories of human killings or rumours of them being man-eaters. As acclaimed science writer David Quammen says, in his book *Monster of God*, which largely details the relationship of man with alpha predators, 'Is it possible to separate *Homo sapiens* from the dangerous inconvenience of alpha predators? Can we have them at all if we're unwilling to suffer among them?'

## Sticking close to the calories

A young leopard carrying a bandicoot for his sundown snack, a leopardess with a broiler chicken in her mouth, another leopard walking away with a langur locked tightly between his canines, one carrying a puppy, another clutching on to a barking deer: these were the photographic glimpses of these cats' daily menus from our camera trapping exercise.

Leopards are diet generalists, meaning they can feed on any kind of meat and on prey of any size. They eat things that any self-respecting tiger would not. Unlike tigers, which prefer large-sized prey species, such as the gaur, the sambar, or the daintier chital, leopards' diets consist of prey species of varying sizes, depending upon where they live. They also lack the strength and the weight of a tiger to bring down larger animals like gaur, though they are occasionally known to kill very large prey. In protected areas where large-sized prey are plentiful, leopards will go after chital, sambar, barking deer, the young ones of wild pig, four-horned antelope, and other similar large- or medium-sized prey. In areas where such large-bodied prey animals are rare, they sustain themselves with small-sized prey such as the bonnet macaque, the langur, the black-naped hare, the jungle fowl and the peafowl.

Studies from Namibia have even shown that female leopards feed on a wider range of smaller prey species, as they need less energy compared to their male counterparts due to their smaller body size. According to the researchers, the females are more restricted in their movements, especially when rearing cubs, and hence this compromise is necessary. Males, with larger home ranges, can find more options and so are more selective.

The researchers arrived at these conclusions through an interesting study: they analysed leopard whiskers by measuring the composition of stable isotopes of carbon and nitrogen found in them. When a leopard consumes prey, the isotope composition of the animal it has fed on is assimilated into the leopard's body and even in its whiskers depending upon the relative abundance of its overall diet. This allowed the scientists to study the leopard's main diet and the variety of prey it may have consumed. The researchers cut off one whisker each from eighteen adult female and eighteen adult male leopards, chopped them into smaller segments of five millimetres and analysed the stable isotope ratios. As leopard whiskers grow at a rate of 0.65 millimetres a day, each segment of the whisker would correspond to approximately eight days of feeding. The 8–10 cm long whiskers allowed the researchers to create a 'feeding history' of approximately 150 days. An interesting foray would be to conduct a similar experiment on men. Would it give any hint at varying diet (both solid and liquid) between weekdays and weekends? Would the diet on weekends be more spirited?

Though leopards are not choosy shoppers, large individuals cannot survive on small prey. Imagine cooking small amounts of food, several times a day to feed the family, and compare that to cooking a substantial amount twice a day—something that will leave the person cooking less stressed and tired. Much the same, a leopard would need prodigious numbers of smaller prey to sustain themselves, and if they merely depended on them, perhaps most of their energy would be burnt out catching small prey.

On an average, leopards must eat up to 5 per cent of their body weight each day, which for the biggest leopard comes to about 4–5 kgs. This amount can be met by feeding on a four-horned antelope or a chital once in every two or three days. Then why would a chital-chasing, porcupine-fighting leopard switch to livestock? It's like switching from eating healthy salad to risky junk food.

But when these packages of meat no longer wander the leopard's habitats then they must look elsewhere for their food. Livestock is perhaps one of the easiest ways to meet their dietary requirement.

This conflict had its beginnings thousands of years ago. Archaeological evidence indicates that livestock was introduced over ten thousand years ago in the fertile valleys of the Tigris and Euphrates of Mesopotamia and the Nile of Egypt. However, new findings based on genetic and archaeological evidence suggest that the first livestock domestication may have happened in the Zagros mountains in Western Iran. The first hunter-gatherers who started experimenting with farming tamed wild game. The mouflon sheep and bezoar goats became their domestic barnyard ungulates; from the aurochs, came the cud-chewing cow. With the domestication of wild ungulates, a new concept of ownership of animals for fresh meat began. The large predators, however, which shared the land with these experimental farmers, began to view their domestic ungulates as possible food. Since then, large predators have been seen as a threat to livelihoods.

There is, of course, a flip side to this story. When humans disturb leopard accommodation, when they encroach upon their habitats, hunt their food for meat, drag or push them out of their ecosystems, their actions increase the risk of conflict. This pattern has been observed with many other species. In addition, we offer a wealth of opportunities to leopards in the form of unguarded livestock, poor herding practices, and chicken farms built right at the edge of leopard habitats.

As per the Indian government's livestock census data, India has 512 million livestock of which 200 million are small livestock (goat and sheep). Livestock draws leopards like a magnet. An estimated 30 million feral dogs live in India. A lot of these canines, too, are converted into cat food annually. Domestic animals make an easy meal for leopards living close to human habitations—their next meal lies snoozing within easy reach, laid out like a buffet.

But the joy of getting an easy meal brings its own challenges and risks—sometimes serious. Occasionally, leopards enter sheep corrals and kill a number of animals in the confusion. This sets up the stage for conflict with humans and adds to the animosity of people. The pressure also builds when they take livestock regularly. Many times, when the owners incur huge losses, they demand that the government capture the animal. Some even kill the offending leopards.

We often encounter examples of the risks leopards face when trying to survive on easier prey or when they live at the interface of human populations and their natural habitat. In January 2016, for instance, a male leopard of three–four years was captured in our camera traps on the edges of the Cauvery Wildlife Sanctuary. In January 2017, exactly a year later, he was found dead, electrocuted by the live fence put across agricultural fields, possibly to prevent wild pigs entering crop fields. Since he was living on the edge of the protected area, his home range included agricultural fields and other human-dominated areas. He had moved away about 5 kms from the boundary of the Cauvery sanctuary, most possibly in search of easy prey. Unfortunately, along with him, another leopard was also found dead at the same location, again due to electric shock. Interestingly, a Fido was the third victim at the same location. In all probability, the leopards had been chasing the dog, and all of them died due to electric shock.

Will communities tolerate wildlife that take their livestock for food? Conflict has many a time left families hungry, communities desperate and the future of leopards uncertain. Though these losses are not new, earlier the battle-axe had a soft side: religion and cultural tolerance. But when social tolerance reaches threshold levels, communities retort. Cultures change constantly. Unfortunately, the traditional reverence that protected wildlife in India is now fading. The thick skin of civilisation, the mystical, magnificent, ancient wisdom that protected wildlife, now seems to have made way for unfathomable spasms of blood. Leopards are scalped, hacked, lit afire, bludgeoned with clubs for killing livestock or, in some instances, for injuring people.

### Victim of conservation success?

In India, after the enactment of the Wildlife Protection Act in 1972, wildlife numbers started to bounce back due to the protection offered against poaching and habitat loss. Poisoning and hunting for sport or for eradication purposes—when leopards, tigers and dholes were seen as lantana-equivalent pests—were legally outlawed. Due to the enforcement of laws, species like the one-horned rhinoceros or the Asiatic lion were almost brought back from the brink of extinction. Species that were not threatened with extinction, like the leopard, also largely benefited due to the legal support, and leopard numbers in India have increased.

Unfortunately, leopards have perhaps become victims of their own success—the people who live along with them, have started to hate them. An axe is constantly suspended over the leopard's head, awaiting an uprising among people against the species.

Why does this conflict happen? We don't have too many answers, and science has not truly given any solution to this increased conflict with people. Scientists, largely based out of urban areas, merely argue that people have to 'live' with leopards. With no leopard troubles of their own, it's easy for them to preach. Conflict occurs far from where these researchers live and write about these issues. Unfortunately, livestock graziers and the communities living in such areas do not enjoy such distance between themselves and the leopards. Writing in English, these armchair activists are also largely not read by those who bear the cost of conflict.

India has nearly five hundred million livestock, almost half of its human population. With agricultural incomes becoming less profitable and more unstable by the day, especially for small and marginal farmers, animal husbandry has become an important source of supplementary income. Livestock farming is the backbone of the livelihood of 72 per cent of India's rural population, and 57 per cent of these households across the country, involving well over 100 million people, have livestock as their only important source of livelihood. If a farmer whose livelihood is dependent on farm animals loses half or all his livestock in one night, does he have the ability to make a comeback? Would he come with an olive branch to save wildlife? Would he be tolerant of wild animals, especially leopards?

On the other side of the story is the burgeoning human population of the country, which demands more and more land for livestock grazing. Today, in most leopard habitats, livestock compete with wild ungulates for forage. They are also the food base in many areas that are devoid of leopards' natural prey. I have a small theory. My theory—really a notion—based on an understanding of leopard population is that we have an inordinate abundance of leopards in some areas due to the presence of excessive livestock. I feel that some of the areas we worked in, like Bhadravathi and Devarayanadurga, had this problem of 'excess' leopards that fed on livestock.

The socio-political economy of pastoralists has also changed in recent times. With the cost of meat going up, the pattern of pastoralism has changed drastically. Entrepreneurs with rural backgrounds who have shifted their base to cities in recent times now see goats as a good investment. They invest in large herds and give the grazing work on contract to poor herders living on the rural side. These entrepreneurs are also the ones who bag government contracts to construct roads, build drains, de-silt tanks and do other similar government-funded work in the rural areas. This provides them with both the financial and political clout to gain power in rural areas in various ways. They also obtain influence by supporting political leaders, who bank on these entrepreneurs for gaining access to vote banks in the rural areas. So, if there is loss of livestock due to large predators, the city-based owners create a ruckus with their newly acquired political influence. Often, they support illegal activities like poaching and forestland grabbing. This sets them up against the forest department. Persistent livestock attacks or one serious injury or human death turns public sympathy against leopards. For the local politicians, leopard attacks are an opportunity to express their dissatisfaction against the forest department. This becomes a vicious cycle of conflict-driven and politically motivated attacks on leopards.

### Injuries, death, and chaos

Animals attack when they feel threatened or cornered. During my days in Tumkur, where I spent most part of my life, I learned a lot about wildlife conservation. I focused not only on natural history but also on the fears and concerns of people who shared their space with wildlife like leopards. I was witness to several instances of leopards entering human habitations and the response of people in such situations. No amount of schooling in wildlife biology could have taught me this field experience.

In June 1998, one incident that occurred at the edge of Tumkur, then a small town with a population about 100,000 people, gave me my first understanding of how injuries happen to people due to no fault of leopards. It also gave me my first taste of how curiosity can kill the cat.

One early morning, I heard that a leopard had been seen inside a house on Garden Road. The location was merely five minutes from my home. Situated on the edge of the town, Garden Road mostly led to coconut farms, rice fields and graveyards. By the time I arrived there, the leopard had come out of the house and fallen into a dry well in an adjoining coconut farm. A big crowd had already gathered at the edge of the farm. The forest department had managed to keep the five hundred-odd crowd away from the animal. They all patiently waited at the edge of farm as though a big movie star would soon arrive. Very thoughtfully, the forest department had summoned an ambulance in case of an emergency.

A small number of people had gathered around the well in which the leopard had fallen. The well seemed to be around twenty-five feet deep, and was lined with granite stone blocks. It was clean, with none of the vegetation growth that is otherwise very normal in open wells. The leopard lay on its dry floor. The monsoon had already set in, so the day was cloudy, protecting the leopard from the harsh sunlight that would have otherwise stressed out the animal a lot more.

About seven–eight of us stood around the well to keep an eye on the animal. We took turns to peer inside at the leopard as we waited for nets to be brought to capture it. A man in shorts and a white vest stood to my right with dry coconut fronds in his hand, fire lit to the ends. Cornered inside the dry well, the animal snarled at anyone with whom it made eye contact. For over an hour, the forest department planned ways to get the animal out; no one knew how to handle this situation. It was perhaps the first such incident in the town.

I thought the animal was tired from all the stress it was under. But I was wrong. Suddenly, the leopard tried jumping the vertical well. 'It will never make it,' I told a forest guard who was standing on the other side of the well. But to our astonishment, after a couple of failed attempts, the leopard made it out. As I watched, the animal jumped vertically about ten feet, held on to the stone-lined wall with its claws, and made another jump. Before anyone could react, it was out of the confines of the well. It lunged at the man with the coconut fronds standing right next to me, and clawed him on his belly. I ducked and missed being injured by a couple of feet. I could clearly see three gashes on the left side of his stomach. He was immediately whisked away in the ambulance. This was my first close encounter of a leopard injuring a person.

Meanwhile, the leopard, confused with so many people around, started running randomly. The crowd that had been standing patiently at the edge of the farm broke loose. Everyone ran behind the leopard, shouting and shooing at the animal as though there was a riot. There was no way the crowd could now be controlled. The baffled animal hid inside a bush and refused to come out despite all the coaxing by people and the police. Finally, an adventurous policeman burst a tear gas shell, forcing the leopard out of the bush.

Running away from people again, the leopard entered a drain that was covered with granite slabs, at the edge of the farm. The granite slabs gave cover to the animal. As soon as it entered the drain, people mobbed the trench on both sides. While the forest officers thought of ways to deal with the situation, a policeman appeared out of nowhere, and with no instructions from anyone sprayed bullets from his automatic rifle into the drain. Everything was over within a few seconds. A couple of brave men in the crowd peeped into the drain and announced that the animal could be seen and was motionless. Another brave man with a C-shaped sickle in his hand, caught the leopard's long tail and pulled it out.

The animal was motionless. A large hole on the right side of its stomach bore testimony to the bullet that had bored through its intestine. Its entrails were hanging out like an entangled rope. Two men held the forelimbs of the dead animal while a third held its back legs. People, armed with sickles, pickaxes and staves, marched behind the animal as it was laid down on a broken wall in the middle of the farm. Several others came to feel the animal before it was finally put in the forest department's vehicle. Luckily, the incident took place before the days of mobile phones or else there would have been a spree of selfies.

The dead leopard's carcass was taken to Ankanahalli, a small forest patch near the town. As it was unloaded from the vehicle and put down on the red mud, a cloud of depression passed over me. I didn't know who was to blame, neither did I know how we could have saved the animal from the mob that had gone berserk. I had no answer to this killing. The policeman had acted on his own. The large crowd had perhaps indirectly put pressure on him. He had probably thought that there would be a series of serious injuries if the leopard came out of the drain, and hence killed it.

Even to this day, we have been unable to change the way we handle situations when leopards enter human-dense areas. Most aspects have remained the same, but the pressure of media personnel to cover such incidents and the illogical desire of people to capture the rare event with their mobile phones has increased several fold, which creates a big hurdle in such operations.

### Biophobia

Humans have long feared many wildlife species. Snakes, lizards, spiders, rats, all are feared for their own reasons. Animal phobia is among the most mystifying and intricately illogical forms of human behaviour.

The fear of spiders and snakes affects millions of people on this planet. These fears are so common that there are even specific terms for them: arachnophobia, the fear of spiders and other arachnids such as scorpions; ophidiophobia, the abnormal fear of snakes.

The tendency to become anxious at the sight of a carnivore, too, is not new, so the distress that the sighting of a leopard leads to does not surprise me. Large carnivores have always seemed ineffably scary to people who find themselves in their vicinity, despite the reality that they do not harm without provocation. The ability of leopards to remain concealed, and the power in their jaws, claws and canines make them a powerful killing machine. It pays to go beyond ordinary caution and fear.

E.O. Wilson, who extensively contributed to the development of new academic specialties in biology, such as chemical ecology, socio-biology and genetic psychology, has dedicated a full chapter to biophobia in his 1984 book *Biophilia*. Wilson explains how primates, as well as humans, react to snakes. Chimpanzees and African monkeys tend to be alarmed in the presence of snakes, whereas lemurs, an indigenous mammal from Madagascar, seem indifferent as there are no dangerous snakes in this island nation. He goes on to explain that aversion to snakes might be an inherent trait, inculcated by natural selection during the process of evolution. It is also activated by an individual's experiences with that particular species. A predisposition against snakes might be built into our genetic heritage. Phobia towards large carnivores may also be genetically influenced. *Encyclopaedia Britannica* has a particularly suitable explanation for this fear: 'These fear responses are the result of evolution in a world in which humans were constantly vulnerable to predators, poisonous plants and animals, and natural phenomena such as thunder and lightning. Fear was a fundamental connection with nature that enabled survival, and, as a result, humans needed to maintain a close relationship with their environment, using sights and sounds as vital cues, particularly for fight or flight response.'

However, there is now a new epidemic of panic. Mere sightings of a leopard near human habitations are reported as conflict by the media. Then, pressure mounts on the authorities to capture and translocate the animal.

We could argue that leopards play an important role in the ecosystem, and they provide these services literally free of cost to humanity. Unfortunately, these days there is no good price for environmental services. Nobody is ready to pay for it. Until the sticky issue of human-wildlife conflict is brought down to tolerable limits, the support of the communities who bear the brunt of conservation will be hard to come by. How can we reconcile the need to conserve leopards with protecting the rights and livelihoods of people who share the environment? Resolving such conflicts is crucial for the survival of leopards and in fact, any conflict-prone species that impacts lives and livelihoods.

Whatever combination of factors trigger leopard conflict, addressing them is imperative for leopard conservation. Many factors contribute to human-leopard conflict, including loss of habitat, limited protection of attractants, loss of natural prey, larger consumption patterns in human society that leads to increase in farming of attractants like chicken that are reared on the immediate boundaries of a leopard habitat and other factors. It's hard to isolate a single reason for the increase in conflict. Conflict might also be related to where and how the leopards live and where and how they have lived.

Then there is the often touted narrative that garbage attracts stray dogs and, in turn, leopards to human-dense areas, and is the sole reason for the human-leopard conflict. This is an overrated proposition and not based on evidence. Though this theory has some relevance in areas where leopards survive adjacent to cities and towns, the large part of human-leopard conflict is peppered across the countryside, where the issue of garbage doesn't come into the picture. Garbage just makes for a convenient villain.

Some experts believe that translocation is the cause of human-leopard conflict and have decided that their research findings have now virtually settled all problems, while others, including myself, have reserved our judgment.

What this shows is that we have little understanding of this phenomenon called human-leopard conflict. The current scientific understanding of human-leopard conflict constitutes pinpricks of light against a dark background.

More work on understanding the dynamics of conflict—including seasonal factors, geographical patterns, circumstances under which conflict occurs and other issues—might give government authorities a chance to predict and understand the causes of conflict and craft policies accordingly. Even then, that will only be the beginning of the fight; implementing them in a complex society like India's will be the biggest challenge.

## 9

# THE CHANCE ENCOUNTER AT
# THE RAINBOW SCHOOL

Andy Warhol, the famed American artist, predicted that everyone would be world famous for fifteen minutes. My turn came in the February of 2016, perhaps.

My parents were leaving from Bengaluru for Tumkur that Sunday afternoon. I put them in an autorickshaw to the central bus station and got back to my work desk at home. For some reason, I was not in the mood to work. I opened my computer and began to watch a Kannada movie. It was one of those predictable plots—love-crime-happy ending—but I forced myself to continue watching. At about three, my phone rang. I remember wondering who it could be on a Sunday afternoon. It turned out to be Kariyappa, a senior forest officer who took a keen interest in forest conservation. He wasted no time in small talk. 'You must have seen the news that a leopard has entered a school. My higher ups have told me to take your help to capture it.'

I told him that I would be there soon and put down the phone. Before I left, just to ensure that it was actually a leopard, I called Arun Sha, a veterinarian who worked with a wildlife rescue NGO, who confirmed that it was indeed a leopard in the school.

As a strange coincidence, many of these incidents of leopards entering human habitations or getting locked up in buildings happen on a Sunday. They seem to have little regard for weekends. As I was preparing to leave, the phone rang once more. It was Kariyappa again. 'There is no leopard in the school. Please don't leave,' he said. I sat back down to continue my movie watching. But in another ten minutes, I had another call from him. He said that the leopard had been spotted again, and I had to come. Arun, whom I called again to confirm, said, 'Yes, sir, we were also told the same, so we had come away for lunch, but we are now heading back to the school.'

I hurriedly stuffed a powerful flashlight and a pair of binoculars into a backpack. This pair of binoculars had been gifted to me by my dear Swiss friend Michel Joye nearly twenty-two years ago, and I always carried them on field trips. Despite the fact that they were battered—the rubber outer coating torn and smelly due to its exposure to weather conditions—I held on to them. I was very fond of them both because of their quality, and because they were given to me by a good friend. They were a 9x40 Steiners, excellent for observing wildlife, virtually unbreakable, and I had spent hundreds, possibly even thousands of hours behind these binoculars. Both the flashlight and the binoculars could be very handy in a situation like this to spot the animal and to help if it got dark.

I booked a cab online. Often, it took the taxi a few minutes to get to us, but on that day the cab driver called and said he was right in front of our apartment. As I walked out of the house I told my wife, 'There is a leopard in a school in Whitefield, and I may get late in the evening.' Little did I realise that it would be a few days before I would return home.

As we travelled towards the destination, I was on my phone, making calls and discussing the situation regarding the leopard. Between two of my calls, the driver asked me, 'Sir, are you headed to that school in Whitefield where a leopard has entered?' When I replied that I was, he immediately clamped his foot on the accelerator and said, 'I know that school, I will take you straight there. We don't need to waste time looking around for the address.'

I spent the rest of the drive calling a few volunteers to check if they were free and would be willing to join. Unfortunately, all of them were busy on that Sunday afternoon. I also emailed the picture of the leopard that had been captured on the closed circuit television to my colleague Rashmi to check if this animal had appeared in our camera traps on the outskirts of Bengaluru.

Normally, it would have taken us more than ninety minutes in Bengaluru for a ride of 22 kms. We were there in exactly forty-six minutes. It was just one of the many remarkable occurrences that day.

When leopards enter highly human dense-areas, such as the outskirts of cities and towns, or get themselves trapped in open wells, crowds gather in a manner that only an immense calamity can summon. When I arrived at the school, there were possibly over a thousand people congregated around the school to get a ringside view of the action. The school had a very large compound, and the big building was partly painted in a gaudy yellow colour. The front wall was adorned with the word VIBGYOR, with each of the letters painted in the corresponding colour of the rainbow.

As I walked through the glass doors of the large building, I met Arun. We immediately went to check the men's urinals, where the leopard was supposedly hiding. Arun is a tall, thick-mustachioed veterinarian. He is largely interested in sloth bears, but helps the forest department in emergency situations with other species as well.

The bathroom had a large ventilator covered with a half broken, paper-thin mesh. When I climbed up and peeped in through it, I caught sight of the tip of the leopard's tail under a washbasin. It was almost certain that the animal would have to be sedated with a tranquilising gun and taken out. If the leopard had been in a building in a farm or near a forest patch I would have suggested that we wait till it got dark, when the leopard could have easily snuck out on its own. But here we didn't have that luxury, as the school was surrounded by hundreds of houses.

We immediately ensured that the door of the urinals was secured and then went on to survey the school building to understand its layout. After a quick assessment of the entry and exit points for the leopard inside the school building, we went out to check the bathroom from the outside.

The bathroom was constructed strangely. There were two walls to the bathroom with a space of about two feet between the two walls. The inner wall had the broken ventilator and the outer wall had no covering to its ventilator. Adjoining the bathroom, within the school compound, was a large swimming pool filled with water to the brim.

I mentally analysed the situation, trying to anticipate the different scenarios that could play out. If the leopard did not try to come out of the bathroom after he had been sedated in there, everything would go well. We could then easily walk into the bathroom, take the sedated leopard out and put him in a cage. But there was another angle: if the leopard became agitated and tried to come out of the bathroom, his only exit route would be this ventilator. In his tranquilised and dazed state, there was a possibility that he could fall in the gap between the two walls trying to jump out through the ventilator. That would be disastrous for the animal as the gap was so narrow that he could get stuck and there would be little we could do to retrieve him. The leopard could easily break his backbone if he fell there. If the leopard did manage to jump out of the ventilator, there was the danger of him falling into the swimming pool, and a remote chance of him drowning due to the effect of the drug. Moreover when the leopard was out, if a panic-driven person, who did not know swimming jumped into the pool, then it would create another critical situation for us to deal with.

We returned inside the building to discuss a plan with the forest authorities. It was decided that we would secure the ventilator before trying to sedate the leopard to ensure that the animal remained inside the bathroom. Then it would be the veterinarian's job to sedate the animal through the ventilator. Dipika Bajpai, the young forest officer who was in charge of Bengaluru, would be the person who would command the entire team so that there was one point of command. After more details were discussed and finalised, we walked out for another examination of the swimming pool area.

Hundreds of people and children had gathered outside the school building. The action was happening in a state capital, but the entire nation's media seemed to be there, jostling for a share of the adventure. Several media personnel had taken over the school compound to get a grandstand view of the action. Some videographers and photographers were precariously clinging onto a frail drumstick tree, waiting for their best shots. It was a bit unnerving.

To avoid any danger of the leopard drowning, I requested the school authorities to empty the water from the swimming pool. The authorities flatly refused. 'Sir, it has one hundred thousand litres of water. We cannot afford to drain it.' Turning to the police inspector, I requested him to clear the crowd and clamp Section 144 (a legal clause under the Indian Code of Criminal Procedure, which prohibits assembly of five or more persons). He immediately retorted that it was not within his jurisdiction to do so. Dipika called the revenue authorities to get Section 144 implemented but only got a tepid response saying that it was a Sunday! The day had already started to come to a close, and it was nearing nightfall. Time was of the essence, as with daylight decreasing, it would be harder to carry out the operation. Again, we requested the police inspector to atleast clear the media personnel who were on the compound. The smart policeman again claimed his helplessness. 'Sir, you will have to handle them. It's difficult for me to convince them,' he said.

I knew that it was important for us to keep the animal calm so the drug could take its effect. But I knew that it was equally vital that we remain calm—such emergency situations require keeping a presence of mind to be able to take balanced decisions in the short period of time available. For some reason, I was extra calm that day.

I was under the impression that my years of experience in working with the media would help me convince them to co-operate. There were about ten media personnel to be spoken to. With my binoculars slung around my chest and the flashlight in one hand, I started talking to them one after the other. Next to me was the smart police sub-inspector. I decided that speaking to the media personnel clinging on to the drumstick tree would be a good first move. 'Sir, which channel do you belong to? If the leopard comes out, there are good chances that you could be injured by it.'

After hearing me out, the reporter said, 'Fine, sir. Will you please share the pictures and video clippings after the operation?' Then he moved away. I felt proud of myself, thinking my words were respected. The next person I tackled retorted immediately, 'Who are you?' From my years of experience working in these situations I had a ready answer for this. Continuing my round of the journalists, I soon reached the corner of the compound. The policeman and a couple of forest personnel continued to followed me.

Curious to know what was happening with the preparations, I turned to check before I tackled the next media person. The forest department personnel were covering the bathroom ventilator with a large green net. The veterinarian, Arun, and his junior, Nirupama, who wore light blue doctors' aprons, were marching around with their dark green tranquiliser guns like disciplined soldiers. Gopi, the volunteer, walked behind Arun carrying the drug kit. Some school personnel with their bright yellow shirts had refused to leave the arena. A few others were busy on their mobile phones, possibly giving live commentary to their friends.

## *The accident*

I was still focused on convincing the media personnel: I was concerned about their safety and also the commotion they could cause if the animal came out. That's when I heard the leopard growl—a sound expressing both rage and desperation. I turned, to find him about twelve feet above the ground, jumping out of the ventilator like an airborne arrow. His front legs were half-folded, but his hind legs and tail were fully stretched. In a fraction of a second, the cat got caught in the large, green net the forest authorities had spread against the ventilator and landed on the ground. But for this net, the leopard would have directly dived into the swimming pool, which was about ten feet from the bathroom ventilator. The small group of people who were near the ventilator, organising various aspects of the rescue, broke loose and ran in all directions. Some entered the small pump room that housed the machinery to pump out water from the swimming pool.

The big cat quickly recovered from the fall and took a left turn and ran towards the small gate that was part of a yellow wire mesh barrier. About seven feet high, this barrier had been erected between the swimming pool and the rest of the school compound in the shape of a large 'L'. Everyone around me, including the media personnel swarming over the compound, had suddenly evaporated into thin air. I waited to see in which direction the leopard would run after he entered the gate. There was a space of about eight feet between the wire mesh barrier and the compound. If the leopard took a left at the gate he would proceed into the large school grounds and possibly exit the school by jumping over the compound.

The first to encounter the leopard was Akshay, the junior veterinarian with Arun. When the leopard leaped towards him, he warded him off using the butt of his non-lethal tranquiliser gun. The big cat was out of the gate, and as I watched him, he turned to his right. 'Oh no! That's going to be in my direction,' I thought. The leopard was now in between the compound and the 'L'-shaped wire mesh barrier. So he would have to run down this narrow corridor before he could find an exit.

My initial plan had been to scout for an escape route after my discussions with the media personnel. This is part of the planning process I always undertake in situations like this. But I had to spend so much time convincing the media that day that I had not yet had the opportunity to do so.

A couple of people whizzed past me. I had no option but to run too. I turned back to get a glimpse of the leopard and kept running. He was headed towards the corner of the compound where one of the cameramen I had been trying to convince had been standing. The leopard tried to climb over the compound at that corner, but it didn't succeed because of the height of the compound wall. As I ran, I saw a tall iron gate to my left and thought I could climb over it to get out of the school compound. That's when I remembered that outside this compound there were children playing cricket. We had to avoid the leopard going out of the school compound at all costs.

I tried clambering on to the ten-foot-tall gate. I managed to climb a bit, but I immediately realised that the top end of the iron bars had very sharp, pointed edges that tapered like the hypotenuse of a triangle. There was no horizontal bar at the top to hold on to, using which I could have jumped over the gate. I tried again to see if I could jump over the gate using my shoulder strength, but in vain. Before I endeavoured again, I thought, 'Let me just see where the leopard is.' That was the moment when, for a split second, my family whizzed past me in my mind. I regained my composure.

When I turned down to see where the animal was, I realised that the leopard was sitting right under me, hind legs folded and forelegs straight. Our eyes met, and his beautiful, brownish-green eyes looked straight into mine. Even in that moment of grave danger, I couldn't resist admiring those beautiful eyes at that close quarter.

But I also knew he was going to come after me. I made a last desperate attempt to climb up the horizontal iron bars that were welded to the gate. That's when I felt the pain in my right buttock. The leopard had jumped and buried his canines into the soft flesh there. I felt his left paw on my left buttock. He again dug in with his canines, and this time I let go my hold over the gate. I fell back with the leopard holding on to my buttocks with its strong canines. Within the blink of an eye I had landed on the soft body of the leopard.

When the leopard pulled me down, I must have landed on him like a ton of bricks. The animal probably weighed somewhere around 50 kgs. I weighed at least 20 per cent more. I rolled over to my right and the leopard to its left. As I sat up, I kept my gaze trained on the leopard. I could understand from the way he was sitting on his hind legs with front legs straight and checking out the wall that jumping out of the compound was clearly on his mind. Four chocolate-brown plastic chairs neatly arranged by the compound wall and some basketballs were obstructing him from jumping over. As the leopard was planning his move, I saw Arun with his tranquilising gun taking shelter behind the L-shaped mesh barrier and running towards me. I shouted at him, 'Arun, go for it.'

'No, sir, it will get back at you if I shoot the dart,' Arun responded.

'It's okay. Just go for it. There are children outside,' I shouted.

The animal had his back to Arun and was still assessing the jump over the compound.

Meanwhile, I had got up and started walking back, with my eyes still trained on the leopard as I didn't want to lose sight of the animal. By then, the binoculars that was strung around my chest was in my right hand—I thought it might come in handy in extreme situations. As I walked back, I saw Arun take aim at the leopard. He was still in the sitting posture with his head lifted up, gauging the compound's height.

The left rump of the leopard was well exposed to Arun. It was the perfect place to give an anaesthetic drug to an animal. I heard the typical 'pluch' sound the $CO_2$-pumped tranquilising gun makes when it is fired. The bright red feathers at the end of the projectile dart flew into the leopard's left rump. As soon as the dart hit him, the leopard curled back towards the dart and snarled in anger. Once it turned back, it saw the perpetrator—Arun. It took three short steps towards Arun and swiped its paws at him but was held back. Arun had saved himself by taking cover behind the mesh barrier. Failing to get to Arun, the large cat turned its attention to its left when it got sight of me.

Our paths were going to converge again. As I walked backwards, keeping an eye on the leopard, my shoes got caught in the rough surface of the tiles, and I slipped and fell. My mind was running at a million miles per hour as I saw the leopard make his way towards me. I knew calm, clear decision-making was the key. For a second, I just relaxed. 'Focus,' I told myself. Perhaps my senses were in overdrive, but for some strange reason I didn't feel like the end of my life was coming towards me one step at a time. I felt a strange sense of peace, despite being confronted with an animal with two sets of strong canines and a short temper. He was over me in four steps and pushed down my left thigh with his right paw. Now I was fully on the ground.

He scraped his long claws on my tummy and chest. In the next couple of moments he had deeply gashed my right hand at a few places. Then he put his right paw near my right armpit and his left paw behind my shoulder and pulled my elbow closer to him. For a moment his muzzle, with the lips pulled back in a snarl, was a few millimetres away from my face. I was as intimate with the long canines and the mottled-pink tongue as anyone could hope to get. His roar echoed in my ears.

*Crunch.* He had bitten through my humerus. '*Ammaaaa!*' I shouted, like anyone does in India while in distress. He dug his canines into my elbow, and sent a searing current of pain through my body. It was excruciating. With a frenzied shake of the head, he shook my arm ever harder, as though he was finishing off prey by holding its trachea till the prey would be suffocated to death. With its four canines embedded deep into my arm, he was violently shaking it. My arm was being thrashed around like it was a rag doll. I felt the dead weight of over 50 kgs hanging on my arm like a sand bag. I fought to keep my wits about me. I instinctively knew this was a real crisis, and I couldn't afford to blank out. Whoever cowed down would lose, I thought. I tried to push the thoughts of being crushed by the animal out of my mind.

Strange though it may sound, being prey gives a very different dimension to understand our study species—a large carnivore. A realisation that we are ultimately a mass of meat.

I could feel the warmth of his breath and his long, stiff whiskers on my arms, shoulders and ribs. He was tidy, disciplined and clean. I did not smell the unbearable smell that some leopards have, most probably linked to ill-health. I have experienced that with a couple of them and the stink does not subside for weeks.

That day I literally experienced what up to then had been a technical term for me—the Bite Force Quotient (BFQ). The BFQ, measured in Pound per Square Inch (PSI), is the regression of the quotient of an animal's bite force in newtons, divided by its body mass in kilograms. A leopard's bite force peaks at a BFQ of 94 PSI. Just for comparison, an adult lion would have a BFQ of 112 while a tiger has 127. So the BFQ of the leopard that day was perhaps not far from the force of an adult lion.

Confrontations in these situations only last a few seconds, but that's good enough. One, two, three, four … a few seconds of contact and it is all over. The canine can cause rapid damage to the windpipe and major blood vessels in those moments. That day death swung before my eyes. But some celestial hand must have turned over the hourglass of my luck just as the grains were running out. I made the split-second decision to stand up. I acted on impulse—an impulse that finally proved to be the difference between life and death. It took all the willpower I could muster to stop the leopard biting me more. But I was clear that I shouldn't pull my elbow from him. It would ensure that large chunks of my muscle would remain in his mouth.

When I first tried to get up, a swipe from his right paw put me down. In that second, I decided I had to fight back. I put all the energy I had into my left hand and tried to get up. This time I was able to stand up, and as soon as I was on my feet I put my left palm on the leopard's neck and pushed him. Like magic, he let go of my arm and turned his back as if nature was on my side. I swung the heavy binoculars in my right hand thinking I would use it to defend myself if the leopard tried to attack again. But luckily, I didn't have to hurt him with my binoculars.

A couple of seconds after the leopard let go of me grumpily, I heard a bullet whizz past, a foot or two from me. Someone had taken a shot at the animal to try to help me. But the bullet, which was traveling at supersonic speed, only narrowly missed me. It landed on the floor just nanoseconds before the leopard came to that particular spot. Spared of his life, the animal trotted into the shower room a few feet away from me.

Within another second, a heavy iron L-angle came crashing at my foot. Someone, again well intended, had thrown a very heavy iron L-angle at me so that I could defend myself against the animal. All I knew was I was lucky to have survived the third attempt at my life within a few seconds.

By then, the veterinarians, Arun and Akshay, had arrived. As I turned around, Gopi, a volunteer with Arun, came down, shouting, 'Gubbi sir is hurt, Gubbi sir is hurt!' Blood flowed down my badly lacerated arm and from several deep wounds on my right hip as I walked out with Gopi's help. People followed me with their mobile phones, trying to capture the moments they were witnessing. I saw a flabbergasted woman's face at a distance. It was the young forest officer who stood there not knowing what to do.

Then I was hurried into a four-wheeler. It left the school premises with many peering inside the vehicle, curious to find out what had happened inside the school campus. We drove for a bit when someone said, 'There's a hospital!' As the vehicle halted in front of the hospital, I hazily made out the word Appo—. Then I was helped into the hospital. Behind me someone spoke to the nurse. 'He's been injured by a leopard and needs urgent medical help.'

'Make him sleep on the bed in the emergency room. The doctor will be there soon,' said the nurse's voice. Seconds seemed to pass by like hours. The pain was increasing, and I could feel the blood flow around the wounds on my hip and hand. After a few minutes I heard an authoritative voice ask, 'What happened to you?'

Someone responded, 'Sir, he's been bitten by a leopard.'

The doctor examined me quickly and said, 'Nothing serious. You just need some first aid.' Then he vanished. Minutes seemed to be more than hours now.

Someone again asked, 'Nurse, is the doctor going to come soon?'

'He's with another patient and will be there soon. You will have to have some patience,' came back the stern response. When the doctor finally returned and re-examined me, he announced, 'There is nothing much. I will give you some local anaesthesia and put some stitches.'

I summoned up the last of my energy to reply, 'Doctor, I think I may need a general anaesthesia. There are lots of wounds.'

'No, no. Not much,' said the highly confident man, and he started pricking me with local anaesthesia at the places I had lacerations in the arm. As soon as the first wound was stitched, the doctor instructed his assistant to pad me up with bandage.

I said, 'Doctor there are more wounds.'

Immediately came the response. 'No, this is good enough.' As soon as the doctor's assistant finished his job I was asked to lift my injured arm. Blood started to drip out of the bandage from some other wound that had not been stitched. The assistant said, 'Sir, looks like there are more wounds somewhere else.' They removed the entire bandage and started stitching another wound.

I tried again. 'Doctor, I think I may need a general anaesthesia, and I am not sure stitching is the best idea as infections can set in. Can I go to a larger hospital?'

It was common sense that animal wounds should be thoroughly washed and left for a couple of days for observation before they are stitched. Leopards don't brush their teeth; their mouth can be covered in bacteria. Get that bacteria in you and you've had it! If not treated properly it can infect the person and can lead to death.

The doctor was not happy this time. He said, 'Are you the doctor or me? I will give you basic care and then send you to a larger hospital.'

My arm was bandaged again and I was asked to lift it. Blood started to drip from another wound. The bandage was again removed, and another wound was stitched. I was losing consciousness but I held on, as I knew this doctor was messing around. Being awake and aware was in my best interest. In the midst of this commotion someone walked to my bed and said, 'Sir, I am from the media. Can you tell me how you're feeling?' I could only smile at this insensitive journalist.

My right arm was swollen and throbbing with pain by this point. I thought I would lose a lot of blood if I continued to lie on the cot.

The doctor said, 'Don't worry. We will only provide you first aid.'

I was not convinced.

After the fourth bandage, there didn't seem to be any blood dripping from the injured arm, and the doctor said I could get up and walk. I tried to tell him there were wounds in my right hip that needed attention, but, as before, the doctor was dismissive. 'No, there are no serious wounds there. You can get up now.'

When I tried getting up, the assistant found the whole bedspread covered with blood, and they realised there were more wounds. I was made to lie down, and my trousers were cut open.

The entire drama of stitching my wounds restarted, but this time they didn't use local anaesthesia. I could feel the pain each time the sharp needles were put through my skin, and I started losing alertness. Still I held on.

Through the pain, I suddenly saw a familiar face—Giridhar Kulkarni, a software engineer who was volunteering with us had arrived at the clinic. He was one of the three people I had sent a message to on my way to the school to check if they wanted to join me.

As soon as the doctor saw Giridhar he raised his voice. 'Who are you? Why are you here?'

'I am the patient's friend,' Giridhar replied. I called Giridhar to my side and told him that I needed to talk to my wife and I would also like to go to a larger hospital and was uncomfortable with this doctor.

I told the doctor, 'Sir, my wife is a doctor as well. Can you please talk to her?'

The doctor finally showed some mercy on me. He asked Giridhar to call my wife and asked me for her phone number.

'990 ... 99000 ... 991 ...' I was unable to recall the number. I always manually input the phone numbers of close family members rather than dialling them directly from the phonebook. Despite that practice, in that critical moment, I was unable to remember my wife's phone number. In those desperate few minutes, I saw another familiar face—Prakash Matada, another one of our volunteers. I called Prakash and repeated what I had earlier told Giridhar, asking him to take me out of this hospital.

Meanwhile I heard the nurse saying, 'Sir, his BP is nearly 240.'

The medical man remained calm. Someone in the room was finally able to get my wife on the line. 'Nurse, you talk to her, and if she asks for the BP tell her it is normal,' said the unruffled doctor. I was really under a lot of pain and this doctor seemed unwilling to accept that he couldn't handle this medical emergency.

Nearly two and half hours of this experimentation went by before I saw a glimmer of hope. Suddenly, a young doctor walked into the room. He calmly said, 'Mr Gubbi, how are you feeling? We have come to take you to a bigger hospital.'

As I looked at the compassionate, smiling, confident young doctor, the relief I felt was palpable. But before the young doctor could go on, the resident doctor stepped in, saying, in a raised voice, 'You can't talk to him until he is discharged from here, and he can't go out without paying his bills.'

I tried to look for my wallet, but obviously couldn't find it; my trousers had been taken away while the doctor was administering his 'first aid'.

Prakash immediately said, 'We will stay on and make the payments. Please let him go.' But the doctor refused.

Prakash continued requesting him. 'I have a credit card. I will stay back and clear his bills.'

But the doctor was not satisfied. 'He can leave only after his bills have been cleared.' It took another twenty minutes for Prakash to complete the payment formalities before I was permitted to be taken out.

The clinic allowed me to be handed over to the emergency doctor who had arrived with an ambulance. As I was rolled out of the clinic on a stretcher, a couple of familiar faces hazily floated by. Poornesha and Ashritha, my colleagues, were standing outside the clinic. I could also make out a few people with large cameras—journalists trying to get footage of me being taken out.

I heard someone saying, as if from a distance, 'He needs urgent medical attention. Let him go.'

Then I was rolled in, and faintly, somewhere in the background, I heard the wail of a siren—not realising that it was the same vehicle I was traveling in.

My memories are fragmented after this. I remember seeing, in a rush of familiarity, the face of my wife when the ambulance door was opened and the stretcher was pulled out. As the stretcher was rolled into the hospital, I remember at least four doctors compassionately talking to me. My next memories are of being wheeled into the operation theatre, its large, bright lights shining above me.

To keep my composure, I tried to talk to the doctor, 'What drugs do you give to anaesthetise us?

The doctor responded, 'What do you use for leopards?'

I replied, 'Keta—.'

But before I could complete the word, I had passed out.

### *The recovery*

I slowly opened my eyes. All around me were many beeping and flashing machines monitoring my vital signs. Someone started to ask me how I was, but even before I'd completed saying, 'I'm fine', I passed out again.

I regained consciousness a couple of hours later. Something surrounding my right leg pumped and released air. A few familiar faces started to hazily appear. After a few hours of being awake, I could assess what was going on around me.

As the doctors came in to change my bandages, I began to understand the extent of my injuries. There were claw gashes on my stomach, forearm and shoulder, all looking quite gory. My right arm had two large wounds on the elbow. The entry wound was the size of a finger, and the exit wound was as big as a thumb. The leopard had bitten right through my arm, and I could see the four clear marks left by the leopard's canines, which had also deeply damaged my arm muscles. There were also three two-inch-long gashes on my right arm.

I was told a bit of my right humerus had been chipped off, and I had broken triceps. There were eight bite marks on my right hip, clearly indicating that the leopard had bitten me there twice. The leopard had bitten right through my buttock—when cleaning solution was put in the top wound, it would come right back out of the bottom wound. A couple of days later, when it was confirmed that there was no infection, the doctors operated again to stitch up all the wounds. They used fifty-five stitches to sew me up. It took many more months of painful treatment, stitches, skin grafts and physiotherapy to put me together again.

While I was at the hospital, I was puzzled about the damage to my mobile phone. But in two days I was able to decipher the mystery. I had kept my mobile phone in my left chest pocket, securely zipped. Exactly at the place where the damaged portion of the phone would have rested, I had a small wound on my chest, a few centimetres below the heart. The phone had saved my lungs from being severely damaged by the leopard's claws.

It was a narrow escape straight out of a movie script, and rivalled some famous incidents: Theodore Roosevelt survived an attempt on his life when the written speech in his pocket stopped the bullet. A pocket watch saved Kamal Ataturk, the revolutionary who founded the Republic of Turkey and was its first president, in 1915.

I was told that the video of the incident had gone viral and it was off to the races at that point. My phone pinged, buzzed and beeped nonstop as it started to receive a day's worth of messages. It practically popped like corn in a kettle. The BBC called, and the American Broadcasting Corporation rang up, as did the CBC from Canada and most Indian leading media houses, all wanting to know what had happened and how.

The news had gone international, and the stories ran for days thereafter. The school itself became the nerve centre of news for several days. The incident had all the ingredients of a Bollywood movie. The story generated large headlines, and newspapers were filled with voluminous columns. I was to learn later that the media, especially the television channels, ran the news for several days. Annually, tens of people get injured by wild animals, including leopards, in India, yet these cases elicit only the most perfunctory interest from the general public and the media.

A few people find pride by associating themselves, almost to the level of proprietorship, with a particular animal species—especially leopards. Apart from the media, this encounter also attracted the attention of some vested interests, who took advantage of the event. A couple of biologists with jaundiced eyes launched diatribes against me. Their opinions came with no actual experience of a situation where they had to capture a leopard that had enter a highly settled area: 'There was no necessity for him to have been there', 'He should have jumped into the swimming pool', 'This was unnecessary bravado'. It looked as though their main objective was to pass on as much tribulation as possible. I had dedicated over twenty-five years of my life to this work, and in the end it seemed I was to be judged on the basis of those 120 seconds. But that sort of cheesy opportunism didn't last long. In situations like these, success is survivability. You win by walking away.

When things finally started calming down, I started to scroll through the messages that had flooded my phone. I had messages from people whom I hadn't heard from for years. One email from a 'wildlife biologist' was particularly funny. He wrote: 'Mr Gubbi, I think you were very lucky. Since you were wearing a full-sleeved shirt, the damages weren't much.' I wondered how a 0.006-inch-thick shirt could protect me against dagger-like canines that were nearly two inches long!

When I checked on the status of the leopard later, I learnt that Arun and his team had been able to capture it after it entered the shower room, once the anaesthesia drug that Arun had fired had taken effect. The animal had been kept in Bannerghatta Zoo, at the outskirts of Bengaluru. But very surprisingly, the leopard had managed to escape from its enclosure in the zoo. I was happy that it was back in its natural habitat, where it belongs to.

The incident has left me with lingering and dangerous mementos. My body suffered a physical beating whose after-effects will last the rest of my life. Across my right arm, belly, chest and hip are the hieroglyphs of the encounter at the school; they join previous ones. Parts of my right forearm continue to be partly numb from the nerve damage inflicted by the leopard's canines. The right arm is not as efficient in its movement as the left is.

This incident has also made my engagement with my subject a bit more personal and not purely academic or conversational. For a leopard to injure a person studying leopards—that seems more than coincidence, doesn't it?

Has being a survivor of a near-death experience with a leopard made me an authority on leopard–human conflict? No. People ask me if the encounter has left me scared. I feel the incident was an aberration. A leopard wandering in human turf is likely to be more unpredictable, more frantic, and such accidents do occur. If anything, I now have greater faith in wild animals. When cornered, any wild animal would do exactly what the leopard did that day.

Though the episode was not a video game, something I could easily walk away from, I never got the gloomy feeling that the curtains were about to come down on my time as a human. We Indians believe in omens—both good and bad. Most people may not believe me when I say that when I arrived I somehow knew things would not go normally that evening.

When I look back on that day, I can hardly believe it happened. The fragile pendulum of life swung; death came right up to my neck and retreated. I had swung between life and death for a few seconds. Now that the uncertain vibration of the moment is gone, it is difficult to express exactly how it had felt. They say you can survive a large cat attack if you keep your wits about you, and this is true. I was also lucky that day, as well as privileged, to receive optimal medical care and attention at the right time.

Post this incident, the sedentary life at home took a toll on my body. I gained eight kilograms in two months—almost 150 grams a day—and my belt size reached thirty-six inches from thirty-two as I developed a watermelon belly. I was now looking fitter for the office than for the jungles. I have decided that leopard bites make you fat. They certainly make it easier to find peace and humour in any situation! Though I have been involved in several occasions when leopards have come into human habitations, this episode stands out, unforgettably!

# 10

# LEOPARDS IN DISTRESS

Robusta coffee, one of the most beloved seed products, which has a number of highly desirable traits, is naturally more resistant to a broader spectrum of threats, and surviving plants pass on their genetic advantages to their young ones. Leopards are like Robusta coffee, successful in adapting to changes in growing conditions.

A resilient species like the leopard, with its delicate beauty and lithe grace, is designed to impress. However, the leopard, which co-habits with its larger cousins such as the tiger and the lion never receives the same concern they do. Instead, its ability to live in close proximity to people has given rise to a false sense of security about the leopard's future.

Leopards face a complex cross-section of conservation threats that are slightly different from other large cats. Decline—due to habitat destruction, hunting of their natural prey, poaching, being driven over by speeding cars, being captured and translocated in the hundreds, being snared, poisoned, torched or clubbed to death, as well as conflict with humans—looms large. The threats leopards face seem to be a chain of seeming impossibilities, as the factors that cause them are often intractable; natural resource extraction, infrastructure development and human-leopard conflict are linked to the economic growth of the nation. This is compounded by the declining tolerance of the society towards nature and wildlife and the failure of the conservation community to provide workable solutions to bring down human-wildlife conflict. That's what makes their conservation so challenging, so complicated and so problematic.

## *Loss of habitat*

In India, nearly 18 per cent of the world's population crowds into merely 4 per cent of the land area. Hence, the demand for land and natural resources is always burgeoning. With India's economy having taken a turn towards liberalisation since the 1990s, more land is in demand to extract natural resources to feed the growing industry and meet the demand for consumer products. Currently, India is one of the fastest-growing economies in the world, and is projected to be the third-largest consumer economy by the year 2025 as per the Boston Consulting Group. All these economic developments come at a cost to wildlife habitats, including that of leopards. In my opinion, the fate of leopards as a species depicts the changes in India's economy.

Today, leopards are threatened by the wholesale destruction of their homes. This ensures that there are solid cracks in the foundations of their future survival. Many such habitats have vanished over the years—at times even within a couple of years—in front of my own eyes. I feel that their loss carries more potent consequences for leopards than several other factors that threaten them today. To me, the future of leopard habitats outside protected areas has never been as uncertain as it is right now. The gradual disappearance of leopards from Chamundi Hills is a classic example.

One such leopard habitat whose base has been shaken is the rocky outcrops of the Deccan. These hillocks are increasingly endangered by bulldozing for granite and minerals like iron ore. Apart from Bengaluru, the nearby towns of Tumkur, Ramanagara,

Kolar and Mandya have all seen a sharp rise in quarrying for granite. The stone quarries around and close to cities stand as mute witness to what were once leopard refuges before they were sacrificed for Bengaluru's burgeoning construction industry. Some of the deep quarry pits that stud the rocky outcrops can easily fit in fifteen-floor buildings. Roads, another pillar of economic and social progress, are also responsible for this toll on leopard habitats. The National Highways Authority of India, the government agency that's responsible for building big highways in the country, has targeted achieving 10 kms of roads a day. The broadening of existing highways has also been taken up on a massive scale. These need an enormous amount of granite, and most of it comes from leopard habitats.

The fate of these habitats is similar to that of the Terai belt of Uttarakhand and Uttar Pradesh, as well as that of the Chitwan Valley in neighbouring Nepal in the mid-1950s. Malaria had kept agriculture expansion away from the fertile floodplains of the Terai. Once the malaria-eradication programme took off, the floodplains attracted millions of people to settle in the Terai, leading to a loss of habitat for tigers, rhinos, elephants, swamp deer, hog deer and other lesser-known wildlife species such as the hispid hare that are dependent on grasslands. Progress has its sacrifices.

The mining and quarrying that has drastically altered, degraded, isolated and destroyed leopard habitats is sometimes legal but often illegal. Every rule is broken with impunity or tripped up by corruption. This quarrying of rocky outcrops remains a vexing problem to leopards outside protected areas or reserved forests and poses a regulatory nightmare for those trying to protect leopard habitats as most of these areas are out of the purview of the forest department, despite having good tree cover. Most times they are even classified as wastelands in government records. The ownership lies with the revenue department, and it issues permits to extract granite for construction and ornamental purposes. The forest department has little legal force to halt this cognisant destruction. Though these rocky outcrops were earlier not protected under any law, they got some reprieve in 1995, when the Supreme Court of India defined the word 'forests', bringing in large swathes of natural forests, including rocky outcrops, under legal protection. They were to be protected by law, honoured at least in principle. But the ground reality is different.

Many of the leopard habitats have also been gouged to extract iron and manganese ore to be exported to countries like China, Japan, South Korea, Malaysia and Indonesia, and for local consumption. Other legal forms of leopard habitat loss include various developmental activities, including wind energy farms. These days, these natural areas are dominated by the deafening sounds of the massive blades of the wind turbines, blanketing the vast orchestra of life. Touted as ecologically green, wind energy holds a very different view from a leopard conservation perspective. Roads constructed for wind energy are hotbeds of snares set for catching all kinds of wildlife that are on the leopard's natural menu.

In a way, it has been a boon that leopards have evolved as habitat generalists. Species that are habitat specialists face a larger threat of extinction. For instance, the endangered wild water buffalo prefers the subtropical and tropical floodplains of Asia that are also highly sought after for rice farming. Today, these powerful ungulates' numbers are less than 2,500, and they survive in isolated patches in India, Nepal, Bhutan, Thailand, Myanmar and Cambodia. There are several such examples of other habitat specialists that have declined in numbers, with some, like the great Indian bustard, even staring at extinction. On the other hand, the leopard, despite suffering habitat loss, does better than its counterpart the tiger, because it can survive in hilly, rocky outcrops, and due to its ecological and behavioural adaptation.

The matter, however, is not so clear-cut. The large-bouldered rocky outcrops only appear to be chains of leopard habitat. In reality, these chains are fragmented and isolated due to the gasping desperation and enterprising scramble of modern India. The wave of granite quarrying and ever-expanding agriculture has turned these rocky outcrops into postage stamp-size parcels. The valleys in between these leopard habitats now teem with stone-crushing industries, farmland and human habitations.

When a species' habitat gets isolated and fragmented, the animal starts surviving with risky compromises and is forced to leave the places it once peacefully lived in. It is coerced into surviving in highly human-modified habitats such as sugarcane fields, maize fields, areca nut, and coconut plantations, which heavily increase the chances of the species coming into contact with people and their livestock, thus bringing them into direct conflict with humans. In such human-modified landscapes, these cats may also increase their predation of livestock, which tends to provoke retaliatory killing and the capture of leopards.

There is a chance that leopards live in these sub-optimal habitats under enormous stress and pressure. Such high stress levels are observed in elephants when they are in human-dominated areas, especially after negative interactions. However, this can be scientifically proven only if the DNA of leopards from agriculture-dominated areas is compared with that of leopards living in natural habitats. There could also be repercussions such as large-scale inbreeding and so forth about which we have very little understanding.

We cannot undermine or ignore the threats of large-scale quarrying, mining and other forms of resource extraction, which now directly compete with the leopards. If humans attribute high economic value to an animal's habitat then such species face far more serious risk than other threats. I was sanguine about the landscape leopards inhabit also because it is not the most suitable for agriculture. All the rocky outcrops created by volcanic oozing are unsuitable for agriculture due to highly undulating terrain, poor soil quality and low and erratic rainfall. In simple words, they're not highly prized real estate. But despite this, the demand for land is such that it has pushed fields ever higher up in the small forest patches where leopards survive.

The issue of habitat loss haunts the country. The situation has escalated due to the state and administration's apathy in implementation and the dilution of wildlife laws. Yet habitat loss has scarcely received more than a sentence or two in recent literature, especially with relation to leopards in India. Devastated habitats may take decades to recover. Thus, conservation efforts should focus on halting habitat loss and improving connectivity between habitat patches, as the conflict situation also largely occurs in those patches that are used by leopards to move between larger natural habitats.

I grew up in dry areas where forests were largely these rocky outcrops that have their own thoughts, textures, and rhythms. I would not like to see them die out.

## Prey poaching—the open buffets

'Food is the burning question in animal society, and the whole structure and activities of the community are dependent upon questions of food supply,' writes Charles Elton, a zoologist from Oxford in the 1920s, in his book *Animal Ecology*. Large carnivores devote a considerable amount of their lifetime to scouting for food and patrolling their territories. For carnivores, plant-eaters are extremely essential. They convert grass, fruits, nuts and other plant material into flesh for the carnivores to survive. Hence protecting these plant-eaters is also an important strategy for large carnivores, including leopard, conservation. But hunting of prey animals for meat consumption remains a dire issue, especially where they survive outside of protected areas.

Forests and rocky outcrops are flush with creatures that many people consider as game. In a way, these areas are a poacher's heaven. Over the years, the sheer amount of evidence of poaching we have found in every forest we have worked in, outside the protected areas, has been daunting. Hunters have penetrated valleys, forest roads and trails to set up snares. They hunt using every means possible—country-made guns, hunting dogs, spears, snares, trip-guns, deadfall traps, explosives kept inside food to lure wild pigs, and nets.

As I discussed earlier, our camera traps have photographed not just wildlife but also several gun-toting poaching teams or hunting dogs pursuing wild ungulates. Men scouting the forests for wildlife are all too common; many hunt boldly in the broad daylight. There has been many a time in remote forest valleys or trails that I have seen people carry away monitor lizards, hare or other prey, but have been unable to do anything. Poaching is like an informal recreation industry around here.

The data from our study sites shows a clear pattern: enforcement against poaching is so lax in these areas that poaching is seven times higher compared to protected areas. It is just a scientific way of objectively confirming what the eye cannot deny.

Sambar and chital have almost disappeared outside the protected areas. Except for small numbers in slightly larger forests such as Bhadravathi, Devarayanadurga, Madhugiri, Kabbal and Narasimhadevarabetta, they have disappeared altogether from most areas we have worked in. One might think that a deer or two, taken here or there is not such a big problem. But poaching, like mining, has an outsized impact. It defaunates the area of leopard food. The Indo-Chinese subspecies of leopards in Cambodia, Laos and Vietnam are heading towards a catastrophe largely due to this very reason—the overkilling of their prey. A similar reason is suspected for the extremely low numbers of the critically endangered Javan and Persian leopard subspecies.

Poaching also leads to other issues. The natural prey outside protected areas is so decimated that, in essence, livestock becomes the best game in town for big hungry predators like the leopard. This is perhaps one of the main causes for leopards to shift to domestic animals, leading to severe friction between people and leopards.

### Direct extermination of leopards

For centuries, leopards have been used as animals of recreation. In the great amphitheatres, the Romans brought leopards from faraway Africa, to be killed in grand spectacle. It is said that in a single day in the Colosseum of Rome more than four hundred leopards were slaughtered.

More recently, between 1605–1906, court rituals in Java involved the killing of tigers and leopards. The rituals involved a fight between a tiger or a leopard, and a water buffalo or a banteng. The tiger or the leopard would be let into a large enclosed place with a buffalo, and both animals were egged on to fight. Eventually, the large cats were gored and crushed to death by the massive ungulate. A second ritual would again involve a tiger or a leopard released into a large square, and ranks of spearmen would spear the cat when it tried to jump over their head to escape. Even to this day, cages are found at the palaces in central Java. Historians say that these rituals may have seriously depleted the stock of leopards in the wild between 1830 and 1870. In Java, leopards were also used to execute criminals.

Well-known environmental historian Mahesh Rangarajan, in his book *India's Wildlife History*, argues that leopards never found conservation refuge in the past as they were simply seen as pests. He has pointed out that between 1875 and 1925 more than 150,000 leopards were bounty-killed in India. Indian rulers often outstripped Britishers in exercising their hunting privileges. Ramanuj Saran Singh Deo of Sarguja, in the current day Chhattisgarh, hunted two thousand leopards and even killed thirteen of them in one night.

In Indonesia, locals killed leopards out of revenge for livestock killing and not merely for bounties. Between 1854 and 1862, a great number of leopards were killed, as the bounty paid out for a leopard was the same as that of a tiger.

Traditionally, the other reason for killing leopards was for their beautiful fur. The leopard has the misfortune of having smooth, beautiful fur with rosettes that can be tanned into premium pelt. Throughout history, original leopard pelt has been worn by warriors to show their powers and by rulers to display their wealth. From the seventeenth to the nineteenth century, leopard skins were one of the key commodities of trade in Ethiopia, and were sent through its ancient trade routes to Sudan, the Mediterranean and the Arabian peninsula, along with gold, forest coffee, honey, wild cardamom, musk and ivory, bringing in economic power to the Kafa province of Ethiopia.

The fashion continued into the twentieth century, adapted by trendsetters and members of the avant-garde, and the leopard print has emerged as one of the world's most distinctive fashion phenomena. Many celebrities and those in power have been known to sport genuine leopard fur robes and accessories—Queen Elizabeth II, American actress Elizabeth Taylor, Zairean president Mobutu Sese Seko and the multitalented diva Eartha Kitt. In 1962, Jacqueline Kennedy wore a genuine leopard-skin coat on an official trip to India and Pakistan, when she accompanied her husband, President John F. Kennedy. What happened next was disastrous. The first lady's fashion statement is supposed to have caused a spike in demand for real leopard skins. It's believed that Oleg Cassini, the renowned designer of Jacqueline's leopard coat, spent the rest of his life consumed with guilt over the harm he had unwittingly caused to leopards in the wild. Over 250,000 leopards are estimated to have been slaughtered as women started to copy Jacqueline, their fashion icon.

In India, during the colonial period, British administrators and English aristocrats took to hunting large cats extensively for their pelts and to keep them as decorative trophies. They prized leopard pelts as much as they did those of the tiger. It was difficult to put a label on who hunted them: those who hunted for sport were royalty, common folk and anyone endeavouring to show off some machismo. Invitation to hunt these large cats became a sort of recreational grease for the Indian royalty. On the eve of India's independence, even the British Royal Band's bass drummers wore leopard skin aprons, an idea that seems to have originated with Emperor Napoleon Bonaparte.

On a summer afternoon in 1998, I visited a family in Kodagu district, the erstwhile Coorg state, in south-western Karnataka. This is a rich, coffee-growing district with a distinct culture, language and people. An ethno-lingual community called the Kodavas, who are very proud of their warrior backgrounds and hunting legacies, are the inhabitants of Kodagu. They speak a language called Kodava thakk. Almost every Kodava home, to this day, owns a license-free gun, a British-era privilege enjoyed by this community legally for the last 158 years but, in principle, for centuries.

The Podamada family lived amidst the coffee plantations in the nondescript village of Devanoor. Their house was a beautiful old building with a palatial appearance. Built in 1938, it was painted an ochre-ish yellow. Anthuriums, and various other ornamental plants, adorned the edges of the house all around. Orchid species hung down in small earthen pots, all accustomed to this heavy rainfall region. The sloping roof with terracotta tiles suited the building to the fullest. A water well with a stone parapet and moss running along the edges of its stone blocks in the courtyard added to the beauty of the house. It was a picture-postcard setting.

Within the house itself, heavy rosewood furniture graced the family's living room. Pure white, laced curtains adorned the windows and doors, giving the entire space a sense of clinical cleanliness. The stuffed trophies of leopards, sloth bears, tigers, leopard cats and sambars stood in stolid silence at various corners of the different rooms. The walls were decorated with the mounted heads of leopards and sambar on rosewood plaques, the horn of the gaur and the chital's pelt. All the trophies had been neatly stuffed and mounted by none other than Van Ingen of Mysuru, the famous taxidermists of Dutch origin, best known for their taxidermy work on leopards and tigers. All these trophies highlighted an era when hunting was the norm. The Podamadas say that they never hunted these animals, but bought them from people who had hunted before the legal ban on hunting came into effect in India in 1972.

Recently, I wanted to go back and visit the family to get another glimpse of the dazzling house and see how the trophies were doing. My efforts to reestablish contact were successful, and I finally got to speak to the younger son, who now lives in Bengaluru, far away from the tranquility of his coffee plantation. He revealed a very shocking fact. The beautiful house I had visited twenty-two years before had been burnt down to ashes in 2012 due to an electrical short circuit. The entire house, its rosewood furniture, and the trophies were all gone with the fire. I had missed my opportunity of revisiting that wonderful house.

The son's fondness for the house was evident in his amiable voice. He told me that he had been fascinated by the way the trophies were mounted in the large workshops of the Van Ingens, whom he used to visit with his dad, as they were family friends. Though he liked the trophies, he categorically stated that 'these things should never be in anybody's home, definitely not in this time and age.'

Not far from where the Podamadas used to lived, are the Palecandas, another Kodava family and coffee planters. The Palecandas live on the south-western edge of the Nagarahole Tiger Reserve, abutting the interstate boundary with Kerala and close to the small sleepy town of Kutta. I had met the eldest son of the family, Palecanda Aiyanna, a middle-aged gentleman interested in wildlife conservation, way back in 1989. Aiyanna's father, Palecanda Madayya, who worked for the British in coffee plantations had been an avid gamesman. Perhaps something he had picked up from the British. Nearly thirty-one years after this meeting, I returned to the coffee plantation at Kutta to meet Aiyanna.

Here was my second disappointment. Sadly, Aiyanna was now deceased. His wife Anita Aiyanna was kind enough to invite me to their beautiful fifty-eight-year-old house, perched on the top of a hillock. The large living room had a very colonial feel with its mosaic flooring and high ceiling. As with most Kodava homes, the house was quaint and spotless. They, too, had trophies of wildlife kept in mint condition—tigers, leopards, leopard cats, sloth bears, gaur, chital, sambar, barking deer, mouse deer and wild pigs.

Aiyanna's younger brother, the grey-haired, seventy-two-year-old, bubbly, highly knowledgeable Palecanda Prabhu, was also present. He perked up as he explained the background of each trophy to me. We sat down with a cup of freshly brewed coffee from his plantation to listen to his anecdotes. A pelt of a tiger with a bullet mark on the forehead, shot in 1948 as it had killed buffaloes and injured a labourer, hung on the wall. A very young stuffed leopard, not more than a few weeks old, stood next to a large leopard trophy. The cub had been mistakenly shot in 1968, in the belief that it had been raiding chicken pens. One trophy that caught my attention was that of a dhole. I had never seen the trophy of a dhole before. This dhole had been hunted with a 0.22 rifle in the neighbouring state of Kerala. An eight-year-old Prabhu had accompanied his father and his father's friend on this 1955 expedition, in which they'd driven a single-cabin Studebaker pickup. Prabhu told me that the Palecandas also got their trophies done by the Van Ingens, who would take six to eight months to get one trophy curated.

Prabhu suddenly got up and vanished. When he returned, he had a timeworn photo album in his hand. The old soul brusquely flipped the pages to show the old, black-and-white photographs of several hunting trips of his father, including those with the British royalty. On one of the pages, he pointed to a white shirt, khaki short-clad young teenager and said, 'That's me.'

Some trophies had been hunted within their estate and some in Kerala with hunting permits. Prabhu's father, Madayya, had meticulously maintained records of all his hunting sojourns, including the permits. One could see Prabhu's childlike enthusiasm when he opened up these records. 'Feather Game License' was a new term I learnt that day, meaning a permit for hunting wild birds.

One missive that particularly caught my attention was a letter written in beautiful cursive. It was an invitation from an Englishman, A.G.G. Barclay, to Madayya, asking him to work for his friend Col. Maurice at his Robusta coffee and orange plantation in Kutta. Along with a pay of Rs 45, a dearness allowance of Rs 35 and Rs 21 of coolie allowance, Barclay tempted him with the 'excellent shikkar (sic) to be had here—better than Mavinkere'. The letter ended: 'He tells me he bought a double barrel hammer gun second hand, in England last year and after paying duty on it in India the total cost was only about Rs 220. Would a hammer gun suit you and if so should I try and get you one when I am in England this year?'

I asked Prabhu what he thought of those trophies. His answer was similar to that of the Podamada's. He immediately retorted, 'Certainly not in these days.'

Despite being banned by some countries, even to this day, in some parts of the world leopards are legally hunted as trophies and for their skins. In 1964, East Africa alone exported fifty thousand leopard skins. A total of 6,138 leopard trophies and skins were exported from different countries between 2015 and 2018, as per the trade statistics provided by the Convention on International Trade in Endangered Species of Wild Fauna and Flora (CITES), an international agreement between countries that came into force in 1974 to ensure that the trade in wild animals and plants is sustainable.

In some countries, not just leopards, but also many species of wildlife including large carnivores are hunted through an annual 'harvest' quota given out by CITES. Bears, lions, mountain lions, African elephants, giraffes, zebras, deer and antelopes species, mountain goats and many other wildlife species are all hunted legally. Many are hunted for their impressive trophies, some because of the incentives proceeds raised from the auction of trophies offer to local communities, some to control species populations, and a few to achieve socially tolerable limits of large carnivores by humans. The culling of wolves in Scandinavia is an example of the last model but not very prevalent in other parts of the world. Though I can't rationally disagree, it's a tedious paradox to me personally.

In many parts of the world, leopards continue to be poached illegally for the black market. In 2003, Chinese customs officials confiscated an illegal shipment from India with 581 leopard skins destined for Tibet. This incident highlighted the size of the problem. Though there was little demand for leopard coats from the fashion industry as earlier, there was a continued demand for their hide from Tibet and Sichuan. Leopard and tiger pelts were used as part of 'chubas', a ceremonial dress worn by the Tibetans and stitched with tiger, leopard and otter skins. It had triggered a systematic, grand-scale poaching operation throughout India of both leopards and tigers. This was revealed by an alarming film made by four undercover agents who travelled to Tibet and Sichuan and exposed the mayhem. However, intervention by His Holiness the Dalai Lama, towards the end of 2005, brought down the demand from this sector of the market. After His Holiness called on the Tibetans to stop using wildlife skins, Tibetans, en masse, set fire to their chubas. The incident showed the strength and influence of religious leaders, who can have a huge impact on wildlife conservation.

Belinda Wright, a wildlife conservationist, who was part of the undercover team, wrote in an article that the Tibetans had found new wealth from the sale of a local caterpillar fungus called yasa gompe (*Cordyceps sinensis*) and a rare golden mushroom, both used in traditional oriental medicine and so highly valued. This wealth had increased the demand for chubas and triggered the killing of the big cats in India. The number of leopards that may have been killed due to this increased demand was gigantic.

Closer to home, in 2008, officers of the Karnataka Police seized twenty-three leopard skins from a house in Hubli, a town in central Karnataka. A student I had taught when she was studying for her Master's degree, now an Indian Forest Service officer, Vanjulavalli Karthick examined these skins through DNA techniques, and she found that many of these skins came from central India. This brought out an interesting aspect. Why were leopard pelts poached in central India brought to the south? Since, prior to this, Hubli was not known as a trading route or a poaching hub, it is possible the poachers used this as a safe house to store the skins before transporting them to their destinations. TRAFFIC, a wildlife trade monitoring network, studied illegal trade in leopard parts in India between 2001–2010. The report they published in 2012 stated that, 'In India, at least four leopards are poached every week.'

The spotted cat is hunted not only for its pelt but also for its bones, tails, claws and whiskers, which are used in traditional Chinese medicine. These are smuggled to the Orient to satisfy the nonsensical belief that these body parts harbour aphrodisiacal qualities. In southern Africa, leopard skins are used during traditional ceremonies and as religious attire by the followers of the Shembe Church, which is a mixture of Christian and Zulu cultures. It is estimated that about eight hundred leopards in South Africa and its neighbouring countries are killed annually to meet this demand. Today, poaching has reduced the Persian leopards to a relic population in the Caucasus. Let's hope the other subspecies of leopards do not take the path of the Persian leopard.

## Wire snares, the silent stragglers

I am incredibly fortunate to see and work alongside the rich Indian wildlife. But through my work, I am also unfortunate to witness the dangers that imperil these incredible animals.

For some strange reason, there has been a litany of leopards entering human dwellings on Sundays. One Sunday afternoon, Arun, the veterinarian who had been with me during the incident with the leopard at the school, telephoned to intimate me that there was a leopard in a farmhouse on the outskirts of Bengaluru. It was tranquilised and taken to the Bannerghatta Zoo. When I arrived at the zoo, I was taken aback looking at the front right paw of this large male leopard, possibly aged about seven years. A wire snare had cut deep into the animal's flesh. The animal had suffered a debilitating injury that had prevented it from hunting. Possibly unable to stalk wild prey, which have better anti-predatory instincts, the leopard must have been pursuing some livestock, an easier prey, and in the melee taken refuge inside the small farmhouse. Though the animal was treated in the zoo, it died an agonising death due to infections, two months after it was taken into captivity. It was perhaps better for the animal, rather than going through the pain of spending every minute of its life in captivity.

In another incident, a telephone call from the forestry authorities, on a summer afternoon in April 2014 made us quickly jump into our vehicle and drive over 170 kms. Sujay, the veterinarian, and my colleague Poornesha accompanied me. When we arrived at the location, the sight was disturbing. A leopard was caught in a wire snare in an areca nut plantation. Though the animal was in the shade of the cool areca palm trees, it looked extremely exhausted due to the wrangling it had done trying to escape from the snare wrapped around its front left paw. We immediately got into action by clearing the crowd. While Sujay prepared the drugs to tranquilise the animal, I started to monitor it through binoculars. Within five minutes of our arrival, I noticed that the leopard had stopped moving. I alerted Sujay and we got closer to the animal for a better view. The animal wouldn't move when we thrust a stick at her. Unfortunately, she had stopped breathing. We had lost one more of these beautiful felines.

Even before we arrived several curious onlookers had gotten close to the leopard to get a better view and to take pictures with their mobile phones, which would have agitated the animal further. In her scuffle to escape the noose the cable would have tightened further, leading to a slow painful death. Perhaps shock and dehydration had also taken its toll.

She was a very healthy adult female. Her coat was a lighter brown than that of other leopards. A thick galvanised iron cable that had been anchored between two wooden poles to catch wild prey had unfortunately ended the life of this four- or five-year-old female. The only consolation was that she was not lactating or else the cubs would have died, an indirect effect of this kind of killing. We returned with a heavy heart and the guilt that we were unable to save her.

Wire snares set to catch wild prey have become a serious threat to these felids in many parts of the country. Snares are easy to set, remain undetected and have lethal consequences. They maim or kill any animal that unknowingly activates the snare. With leopards, strangulation, internal haemorrhaging, damage to the intestine, dehydration, and shock normally kill the cat. There seems to be a worryingly high number of incidents of leopards being trapped in wire snares in the country, and sadly many animals die as a result of this indiscriminate hunting method. In Karnataka state alone during a ten-year period, we recorded a total of sixty-seven leopard deaths due to these silent killers. There could be more that never got detected. The highest number of leopard deaths occurred outside their natural habitats, in agricultural fields and other human-dominated areas, depicting the risk these cats face in such landscapes. Our research showed that as human population densities crossed over 275 people per sq km, the threat of snares to leopards also increased. This showed that though leopards may survive in human dominated landscapes the threats they face were also higher.

Many times, even when leopards are rescued from snares and brought to captive facilities, they die due to the serious injuries and trauma they incur during the agonising hours spent in the snare. Even if they survive, the captive facilities are far and few, and the existing ones are overcrowded. Crammed in small ten feet by ten feet enclosures, where their physical and social environment is bleak, they suffer from the slow and perplexing misery of their solitude. The leopard's plight in captivity is not something the free cat would enjoy.

Over the years I have witnessed tigers, sloth bears, elephants, dholes, sambar, chital, and many other forms of wildlife die due to wire snares. Many die across the country due to this 'little piece of wire'. Often, we have silently suffered, as the authorities have taken no interest in the information provided by us about wildlife walking around with snares.

## *Automobiles—the new leopard predators*

India's ambitions to transform itself into an economic powerhouse and to preserve the country's wildlife and their habitats are often counterintuitive goals.

At one time, the single-carriageway road between Bengaluru and Mysuru, which was then called the State Highway 17, had large canopied rain trees (*Samanea saman*), banyan (*Ficus bengalensis*), peepul (*Ficus religiosa*), tamarind (*Tamarindus indica*) and other similar trees dotting the roadside. Almost the entire stretch of the highway was like being under a giant green umbrella, providing a cool drive even at the height of the summer. Lush green rice paddies provided a welcome break to the eyes during hot summer periods. The story of this road, now the National Highway 275 (NH 275), in many ways is the story of India's changed relationship with nature and wildlife.

When the widening of this highway started in the mid-2000s, the stretch lost all these magnificent trees. More and more vehicles zipped down this highway as Bengaluru's population boomed, and many well-off city residents sought to spend holiday time in the quiet green surroundings of Kodagu and Mysuru and in other spots in the neighbouring states of Kerala and Tamil Nadu. As disposable incomes rose and the tourism sector began expanding into those areas, more and more people started using this highway. Besides, the job opportunities in Bengaluru brought many Mysureans and people from Kerala and Tamil Nadu to the city, with many of them traveling to visit families over weekends and holidays. The road became an endless traffic-clogged area and the vehicular traffic density increased massively within a span of a few years. In addition, mini-malls, food courts, restaurants and industries developed all along the highway, acting as human barriers that blocked the movement of leopards from one patch of their habitat to the other.

The NH 275 also plays a key role in connectivity: it is a key node in the movement of goods from Kerala to Karnataka and vice-versa. This brings in hordes of large-sized vehicles that will kill anything that gets close to them. A video shot by an unknown amateur photographer on the Bengaluru–Mysuru highway in Karnataka went viral among wildlife communities in October 2016. The video shows a leopard desperately and hurriedly crawling by, dragging its hind legs, to cross the highway amidst the dazzling headlights of vehicles. It had certainly been hit by a speeding vehicle that had paralysed the lower half of its body and had bled internally due to the accident. The big cat didn't survive the mishap.

Highways, when they pass through wildlife habitats, pose a serious problem to leopards. Many have come under the wheels of speeding vehicles. The highest number of large cats bumped off by speeding vehicles seem to be leopards. In Iran, road accidents are the second-largest cause of unnatural mortality of the endangered Persian leopards, after illegal hunting.

Large cats, both leopards and tigers, wait at road edges to find an ideal occasion to run across. Despite thousands of years of ecological evolution that has built them for speed, these animals find themselves no match for modern-day vehicles and driving. Few of us have the patience to drive slowly through forests. Despite driving slow, I once got too close to a sloth bear inside Nagarahole Tiger Reserve when the animal dashed out of a bush. A curve had blinded both the animal and me.

Snaking south-west from Bengaluru, the NH 275 cuts through leopard habitats, and ends up being a hotbed of mortality for the spotted cat. Between 2014 and 2017, ten leopards were killed in vehicular-related accidents on this highway. A leopard was killed every fourth month on this road. Such incidents are not rare in the country now. The NH 275 is being further expanded and will take away more leopard habitats soon. Already, the few, barely visible boards that warned drivers of leopard crossing have been taken away for road expansion.

As the country goes through an economic turnaround, high-speed roads seem to be an important component of development infrastructure. In this situation, we will see increased multi-lane highways with barriers between the lanes. This would fragment wildlife habitats and literally stop the movement of wildlife between different habitat patches. Jeopardising the ability of leopards to move between different habitat patches also forces low genetic diversity, curtailing the long-term persistence of the species.

Extreme caution is necessary while driving on roads through forests. But far more impactful would be making roads wildlife-friendly: One solution that seems to work for other felid species is to install wildlife crossings in identified locations. These have been successfully tested in North America and Europe. Highways should also be diverted away from large protected areas where such alternatives exist.

### Creating leopard habitats

In August 1994, a small group of us wildlife enthusiasts had travelled on mopeds to Maidenahalli, a grassland area in my home district of Tumkur that harbours blackbucks. Monsoon had turned the landscape, which is generally dry brown, to a lush refreshing green. As we munched our meagre lunch sitting beside a small gully, we heard some rustling amongst the bushes and saw some movement. We remained motionless, expecting some small wildlife to appear. I immediately reached out for my binoculars and pressed the eyepiece against my face. To our joy and astonishment, we saw a lanky wolf slowly trotting towards us. But, it was not alone; there was a second head popping out of the bush. The number of heads continued to increase. One, two, three, and our count reached a total of six! We were ecstatic.

But, our excitement was short-lived. Within minutes, a khaki-clad forest watcher appeared on the scene with a double-barrelled shotgun. As we watched, he aimed his gun at the wolves. I was shocked but jumped and held the barrel of the gun and shouted, 'What are you doing?'

In reply to my query the guard said, 'These dirty wolves eat up all our deer (blackbucks), so our ranger has ordered me to eliminate all of them, sir.' I felt like I had been hit by a thunderbolt. This was the ignorance of the authorities responsible for saving our wildlife. They didn't know, even twenty-two years after the passing of the Wildlife Protection Act, that the Indian grey wolf was protected under Schedule I of the law, giving it the highest protection.

We managed to stop the forest watcher from carrying out his ludicrous act and brought it to the notice of Krishne Gowda, the deputy conservator of forests. He was the highest forestry authority in the district. My newly acquired moustache must have brought me some respect among government officials, for they had begun to take me more seriously. Krishne Gowda immediately called the local ranger and asked him to stop this insane action.

After the sighting of the wolves, we worked towards getting legal protection for the area. After four years of running around and convincing officials, the grassland-scrubland area, which had been under the ownership of the revenue department, was handed over to the forest department when a pro-conservation revenue officer Gopalkrishne Gowda took charge as the deputy commissioner of the district. Subsequent visits to the place always revealed signs of wolves or reports of wolves' presence from the local forest department watchers or shepherds. It was quite satisfying that the land was now dedicated to the protection of the wolf, the Indian fox, the blackbuck and several bird species that survived in the dry grasslands.

Nearly twenty-one years after I saw the wolves in Maidenhalli I returned to this area to do my camera trapping work in 2015. By then, the government had gazetted the area as the Jayamangali Conservation Reserve, a legal status that brought some additional protection for the land. I was, however, disappointed when I got the results from the data curation after the fieldwork. While we captured images of the Indian fox, the jackal, the sloth bear, the rusty-spotted cat, the blackbuck and a few other wildlife, we missed getting any wolf pictures. But unexpectedly, and to my utter shock, we got leopard images on our camera traps. Earlier, during my two decades of visits to this place, I had never seen signs of the leopard in Maidenahalli.

Earlier, these grasslands had very little of the tree cover that's preferred by leopards. Instead of protecting the grasslands, the forest department had carried out afforestation drives and 'created' forests. Besides, because of the protection provided against grazing the vegetation had become denser, a habitat difficult for the wolves to survive. Leopards had perhaps moved into this area due to the cover the trees offered. Had the wolves made way for the leopards in this habitat? Do leopards exclude other large competing carnivores such as the wolf, once the habitat is turned in their favour? The way this area has been handled is an excellent example of the unscientific management of wildlife habitats.

In January 2017 we returned to Maidenahalli and again set our camera traps. I wanted to repeat the camera-trapping exercise in a few selected sites, including Maidenahalli, as repetition is essential to science. Even though in wildlife biology no particular question can be answered to two decimal places of precision, unlike pure math or physics, repetition gives increased confidence of accuracy. This time, to our amazement we got chital, a deer species of the forests, in our camera traps. Whether this species has colonised on its own or it has been introduced by someone is an intriguing question. There was even a chital fawn with a mother, an indication that the animals were even breeding.

We again spotted leopards but no wolves. The tree and bush cover in the area was just over the size of one of the large shopping mall parking lots that are often seen in North America or Europe. Yet our camera traps documented three individual leopards within sixteen days. This is a staggering number of leopards in a small area of three sq kms.

In its zeal to grow more trees, the forest department has converted natural grassland and scrubland into forests, often with exotic tree species. Though leopard habitats have been unintentionally and artificially created, we have, unfortunately, lost the wolf habitat. The same has happened in the Ranibennur Wildlife Sanctuary in central Karnataka, where the grasslands have been converted into a woodland of eucalyptus trees. In the process, the grasslands that were home to the critically endangered great Indian bustard are now lost. I'm still keeping my fingers crossed that we see the pack hunters again during our next camera trapping exercise at Maidenahalli.

Dry lakebeds and natural grasslands near villages have been planted with trees, enticing leopards closer to human habitations and causing human-leopard conflict. This is another unintended and ignorant outcome of artificially creating leopard habitats. Whether there is a direct correlation between these two trends is currently speculative, but a longer study would nail it down.

## Disease

In May 2015, a two-year-old female wild Amur leopard, a critically endangered subspecies, turned up at the side of a road in eastern Russia. This cat, rarely sighted in the wild, exhibited very strange behaviour. It was disoriented, underweight, showed no fear towards people and vehicles, and was indifferent towards its surroundings. Not a natural behaviour for a wild cat. The animal was immobilised and taken to a care facility. Sadly, the beautiful cat had to be euthanised for humane reasons, as it had developed a severe neurological disease that couldn't be cured with medicine. With less than eighty Amur leopards left in the wild, the loss of even a single individual is a devastating loss to the population.

The findings of the team were surprising as the leopard was diagnosed to be infected by Canine Distemper Virus or CDV, a pathogen that affects many animals, including canids. This disease occurs in social cats like lions, but rarely occurs in solitary cats. In 1994, a CDV outbreak in Tanzania killed over 1,000 lions in the Serengeti National Park. The only surviving population of Asiatic lions found in Gujarat was affected by CDV in 2018, killing twenty-seven of these endangered lions. Six leopards were also found to be infected by CDV at the same site. CDV has been diagnosed in the Siberian tiger since 2001, and by 2013, CDV had infected 15 per cent of the 400 Siberian tigers in Russia's Far

East. Recently, in April 2020, two Malayan tigers were found to have contracted CDV in the Johor state of Malaysia.

Poultry farms at the edge of leopard habitats have increased, and our camera traps at times capture leopards walking away with broiler chicken in their mouths. This exposes the big cat to the highly pathogenic Avian Influenza (AI). There have already been instances of domestic cats being infected by AI in New York. Similarly, two leopards and two tigers contracted AI in Suphanburi Zoo, Thailand, as they had fed on infected poultry carcasses, and developed severe pneumonia as a result.

As leopards survive close to human habitations and many of them feed regularly on unvaccinated domestic dogs and poultry, there are increasing possibilities that some leopards could acquire CDV or AI. At least to date in India, epidemics don't seem to be an issue with leopards. However, this is a little-studied subject. A study in 2018 documented that 86 per cent of feral dogs around the famed Ranthambhore National Park in Rajasthan carried CDV antibodies in their bloodstream.

Though AI is yet to be ascertained in wild leopards in India, could diseases act as an important threat to this feline in the future as leopards are more and more interfacing with human habitations? Leopards continue to be threatened by a variety of problems, and if diseases add to this list it can prove detrimental to the species. More studies on diseases in leopards could set the stage for understanding this potential problem.

### Tourism as a potential threat

In recent times, leopards have also become fashionable, boutique carnivores in some parts of the country. In the northern state of Rajasthan, Bera, a nondescript area, has emerged as a hotspot for leopard tourism. It has become a powerful magnet for the nature tourism industry in the area. However, it is alleged that the tourism lodges bait leopards with livestock and that's perhaps the reason why these shy cats are seen here so easily.

In the same state, adjoining the state capital of Jaipur, is another leopard reserve that lures in hordes of tourists and photographers. Part of the Aravalli hill ranges, the Jhalana Leopard Reserve is a 20 sq km reserve surrounded partly by the city of Jaipur. Here, the focus of tourism is the leopard, bringing in revenue to the government and jobs to people.

Down south, too, leopards are drawing tourists to a couple of reserves. Living in crowded cities, doing stultifying work and apparently with extra cash, a class of citizens has arisen that is inevitably bored with their sedentary life. The IT boom in Bengaluru that has destroyed leopard habitats has also brought in enthusiasts vying to photograph these stippled felines in Nagarahole and Bandipur Tiger Reserves in southern India. These areas draw large numbers of photography enthusiasts with expensive hardware, who vie to capture a black leopard resting or playing on a large tree. The last decade has witnessed the spawning of a major tourism industry around these areas. A leopard resting or playing on a large tree has seemingly become a gold mine for tourism lodges. This is where a photographer could get a picture postcard shot of the leopard in India despite them being widespread.

Tourism can potentially bring in focus on leopard conservation, but it should not end up as a stumbling block like it has with tigers. In many areas of the country, tiger tourism is a key lobby that determines several aspects of management of tiger reserves in addition to creating problems for the very species it earns its revenue from. Let's hope leopard tourism does not take the route that tiger tourism has.

## 11

# THE FUTURE OF THE LEOPARD

Early morning on the backwaters of the Kabini reservoir in the famed Nagarahole Tiger Reserve, a thin layer of mist covered the dry forests. As we were going past a majestic banyan tree (*Ficus bengalensis*), something moved in the large branches. A young leopard was peering straight into our eyes. After staring at us for a few seconds, the young cat ran down the tree and vanished into the bushes. A couple of minutes later, the mother climbed down the tree and went looking for the cub. As we waited for her to reappear from the bushes, we saw her climbing up a tree a few metres away. She got on to a large fork in the tree and started calling out to her cub, gazing in the direction where the cub had run.

I watched her call for a few minutes—a leopard in search of her future.

My research has given me intriguing glimpses into leopard biology. I have arrived at some tentative answers about conflict and leopard numbers. Though scientific knowledge is necessary, it is far from sufficient. The outcomes of wildlife science are not perfect and represent constant learning. The existence of leopards in the future, especially outside protected areas, will be fundamentally shaped by economic changes in leopard habitats, attitudes of people towards co-existing with a large carnivore, and the measures the government takes to tackle and bring down conflict to tolerable limits.

The lives of leopards in India are not of statis, peace and stability but rather of turbulence and churning. Biodiversity, especially outside protected areas, is a big deal in the field of wildlife academics and conservation, but sustaining it requires a huge effort.

The survival of large predators is a great barometer of our maturity as a species. We may survive the ecological impact if they come to a crashing halt. But though this may not threaten our survival, we will end up in a bleak world.

I hope leopards, one of nature's great beauties, will continue to roam the rocky outcrops of Karnataka, as well as the rest of the country and their entire distribution range with unrestricted freedom. But this dream hinges on the economy seeing leopard habitats as something other than feedlots for quarrying and mining. We do not want to live in a zoologically impoverished world. Our children's bedtime stories cannot be so bleak that we will be unable to read out tales of living leopards. It is up to us to decide what kind of ecosystem we want to have in the future.

It is said that by the year 2150, 10.8 billion people will weigh upon this planet, and the growth curve will level off. Unfortunately, by then, the alpha predators, including leopards, may also cease to exist in the wild.

Leopards' evolutionary adaptations and hardy genes haven't prepared them to face the kinds of anthropogenic crisis they do today—the rapid, irreversible changes to their habitat and food sources. The deadly cocktail of threats they face, including denuded habitat, indiscriminate hunting of their prey, direct extermination, conflict with people and mortality due to vehicular accidents, make leopards the most persecuted big cat in the world. Though leopard numbers are greater than that of other *Panthera* species, precaution is necessary to ensure that they are not pushed to the same status of other big cats. Concerted international effort is required to ensure that this spotted cat does not go the way some of its felid cousins have. The leopard certainly needs a way to go before rivalling tigers as one of the most loved cats in the world.

I truly hope that in the twenty-second century we find as many leopards roaming this country as we do today. However, this needs involvement and fuelling conservation not merely through science but through on-ground efforts by ecologists, wildlife enthusiasts, photographers, filmmakers, media personnel and everyone keenly interested in saving nature. Science is like the tangier delights of food, adding variety and flavour to the diet, while conservation is like cod liver oil, essential for sustenance and building strength. Much like poetry, in conservation what matters is saying what we see, and the need of the hour is that we speak up about the threats these graceful cats face.

Many questions related to leopards remain unanswered to this day. We know only a thing or two about these graceful cats. If our work and this book contribute even a nickel's worth to help conserve this felid species, my team and I would be delighted.

# SOME LEOPARD FACTS

## Classification

Class: Mammalia
Order: Carnivora
Family: Felidae
Genus: Panthera
Scientific name: *Panthera pardus* (Linneaeus, 1758)

Currently, leopards are classified into nine subspecies: *Panthera pardus fusca, Panthera pardus nimr, Panthera pardus saxicolor, Panthera pardus pardus, Panthera pardus kotiya, Panthera pardus delacouri, Panthera pardus melas, Panthera pardus japonensis and Panthera pardus orientali.*

## Body size and structure

Head–body length: Male: 91–216 cms, Female: 95–190 cms
Tail: 51–101 cms
Shoulder height: 55–89 cms
Weight: Male: 20–90 kgs, Female: 17–42 kgs

## Life history traits and ecology

Gestation period: 90–106 days
Litter size: 1–3 cubs

Age at dispersal: 12–18 months
Maximum recorded life span: 19 years in the wild, 23 years in captivity

## A leopard by another name ...

(The names listed are selective and not exhaustive. This compilation is from various sources.)

Scientific name: *Panthera pardus*
English: Leopard, panther
Hindi (India): Tendua
Sanskrit: Dvipin, Pradaku
Kannada (Karnataka, India): Chirate, dodda naayi, chitte huli, kiruba
Tamil (Tamil Nadu, India): Chiruthai puli
Telugu (Andhra Pradesh, India): Chinna puli
Malayalam (Kerala, India): Pulli puli
Assamese (Assam, India): Nahar patukia bagh
Odia (Odisha, India): Kalarapataria Bagha
Marathi (Maharashtra, India): Bibaṭyā
Bangla (West Bengal, India): Chitabagh
Gujarati (Gujarat, India): Dīpaḍō
Bangla (Bangladesh): Gulbagh
Nepali (Nepal): Chituwa
Burmese (Burma): Kyarr sait
Thai (Thailand): Seūxdāw
Malay (Malaysia and Indonesia): Harimau bintang
Sumatra (Indonesia): Macan tutul
Laotian (Laos): Seu dav
Khmer (Cambodia): Khlarkhen
Korean (Korea): Yobeom
Vietnamese (Vietnam): Báo
Mandarin (China): Bào
Russian (Russia): Leopard
Arabic: Namir
Farsi (Iran): Palang

# REFERENCES

Akthar, M., Agarwal, P. K., & Srivastava, R. C. (2018), 'Living cycads in India: Preliminary report', *Indian Journal of Plant Sciences 7(4), 12-18.*

Allen, W. L., Cuthill, I. C., Scott-Samuel, N. E., & Baddeley, R. (2011), 'Why the leopard got its spots: Relating pattern development to ecology in felids', *Proceedings of the Royal Society B. 278, 1373–1380.* http://doi.org/10.1098/rspb.2010.1734

Ambekar, M., Murthy, A., & Mirza, Z. Z. (2020), 'A new species of fan-throated lizard of the genus Sitana Cuvier, 1829 (Squamata: Agamidae) from northern Karnataka, India', *Bonn Zoological Bulletin, 69(2), 157-164.*

Andheria, A. P., Karanth, K. U., & Kumar, N. S. (2007), 'Diet and prey profiles of three sympatric large carnivores in Bandipur Tiger Reserve, India', *Journal of Zoology, 273(2), 169–175.*

Atkins, J. L., Long, R. A., Pansu, J., Daskin, J. H., Potter, A. B., Stalmans, M. E., Tarnita, C. E., & Pringle, R. M. (2019), 'Cascading impacts of large-carnivore extirpation in an African ecosystem', *Science, 364 (6436), 173–177.*

Balaji, A. (2018), 'The felines of Tutankhamun: Leopard changes its spots to turn black panther?', *Ancient Origins,* https://www.ancient-origins.net/history/felines-tutankhamun-leopard-changes-its-spots-turn-black-panther-part-009969

Balme, G. A., Slotow, R., & Hunter, L. T. B. (2009), 'Impact of conservation interventions on the dynamics and persistence of a persecuted leopard (*Panthera pardus*) population', *Biological Conservation, 142(11), 2681–2690.*

Bhatt, P.M. & Wright, I. (2009), 'Livestock towards livelihood of small farmers in India', In: *Agriculture year book 2009,* pp. 116-118. International Livestock Research Institute. Nairobi, Kenya.

Boomgaard, P. (2001), *Frontiers of Fear: Tigers and People in the Malay World. 1600-1950*, Yale University Press, New Haven, USA & London, UK.

Braczkowski, A. R., O'Bryan, C. J., Stringer, M. J. Watson, J. E. M., Possingham, H. P., Beyer, H. L. (2018), 'Leopards provide public health benefits in Mumbai, India', *Frontiers in Ecology and the Environment. 16(3), 176-182.*

Brain, C. K. (1970), 'New finds at the Swartkrans Australopithrcine site', *Nature 225. 1112–1119.* https://doi.org/10.1038/2251112a0

Chakrabarti, S., & Jhala, Y. V. (2019), 'Battle of the sexes: a multi-male mating strategy helps lionesses win the gender war of fitness', *Behavioral Ecology. 30(4), 1050–1061.*

Chhangani, A. K., & Mohnot, S. M. (2006), 'Ranging behaviour of hanuman langurs (*Semnopithecus entellus*) in three different habitats', *Primate Conservation. 21, 171-177.*

Corbett, J. (2018), *The Hour of the Leopard*, Aleph Book Company, New Delhi, India.

Department of Archives (2001), Selections from the records of the Mysore palace. Government of Karnataka, Bangalore, India.

Divyabhanusinh (1993), 'On mutant leopards *Panthera pardus* from India', *Bombay Natural History Society 90, 88-89.*

Divyabhanusinh (1999), *The End of a Trail: The Cheetah in India*, Oxford University Press, New Delhi, India.

Dutta, T., Sharma, S., Maldonado, J. E., Wood, T. C., Panwar, H. S., & Seidensticker, J. (2013). 'Fine-scale population genetic structure in a wide-ranging carnivore, the leopard (*Panthera pardus fusca*) in central India', *Diversity and Distributions 19(7), 760–771.*

Elton, C. S. (1927), *Animal Ecology*, 1st edn 1927, Sidgwick and Jackson, London.

Gottelli, D., Wang, J., Bashir, S. & Durant, S.M. (2007), 'Genetic analysis reveals promiscuity among female cheetahs', *Proceedings of the Royal Society B: Biological Sciences, 274, 1993–2001.*

Gubbi, S., Poornesha, H.C. & Madhusudhan, M.D. (2012), 'Impact of vehicular traffic on use of highway-edges by large mammals in a south Indian wildlife reserve', *Current Science 102(7), 1047-1051.*

Gubbi, S., Reddy, V., Nagashettihalli, H., Bhat, R., & Madhusudan, M. D. (2014), 'Photographic records of the Ratel *Mellivora capensis* from the southern Indian state of Karnataka', *Small Carnivore Conservation 50*, 42–44.

Gubbi, S, Poornesha, H. C., Daithota, A. & Nagashettihalli, H. (2014), 'Roads emerging as a critical threat to leopards in India?' *CatNews 60, 30-31.*

Gubbi, S., Mukherjee, K., Swaminath, M.H., & Poornesha, H.C. (2016), 'Providing more protected space for tigers in the Western Ghats, southern India', *Oryx 50(2), 336 – 343.*

Gubbi, S., Poornesha, H. C., Nagashettyhalli, H., & Kolekar, A. (2016), 'Safely handling situations when leopards enter human dense areas', Nature Conservation Foundation, Mysore, India.

Gubbi, S., Kolekar, A., Chakraborty, P., & Kumar, V. (2019), 'Big cat in well: an unconventional threat to leopards in southern India', *Oryx. 54(5),* 658-660. doi:10.1017/S0030605319000280

Gubbi, S., Nagashettihalli, H., Suthar, S., & Menon, A.M. (2019), 'Report on monitoring of leopards at Biligiri Rangaswamy Temple Tiger Reserve in Karnataka', Nature Conservation Foundation, Mysore, India.

Gubbi, S., Nagashettihalli, H., Suthar, S., & Menon, A.M. (2019), 'Leopards of Bannerghatta National Park: A camera-trapping exercise to estimate abundance and densities of leopards', Nature Conservation Foundation, Mysore, India.

Gubbi, S., Sharma, K., & Kumara, V. (2020), 'Every hill has its leopard: Patterns of space use by leopards (*Panthera pardus*) in a mixed use landscape in India', *PeerJ. 8:e10072* https://doi.org/10.7717/peerj.10072

Gubbi, S., Kolekar, A., & Kumara, V. (2020), 'Policy to on-ground action: Evaluating a conflict policy guideline for leopards in India', *Journal of International Wildlife Law & Policy. 23(2), 127-140.* doi: 10.1080/13880292.2020.1818428

Gubbi, S., Ramesh, S., Menon, A., & Poornesha, H. C. (2020), 'The lone wolf: New distribution update of the Indian grey wolf (*Canis lupus pallipes*) in southern India', *Canid Biology & Conservation 22(6), 21-24.*

Gubbi, S., Suthar, S., Girish, M. N., & Menon, A.M. (2020), 'Rosettes in Chikkaballapur: Estimating leopard densities and abundance through camera trapping', Nature Conservation Foundation, Mysore, India.

Gubbi, S. (2020), 'Ecology and conservation of leopards in protected and multiple use forests in Karnataka'. PhD Thesis. Kuvempu University, Shankarghatta, India.

Gubbi, S., Kolekar, A. & Kumara, V. (2021) 'Quantifying wire snares as a threat to leopards in Karnataka, India'. *Tropical Conservation Science*, https://doi.org/10.1177/19400829211023264

Habib, B., Shrotriya, S., Sivakumar, K., Sinha, P. R., & Mathur, V. B. (2014), 'Three decades of wildlife radio telemetry in India: a review', *Animal Biotelemetry. 2(4).* https://doi.org/10.1186/2050-3385-2-4

Hamalainen, A., Broadley, K., Droghini, A., Haines, J. A., Lamb, C. L., Boutin., S., & Gilbert, S. (2017), 'The ecological significance of secondary seed dispersal by carnivores'. *Ecosphere. 8(2), e01685.*

Hayward, M. W., Henschel, P., O'Brien, J., Hofmeyr, M., Balme, G., & Kerley, G. I. H. (2006). 'Prey preferences of the leopard (*Panthera pardus*)', *Journal of Zoology 270(2), 298–313.*

Hedges, L., Lam, W. Y., Campos-Arceiz, A., Rayan, D. M., Laurance, W. F., Latham, C. J., Saaban, S., & Clements, G. R. (2015), 'Melanistic leopards reveal their spots: Infrared camera traps provide a population density estimate of leopards in Malaysia', *Journal of Wildlife Management. 79(5), 846–853.*

Hunter, L. (2015). Wild Cats of the World. Bloomsbury, London, UK & New York, USA.

Jacobson, A. P., Gerngross, P., Lemeris, Jr. J. R., Schoonover, R. F., Anco, C, Breitenmoser-Würsten, C., Durant, S.M., Farhadinia, M.S., Henschel, P., Kamler, J.F, Laguardia, A., Rostro-García, S., Stein, A.B., & Dollar, L. (2016), 'Leopard (*Panthera pardus*) status, distribution, and the research efforts across its range', *PeerJ 4:e1974.* https://doi.org/10.7717/peerj.1974

Judas, J., Paillat, P., Khoja, A., & Boug, A. (2006), 'Status of the Arabian leopard in Saudi Arabia', *Cat News Special Issue 1.*

Kansal, S. (1997), 'Factors determining Indian sugar production and its comparative advantage. Sugar and Beverages Group, Commodities and Trade Division', Food and Agriculture Organisation, http://www.fao.org/3/X0513E/x0513e16.htm. Accessed on 30-12-2020

Koehler. J. (2017), *Where the Wild Coffee grows: The Untold Story of Coffee from the Cloud Forests of Ethiopia to Your Cup*, Bloomsbury, London, UK.

Lal, P. (2016), *Indica: A deep natural history of the Indian subcontinent*, Penguin Random House India Pvt. Ltd, Gurgaon, India.

Lingaraja, S. S., Chowdhary, S., Bhat, R., & Gubbi, S. (2017), 'Evaluating a survey landscape for tiger abundance in the confluence of the Western and Eastern Ghats', *Current Science 113(9), 1759 - 1763.*

Mondal, K., Bhattacharrjee, S., Gupta, S., Sankar, K., & Qureshi, Q. (2013), 'Home range and resource selection of 'problem' leopards translocated to forested habitat', *Current Science. 105(3), 338-345.*

Mondol, S., Sridhar, V., Yadav, P., Gubbi, S., & Ramakrishnan, U. (2015), 'Tracing the geographic origin of traded leopard body parts in the Indian subcontinent with DNA-based assignment tests', *Conservation Biology 29(2), 556–564.*

Mourya, D. T., Yadav, P. D., Mohandas, S., Kadiwar, R. F., Vala, M. K., Saxena, A. K., Shete-Aich, A., Gupta, N., Purushothama, P., Sahay, R. R., Gangakhedkar, R. R., Mishra, S. C. K., & Bhargava, B. (2019), 'Canine distemper virus in Asiatic lions of Gujarat state, India', *Emerging Infectious Diseases 25(11), 2128–2130.*

Nagalingum, N. S., Marshall, C. R., Quental, T. B, Rai, H. S., Little, D. P. & Mathews, S. (2011). 'Recent synchronous radiation of a living fossil', *Science, 334, (6057), 796-799.* DOI: 10.1126/science.1209926

Nagendra, H. (2016), *Nature in the City: Bengaluru in the past, present and future*, Oxford University Press, New Delhi.

Nicholson, F. A. (1887), *The Manual of the Coimbatore district in the Presidency of Madras*, Madras, India.

Odden, M., & Wegge, P. (2009), 'Kill rates and food consumption of leopards in Bardia National Park, Nepal', *Mammal Research 54, 23–30.*

Oregon State University (2011), 'An ecosystem being transformed: Yellowstone 15 years after the return of wolves', *Science Daily*, 21 December 2011. www.sciencedaily.com/releases/2011/12/111221140710.htm.

Painter, L. E, Beschta, R. L., Larsen, E. J., & Ripple W. J. (2018), 'Aspen recruitment in the Yellowstone region linked to reduced herbivory after large carnivore restoration', *Ecosphere 9(8),* https://doi.org/10.1002/ecs2.2376

Patil, B. S., Siddaiah,, Ravichandra, V., & Yashvanth, V. (2015), *Bengaluru: Way Forward*, Bengaluru: Expert Committee, BBMP Restructuring, BBMP.

Quammen, D. (2000), *The Boilerplate Rhino: Nature in the Eye of the Beholder*, Scribner, New York, USA.

Quammen, D. (2003*), Monster of God: The man-eating predator in the jungles of history and the mind*, W.W. Norton & Company, Inc., New York, USA.

Rangarajan, M (2001), *India's wildlife history*, Permanent Black, New Delhi India.

Raza, R.H., Chauhan, D.S, Pasha, M.K.S & Sinha, S. (2012), 'Illuminating the blind spot: A study on illegal trade in leopard parts in India (2001-2010)', TRAFFIC India/WWF India. New Delhi, India.

Ripple, W. J. & Beschta, R. L. (2011), 'Trophic cascades in Yellowstone: The first 15years after wolf reintroduction', Biological Conservation, 145(1), 205-213. doi:10.1016/j.biocon.2011.11.005

Rostro-García, S., Kamler, J. F., Crouthers, R., Sopheak, K., Prum, S., In, V., Pin, C., Caragiulo, A., & Macdonald, D. W. (2018), 'An adaptable but threatened big cat: Density, diet and prey selection of the Indochinese leopard (*Panthera pardus delacouri*) in eastern Cambodia', *Royal Society Open Science 5: 171187*. http://dx.doi.org/10.1098/rsos.171187

Sidhu, N., Borah, J., Shah, S., Rajput, N., & Jadav, K. K. (2019), 'Is canine distemper virus (CDV) a lurking threat to large carnivores? A case study from Ranthambhore landscape in Rajasthan, India', *Journal of Threatened Taxa 11(9), 14220–14223*.

Singhi, A., Jain, N., & Sanghi, K. (2017), 'The new Indian: The many facets of a changing consumer', Boston Consulting Group. Mumbai, India.

Skinner, J. D. & Chimimba, C. T. (2005), *The Mammals of Southern African subregion*, Cambridge University Press, Cambridge, UK.

Stein, A.B., Athreya, V., Gerngross, P., Balme, G., Henschel, P., Karanth, U., Miquelle, D., Rostro-Garcia, S., Kamler, J.F., Laguardia, A., Khorozyan, I. & Ghoddousi, A. (2016). *Panthera pardus* (errata version published in 2016). The IUCN Red List of Threatened Species 2016: e.T15954A102421779. http://dx.doi.org/10.2305/IUCN.UK.2016-1.RLTS.T15954A50659089.en. Downloaded on 17 March 2018.

Stolzenburg, W. (2008), *Where the Wild Things Were: Life, death, and ecological wreckage in a land of vanishing predators*, Bloomsbury, New York. USA.

Sulikhan, N. S., Gilbert, M., Blidchenko, E. Y., Naidenko, S. V., Ivanchuk, G. V., Gorpenchenko, T. Y., Alshinetskiy, M. V., Shevtsova, E. I., Goodrich,

J. M., Lewis, J. C. M., Goncharuk, M. S., Uphyrkina, O. V., Rozhnov, V. V., Shedko, S. V., McAloose, D., Seimon, T. A., & Seimon, T. A. (2018), 'Canine distemper virus in a wild Far Eastern leopard (*Panthera pardus orientalis*)', *Journal of Wildlife Diseases 54(1), 170–174.*

Suthar, S., Menon, A., & Gubbi, S. (2020), 'An extension of known range of Brown Mongoose *Urva fuscus* from Southern India', *Small Carnivore Conservation 58, e58007*

Uphyrkina, O., Johnson, W. E., Quigley, H., Miquelle, D., Marker, L., Bush, M., & O'Brien, S. J. (2001), 'Phylogenetics, genome diversity and origin of modern leopard, *Panthera pardus*', *Molecular Ecology 10(11), 2617–2633.*

Van Bockhaven, V. (2018), 'Anioto: Leopard-men killings and institutional dynamism in northeast Congo, c. 1890-1940', *The Journal of African History* 59(1), 21-44.

Van Neer, W., Udrescu, M., Linseele, V., de Cupere, B., & Friedman, R. (2015), 'Traumatism in the wild animals kept and offered at Predynastic Hierakonpolis, Upper Egypt', *International Journal of Osteoarchaeology 27(1), 86-105.* doi:10.1002/oa.2440

Vijayakrishnana, S., Kumar, M. A., Umapathy, G., Kumar, V., & Sinha, A. (2018), 'Physiological stress responses in wild Asian elephants *Elephas maximus* in a human-dominated landscape in the Western Ghats, southern India', *General and Comparative Endocrinology 266, 150-156.*

Voigt, C. C., Krofel, M., Menges. V., Wachter, B., & Melzheimer, J. (2018), 'Sex-specific dietary specialization in a terrestrial apex predator, the leopard, revealed by stable isotope analysis', *Journal of Zoology 306(1), 1–7.*

Weldon, J. (2018), *Fierce: The History of Leopard Print*, Harper Design. New York.

Wilmers, C. C., Isbell, L. A., Suraci, J. P., & Williams, T. M. (2017), 'Energetics-informed behavioral states reveal the drive to kill in African leopards', *Ecosphere. 8(6), e01850.* https://doi.org/10.1002/ecs2.1850

Wilting, A., Patel, R., Pfestorf, H., Kern, C., Sultan, K., Ario, A., Peñaloza, F., Kramer-Schadt, S., Radchuk, V., Foerster, D. W., & Fickel, J. (2016), 'Evolutionary history and conservation significance of the Javan leopard *Panthera pardus melas*', *Journal of Zoology 299(4), 239–250.*

Wilson, E. O. (1984), *Biophilia: The Human Bond with Other Species*, The Harvard University Press, Cambridge, Massachusetts, and London, England.

# ABBREVIATIONS

| | |
|---|---|
| AI | Avian Influenza |
| BCE | Before the Common Era |
| BRT | Biligirirangaswamy Temple Tiger Reserve |
| CDV | Canine Distemper Virus |
| CMS | Centimeters |
| COVID-19 | Coronavirus Disease-2019 |
| DCF | Deputy Conservator of Forests |
| DNA | Deoxyribonucleic acid, is the molecule that contains the genetic code of organisms. |
| GPS | Global Positioning System |
| HR | Human Resource |
| IUCN | International Union for Conservation of Nature |
| IT | Information Technology |
| KG | Kilogram |
| MM Hills | Malai Mahadeshwara Hills |
| NH | National Highway |
| PA | Protected Area |
| PCCF | Principal Chief Conservator of Forests |
| SH | State Highway |
| SQ KMS | Square Kilometers |
| VHF | Very High Frequency |

# GLOSSARY

Abundance – Total number of individuals or objects of interest in a defined area and time (e.g. number of tigers in Karnataka during 2020)

Cenozoic – This is the third documented era in the history of Earth. It began about 65 million years ago and continues into the present.

Density – Number of individuals or objects per unit area (e.g. number of elephants per square kilometre)

Distribution – An area where animals or objects of interest are found

DNA – Deoxyribonucleic acid, the substance comprising the genetic material and the hereditary information passed from parents to offspring.

Home range – The area traversed by an individual animal in its normal activities of food gathering, mating, and caring for the young.

Ice age – An ice age is a period of colder global temperatures and recurring glacial expansion. This period began about 2.6 million years ago and lasted until about 11,700 years ago.

Landscape – An area of land that contains a mosaic of habitat patches.

Mesozoic – It's the second of Earth's three major geologic eras and began 252 million years ago and ended 66 million years ago. Best known as the time of dinosaurs, the ancestors of major plant and animal groups that exist today first appeared during the Mesozoic era.

Musth – It refers to a set of physical and behavioural characteristics displayed periodically by adult male elephants. This condition is associated with increased aggressiveness, restlessness, significant weight reduction and markedly elevated androgen levels in adult male elephants.

Pliocene – The Pliocene epoch is the period in the geologic timescale that extends from 5.3 million to 1.8 million years before present.

Pleistocene – Pleistocene, the time period that spanned from 1.8 million to 10,000 years ago.

Ruminant – Ruminant herbivores have a unique digestive system with four-chambered stomachs. Ruminants do not completely chew the grass or vegetation, they eat but partially chew the food which goes into the large rumen where it is stored and broken into cud. They include cattle, sheep, goat, buffalo, giraffes, deer, etc.

Terai – The Terai is a lowland region in northern India and southern Nepal on the foothills of the Himalayas, the Sivalik Hills and north of Indo-Gangetic plains. The Terai is characterised by tall grasslands, sal forests and clay-rich swamps.

# ACKNOWLEDGEMENTS

At times, I sat at the Yerekatte waterhole on the foothills of Kote Boli, a large hillock with a grassy top at the edge of BRT Tiger Reserve writing or thinking of these stories. In the stillness of the forest, I listened to the conspicuous metallic *tuk, tuk, tuk* sound of the barbet the melodious singing shama, one of the most beautiful singers of the forests and the alarm barking of the muntjac. I saw the gingerly chital coming in for a mid-afternoon drink the sambar wallowing in mud sprayed with its urine to smear the mud to attract individuals of the opposite sex and dholes chasing chital into the waterhole. The aggressive bicoloured ant scurried on the rocks endlessly like a hermit looking for something, which I never could make out. Flap-shelled turtles swam on the surface of the water, occasionally poking their pig-nosed faces out of the water, white-throated kingfishers dived like arrows into the water and reappeared with frogs or fishes in their beaks.

The place had a dazzling bird life. A metallic brown, very attractive female Asian paradise flycatcher with its long ribbon-like tail would at times land graciously on the branches of the jamun tree. After carefully scanning the surroundings, a few seconds later, she would dive to get an occasional morsel of an insect and land on the nearby sandalwood tree. Her long tail resembled a ballerina with a long tape. A green imperial pigeon ate small lumps of mud at the water's edge while a white-bellied drongo perched on a dry tree branch would sometimes take a plunge into the cool waters for a mid-afternoon bath.

A lot of wildlife action took place around me as I keyed in these stories. All of this was possible due to the warmth extended by the owner of this paradise—Gautam Kadam. I could write and edit a whole lot more when I sat down at his watchtower than I could at any other place, thanks to Gautam's generosity.

I have had the pleasure of working with some extraordinary colleagues, donors, individuals and friends. I am extremely grateful to those who have supported my work for several years. IUCN-KfW, Elephant Family, British Asian Trust, Whitley Fund for Nature, the Rhino and Tiger Conservation Fund of the US Fish and Wildlife Service, the Singhal Foundation, H&M Foundation, Kaplan Graduate Fellowship, Prince Bernhard Fund for Nature, and the Rufford Foundation have all provided financial support for various aspects of my research and conservation work.

I have accrued a lengthy list of people to thank for their support, encouragement, patience, and generosity. Without the wonderful support of some individuals including Ganesh Ramani, Ruth Ganesh, Venkat Krishnan, I would not have been able to advance my work on leopards. Jörn Rohde and Margit Hellwig-Bötte, German Consul General, German Consulate, Bengaluru extended their generous backing to our work to whom we are greatly indebted.

There are so many friends in the conservation field who shared insights, thoughts, and encouragement that made me see the values of this work, long before it was complete. My special thanks to the devout, preternaturally tolerant, intelligent academic M.D. Madhusudan for his help as always. I am enormously indebted to A.J.T. Johnsingh, Mahesh Rangarajan, Nigel-Leader Williams, Suresh Chandra, Bivash Pandav, Koustubh Sharma, Srikanth Seshadri, Kannan A.S. and Ramprasad Ramanna for their friendship and ecological, societal, statistical and technological insights.

Our small, committed field team, which is more like a cottage industry is driven by youthful idealism and a fondness for wildlife conservation. Though our team is no match for the hugely funded, highly qualified, large conservation organisations, well-wishers say we have set gold standards in conservation work. The team has slaved virtually around the clock, even working with oil lamps at night. As a team, we have undertaken back-breaking work, sweaty and dirty with temperatures at times soaring above 40 degrees centigrade. An enormous heartfelt thanks to this entire team.

I express my indebtedness to this team who worked with me and some are mentioned in this book—Amrita Menon, Aparna Kolekar, Ashritha Anoop, Ashoka H.P., Ashwin George Philip, Gaurav P.J., Girish M.N, Gnanendra L., Harish N.S., Kiran Prabhu, Nishandh M., Prakasha H.M., Poornesha H.C., Praveen T.V. Rashmi Bhat, Ravidas G. Gavada, Ruma K. Kundurkar, Sandesh A. Naik, and Shravan Suthar. Very sadly, our ever-loving cook Lokesh passed away recently, and I will fondly remember him for the care he showed during our fieldwork and for all the wonderful dishes he was good at preparing.

I thank the Nature Conservation Foundation and all my colleagues there for the support that helped me pull the cart through, and I hope to the fullest.

I want to express my deep gratitude to the bevy of scientific researchers whose work fill the bibliography. I am thankful to Vijaya Kumara and the entire staff of the Wildlife and Management Department of the Kuvempu University.

The Karnataka Forest Department who gave me permissions and supported our work in the wild areas of the state not just for my biological monitoring part but for many other aspects. In particular, I thank B.K. Singh, Dipak Sarmah, G.S. Prabhu, Ravi Ralph, Vinay Luthra, C. Jayaram, Sanjai Mohan, Ajay Misra, Subhash K. Malkhede, P. Shankar, V. Karikalan, Vasanth Reddy, Javeed Mumtaz, V. Yedukondalu, Prashant Shankhinamath, S. Ramesh, H.C. Girish and many others.

My sincere thanks to all the kind persons including Ananth Subramanian, Arun Simha, Arun Bastin, Deon De Villiers, Ganesh Raghunath, Geetha Srinivas, Phillip Ross, Praveen Siddannanavar, Shaaz Jung, Shreyas Kumar Shenoy, Steve Winter, Sudhir Shivaram and Vinay S. Kumar who have allowed me to publish one or more of their wonderful photographs. I would like to mention my special thanks to Sangeetha Kadur who worked on the wonderful illustrations in this book.

Karthik Venkatesh served as the patient, wise editor of several drafts and I thank him for his unwavering faith in this project from proposal to press. I was fortunate to have Dipanjali Chadha who assisted in editing the draft of the book. I also thank A.J.T. Johnsingh whose inputs spared me some embarrassing gaffes.

Some names that should have appeared here have either been lost or simply forgotten. My humble apologies to those so unwittingly omitted, along with my thanks

None of this would be possible, or particularly enjoyable, without the love and support of my family. My last word of thanks goes to my fellow life travellers, for their usual forbearance and their company: my parents, parents-in-law, siblings, my beloved wife Suma and loving son Ninaadha.

Finally, I cannot help but marvel at these regal leopards, not only for their unabashed majesty, but also for the remarkable lessons they have taught me.